The Gourmet Jewish Cookbook

The Gourmet Jewish Cookbook

Denise Phillips

More than 200 Recipes from Around the World

Thomas Dunne Books
St. Martin's Press
New York

THOMAS DUNNE BOOKS.
An imprint of St. Martin's Press.

Food photography by Ilian Iliev

www.thomasdunnebooks.com
www.stmartins.com

Library of Congress Cataloging-in-Publication Data

Phillips, Denise.
    The gourmet Jewish cookbook : more than 200 recipes from around the world / Denise Phillips. —
First U.S. Edition
        p. cm.
    Includes index.
    ISBN 978-1-250-04593-5 (hardcover)
    ISBN 978-1-4668-4607-4 (e-book)
    1. Jewish cooking. I. Title.
    TX724.P482 2014
    641.5'676—dc23

                                                                                2014010791

St. Martin's Press books may be purchased for educational, business, or promotional use. For information on bulk purchases, please contact Macmillan Corporate and Premium Sales Department at 1-800-221-7945, extension 5442, or write specialmarkets@macmillan.com.

First published in Great Britain by The Robson Press, an imprint of Biteback Publishing Ltd

First U.S. Edition: September 2014

10   9   8   7   6   5   4   3   2   1

This book is dedicated to the two matriarchs in my family: my mother, Audrey Kostick, and my mother-in-law, Rica Green. Both are 'Aishet Chayils' – Jewish Women of Worth – as well as being wonderful grandmothers and they are adored by the whole family.

Welcome to The Gourmet Jewish Cookbook!

It is over twelve years since I published my first cookbook, *Modern Jewish Cooking with Style*, and more than twenty years since I became a professional Jewish chef. In that time there have been so many changes in the food world, many of which have been of great benefit to the Jewish cook and as a result they feature strongly in this new and unique collection of recipes.

An explosion of new ingredients ...

Supermarkets, markets and kosher shops are bursting with new herbs, spices, fruits and vegetables that can enhance the flavour and appearance of our food. Coconut milk, soya yoghurt, rice milk, soya cream and non-dairy cream cheese enable the strictly kosher cook to adapt those previously impossible recipes, for example those that include both meat and dairy in the same recipe, such as lasagne. Our culinary repertoire has been expanded enormously by many new specialist ingredients from Israel and the USA that are now on the shelves of kosher shops.

Eating out/eating in ...

There are now so many restaurants to choose from with cuisine from everywhere in the world and at every price. They provide cooks with the inspiration to return home, find the recipe and make it themselves. Many of my new recipes in this book support the philosophy that 'dining in is the new eating out'.

It's a small world ...

Jews love to travel and to eat. Today you really can go anywhere in the world as a tourist. Thanks to outreach groups such as Chabad you can be kosher in almost every country. So Jews are holidaying everywhere, trying out different foods and being exposed to the diets of different cultures. The desire to experiment when you return home is a natural development – I hope my book will give you the scope to do this.

Free from ...

We seem to live in the Age of the Allergy. As medical knowledge increases we have been able to improve the quality of people's lives simply by excluding certain problem ingredients. Sugar substitutes and gluten-free flour are just two items helping individuals access a more normal diet, and improved non-dairy substitutes are great products for making recipes that would otherwise not be kosher. Many people believe that eating fewer or no animal products is best both from a moral and a health viewpoint. In the chapter called 'Free From', I have suggested many options – however, a large number of other recipes in the book also fit this category.

However, not everything changes …

Most Jews are still traditionalists and follow the Jewish festival calendar and enjoy the old favourites. My book allows room for all this – I have adapted a number of classic recipes and suggested interesting variations and special menus.

Jews are an ancient people living modern lives. Jewish continuity means that whilst nothing stays the same, nothing really changes. Enjoying good food is certainly a constant in my life and those of my family. As it says in the Talmud:

'*There can be no joy without food and drink.*'

I hope that you enjoy my book.

Denise Phillips, July 2012

Notes on Recipes

Always read through the whole recipe before you start cooking. Check the list of ingredients and possible substitutes and have everything ready and measured before you start. Having ingredients measured and the correct equipment to hand will make the whole experience faster and more efficient.

Ingredients are given in metric and imperial measures. Use either set of quantities but not a mixture of both in any one recipe, or the results may not be as intended.

All spoon measures are level.

1 tsp = 5 ml; 1 tbsp = 15 ml

Eggs are large unless otherwise stated.

Only freeze those dishes that are so indicated. Ideally always cook and enjoy fresh dishes.

Each recipe has been given approximate preparation and cooking times. The preparation time includes weighing, peeling, chopping and rolling out – in fact anything that is hands on or requires close attention before cooking.

The cooking time is the length of time when the dish (or part of the dish) can be left in the oven, under the grill or on the hob unattended. Set a timer to remind you to check. During this time you may be able to prepare other parts of the dish or meal that will speed up the total time taken to complete the recipe. Multi-tasking in the kitchen needs concentration and planning at first, but it will bring its own rewards.

Ovens should be pre-heated to the specified temperature – if using a fan-assisted oven, follow the manufacturer's instructions for adjusting the time and the temperature.

Cake tins vary in size. A cake in a deeper tin will take longer to cook. If you alter the size of the tin, the cooking time will vary.

All ingredients are kosher. Some 'milky' recipes may be made parev by substituting non-dairy products. Dishes suitable for Passover are indicated and many can be adapted by using specific Kosher for Passover products.

Fresh herbs should be used wherever possible.

Sugar is caster unless stated.

Mustard is always ready-made unless stated.

Measurements for both herbs and spices are according to my preference; please adjust to your taste.

Key

Parev	PAREV	Shabbat	SHABBAT
Dairy	D	Pesach	P
Meat	M	Vegetarian	V
Rosh Hashanah	RH	Yom Tov	YT
Chanukah	CHANUKAH	Gluten-Free	GLUTEN-FREE
Shavuot	SHAVUOT	Dairy-free	DAIRY-FREE
Succot	SUCCOT	Diabetic Friendly	DIABETIC FRIENDLY

What is kosher?

'Kosher' means fit or proper and is derived from the Hebrew word 'Kashrut'. This is the body of Jewish law which deals with what Jews can and can't eat, and how to prepare and eat what is allowed.

The origins of the rules of Kashrut are found in the Torah, the first five books of the Jewish Bible, The Old Testament. The reasons for these rules are not given and for thousands of years Jews have debated 'why keep kosher?' Possible explanations include health benefits, environmental considerations, to reach holiness through self-control, to practise religious ritual and to be separate from other groups. The debate is ongoing – the short answer most Jews accept is simply because the Torah says so. For an observant Jew no further reason is needed.

There are three categories of kosher food:

Meat

Only animals which have split hooves and chew the cud are permitted. Cows and sheep are fine – pigs, horses and rabbits are not. Kosher poultry includes chicken, turkey, geese and duck. Animals which can be consumed are ritually slaughtered and no blood can be eaten.

Dairy

Dairy products from kosher animals are allowed. However, these cannot be mixed with meat or poultry in the same recipe, at the same meal or even on the same plates. So kosher households have two sets of everything to do with food preparation and delivery, from pans and plates to tea towels and dish cloths.

Parev

Foods with no meat or dairy content are called 'parev' and are neutral. All eggs, fruits, grains and vegetables are parev and may be served with meat or milk meals.

Fish is not classified as a meat, but we are only allowed to eat fish that have fins and scales, such as tuna, salmon, cod and herring. Shellfish of any sort and other 'scavengers' are forbidden. Whilst fish is parev, it is not served on the same plate or within the same dish as meat – which means, for instance, that you can't use something like Worcestershire sauce to add flavour to a beef stew, because it has anchovies in it.

Spirits and alcohol made from grains are kosher. However, there are specific guidelines for wine and wine-products such as brandy. To be kosher, wine has to be prepared from grape to bottle under Rabbinic supervision.

Nowadays a lot of our food is packaged or processed and it can be hard to know the source of the ingredients, how they have been manufactured and whether they are all kosher. To assist the shopper, there is a system of certification which involves the Rabbinic authorities scrutinising products made for the Jewish and non-Jewish market to ensure that all the ingredients and all the processes meet approved standards. There are various issuing authorities but one of the biggest is the KLBD.

Shabbat and Yom Tov Cooking

Because we are not allowed to 'work' on Shabbat and Yom Tov there are strict rules in Kashrut regarding food preparation including storing and heating and reheating on these days. The general principle is to prepare in advance a selection of dishes which can either be eaten cold or kept warm for a long time. For further guidance consult your local community Rabbi.

Acknowledgements

Writing a cookbook requires a great deal of time, creativity and of course, eating. I am blessed with three wonderful children, Abbie, Samantha and Nicholas, all of whom love to try my new creations and provide constructive criticism. Special thanks go to my husband Jeremy who never complains about the unusual dinner combinations that he receives after a day's food photography and experimentation; he just gamely asks, 'Is it milk or meat?'

Also thanks to Marsha Schultz who has spent many hours checking and reviewing my recipes and introductions as well as always being there at the end of the phone to discuss foodie ideas. Her honest opinion is greatly valued. Her husband Martin also deserves recognition for letting her spend so much time with me.

My good friend Lynne Misner has also been very supportive and her help and encouragement are much appreciated.

For a cookbook to be a success the recipes must work well in all circumstances and I owe a big thank you to my small army of testers who have made and evaluated every one of these recipes:

Abbie Phillips, Alex Galbinski Newman, Angel Gordon, Annabelle Hodgkinson, Audrey Kostick, Aviva Wilford, Barbara Hodgkinson, Catharine Ross, Claire Barsam, Debbie Bello, Debra Kasler, Emma Viner, Gail Garcia, Gilly Shulman, Helen Carr, Jane Rome, Janice Fairfield, Jenny Bracey, Karen Golanski, Katy Jones, Lauren Schogger, Laurie Sherman, Lindsay Treger, Liz Maykels, Lynne Misner, Marsha Schultz, Michele Gilford, Pearl Moore, Philip Ettinger, Rachel Sinclair, Reena Joseph, Reva Demant, Sharon Phillips, Shelley Levy, Simone Leboff, Sue Morgan, Vivien Collins, Vivien Morris, Yael Jackson.

I am thrilled with the photographs that Ilian Iliev produced for this book. We cooked and photographed thirty recipes in three days – a marathon task with exceptional results.

With all the cooking comes the washing up and cleaning and I could not work at the pace that I do without the help of Silvia Burlui.

A special thank you must also go to my Uncle Sidney from South Africa who sent me emails full of vivid descriptions of Jewish foodie life in the 'Old East End' during the early 1930s.

I would also like to thank Rabbi Dr Moshe Freedman of Northwood United Synagogue for ensuring that the Kashrut and religious content of the book is correct. In addition, every Monday I expand my Jewish learning with two special teachers, Chaya Borden and Lesley Glassberg – both nourish my spiritual spark and enable me to bring so much Jewish passion to the recipes. I particularly like the following commentary:

'If three have eaten at a table and have not spoken words of Torah there, it is as if they have eaten of offerings to the dead idols. But if they have spoken words of Torah it is as if they have eaten from the table of God Himself.'

— Ethics of the Fathers, chapter 3 verse 4

As this book includes recipes from around the world, I would like to thank Chabad, who operate an amazing service of outreach for visiting Jews all over the globe and have been a great source of information, especially on isolated Jewish communities.

Finally, I would like to thank Jeremy Robson, my publisher.

Contents

The Gourmet
Jewish Cookbook

Chapter 1

In the Beginning

_

Starters, Breads and Soups

In the Beginning

The opening dish of the meal sets the scene and mood and very often provides a great opportunity for a theme. Balance is essential so that guests can do justice to the forthcoming main course and dessert. The simplest recipe can be the best as long as ingredients of prime quality are chosen for their colour, flavour and texture.

All Jewish people love mixed hors d'oeuvres; Sephardi and Mizrachi communities enjoy meze including hummus, baba ganoush, tabbouleh and pitta bread whilst Ashkenazim feast on 'vorspeisen' including chopped liver, herring, egg and onion and pickles.

This chapter includes very tasty little dishes which complement each other and are totally up to date. Put two or three of them together to create a thoroughly modern Jewish fusion meze!

Many of my starter recipes can be served hot, cold or warm which makes life easier for the cook to serve and enjoy.

Starters
- Dainty cherry tomato tarts
- Smoked aubergine pâté – Moutabel
- Smoked salmon and dill frittata
- Stuffed mushrooms with hazelnut gremolata
- Herb omelette
- Mini spinach and pine nut pies
- Lemongrass fish cakes with lime mayonnaise
- Mini corn fritters with guacamole
- Roasted beetroot with goat's cheese layers
- Onion bhaji

Soups
- Carrot and apple soup
- Italian tomato and bread soup
- Sweet potato and chestnut soup with garlic croutons
- Beetroot and carrot soup with coriander oil
- Tricolour minestrone
- Roasted red pepper and carrot soup
- Cinnamon and pumpkin soup

- Chinese chicken and sweetcorn soup
- Udon noodles with egg broth and ginger
- Wild mushroom and leek soup
- Turkish red lentil and carrot soup

Breads

- Onion bread
- Granary bread
- Sesame bread
- Tomato and basil bread
- Cheese and beer bread
- Herb pitta bread sticks

Dainty Cherry Tomato Tarts

PAREV SUCCOT (V)

Info
- Preparation Time: 30 minutes
- Cooking Time: 12 minutes
- Makes: 6 tarts
- Can be made in advance

Ingredients
- 375g/13 oz ready-rolled puff pastry
- 1 egg, for glazing

✡

- 150g/5 oz/½ cup cream cheese mixed with 3 tbsp fresh herbs – basil, chives, coriander or mint (use Toffuti non dairy cream cheese for a parev option)

✡

- 300g/11 oz/2 cups cherry tomatoes cut in half (you will need about 8 per tartlet)
- salt and freshly ground black pepper

✡

- To serve: extra virgin olive oil

These little tarts are a great starter or an accompaniment to a fish or meat meal any time. They are quick to make and can be made in advance. I have used cream cheese on the base but if you prefer, try sun-dried tomato paste or tapenade (chopped olive spread). I suggest that you make double the quantity, as extra friends and family always seem to turn up when these delicious items are on the table.

Method
- Pre-heat the oven to 220ºC/425ºF/Gas mark 7.
- Cut the ready-rolled pastry in half. Cut each half into three rectangles.
- Line a baking tray with baking parchment.
- Put the pastry rectangles on the baking tray and score a border into the pastry about 2 cm/1 inch from the edge.
- Glaze the pastry with the beaten egg.
- Spread the cream cheese and herb mixture over the pastry rectangles, keeping within the border.
- Place the tomato halves on top of the cream cheese mixture in rows.
- Season with salt and black pepper.
- Bake for 10–12 minutes or until golden brown.

To serve the stylish way: Serve either hot or warm and drizzle over some good-quality extra virgin olive oil and some ground black pepper.

Smoked Aubergine Pâté – Moutabel

PAREV **V** **DAIRY-FREE** **GLUTEN-FREE**

Info
- Preparation Time: 10 minutes
- Cooking Time: 15 minutes plus 10 minutes cooling
- Serves: 4–6
- Will keep for a couple of days in the fridge

Ingredients
- 8 large aubergines

✡

- 2–3 small cloves garlic, peeled and crushed
- ½ tsp salt
- 3–4 tbsp lemon juice
- 2½ tbsp tahini

✡

- Garnish: Chopped parsley, pinch of cayenne, 1–2 tbsp extra virgin olive oil, pomegranate seeds, chopped walnuts, 1 red pepper, deseeded and cut into small diamond shapes

In this dish, the secret of the smoked flavour comes from open flame-grilling. Moutabel is found on nearly every Middle Eastern table as part of the starter or meze selection.

I was first shown how to make this recipe when I was in Istanbul but have adapted it slightly to fit my personal tastes.

Istanbul has an amazing spice market and a long Jewish heritage. The Jews fleeing the Spanish and Portuguese Inquisitions of the sixteenth and seventeenth centuries were welcomed into the Ottoman Empire which had its capital in Constantinople (the old name for Istanbul). During World War Two, Turkey served as a transit point for Jews fleeing Europe and, although there were some problems, a number of sympathetic Turkish diplomats went out of their way to save many thousands of Jews.

Today the Turkish Jewish community is very small but its history is portrayed in a wonderful Jewish museum in Istanbul, which is well worth a visit.

Delicious examples of Jewish Turkish cuisine include stuffed and baked vegetables, recipes made with chickpeas, lentils, bulgur wheat and more rice than potatoes. Many of the meat dishes incorporate dried fruit and are garnished with pine nuts. Spices like cumin, coriander, cinnamon, saffron, turmeric and fresh herbs including parsley, mint, coriander and dill are very popular.

Chef's Tip: Cover the hob with foil as burning the aubergine tends to be quite messy.

Method
- Cover the hob with foil leaving holes for the flames.
- Place the aubergines over a medium open flame. Use tongs to turn regularly to ensure even cooking. This is the best way to obtain that smoky flavour. The skin will blacken and shrivel with the heat. Cook until the skin is soft all over.

- Leave to cool for about 10 minutes.
- Peel the skins away and discard. Cut the aubergine into small pieces and mash with a fork. It is good to have some texture left.
- Gradually add the garlic, salt, lemon juice to taste and then the tahini.

To serve the stylish way: Garnish with the chopped parsley, sprinkle with cayenne pepper and drizzle over the olive oil. Top with some pomegranate seeds, chopped walnuts and red pepper.

Smoked Salmon and Dill Frittata `PAREV` `DAIRY-FREE`

- Preparation Time: 25 minutes
- Cooking Time: 20 minutes
- Serves: 6

✡

Ingredients
- 150g/5 oz dried fusilli pasta

✡

- 1–2 tbsp vegetable oil, to grease ramekins

✡

- 6 eggs, lightly whisked
- 250ml/9 fl oz/1 cup milk or single/soya cream (Alpro)
- 150g/5 oz smoked salmon, roughly chopped
- zest of 1 lemon
- 3 tbsp roughly chopped dill
- salt and freshly ground black pepper

✡

For the pickled cucumber salsa
- 3 pickled cucumbers, drained
- ½ fresh cucumber, cut in half
- 1 tbsp lemon juice
- 1 tsp sugar
- 1 tbsp finely chopped fresh dill
- 1 tbsp extra virgin olive oil

✡

- Garnish: 1 lemon, cut into wedges, sprigs of fresh dill

Frittata is an Italian open-faced omelette dish that can be made in advance and reheated gently when required. It is a creative way of using spare cooked pasta. I have made individual portions which make an impressive starter but one large frittata inside a cake tin would work equally well – cut into thick wedges to serve. I have accompanied it with a pickled cucumber salsa.

Method
- Cook the pasta according to the packet instructions and drain well.
- Line the base of six ramekins with non-stick baking parchment. Grease the sides with a little vegetable oil.
- Mix the eggs and milk or cream together. Stir in the smoked salmon, lemon zest and dill and season well with salt and pepper. Add to the pasta.
- Pre-heat the oven to 200°C/400°F/Gas mark 6.
- Using a large spoon, ladle the mixture into the prepared ramekins.
- Bake for 20 minutes or until golden.
- To make the salsa, finely chop the pickled cucumbers. Using a spoon, remove the seeds from the fresh cucumber and then finely chop and combine with the pickled cucumbers.
- Stir in the lemon juice, sugar, dill and extra virgin olive oil.

To serve the stylish way: Invert the ramekins on to a plate and serve with the pickled cucumber salsa. Garnish with a wedge of lemon, sprigs of fresh dill and a dusting of black pepper.

Stuffed Mushrooms with Hazelnut Gremolata

DAIRY-FREE   **GLUTEN-FREE**

PAREV   **P**   **V**

Info
- Preparation Time: 10 minutes
- Cooking Time: Approximately 20 minutes
- Serves: 8

✡

Ingredients
- 8 medium Portobello mushrooms (or any large flat mushroom variety), stems removed
- olive oil

✡

For the gremolata
- 200g/7 oz/1 cup whole hazelnuts
- 2 cloves garlic, finely chopped
- 2 tbsp finely chopped fresh flat-leaf parsley
- 2 tbsp finely grated lemon zest
- salt and freshly ground pepper

✡

- Garnish: Rocket salad

This recipe has become a firm favourite at many Yom Tov meals and dinner parties. As well as being delicious it also ideal for serving large numbers as it is straightforward to make and to serve. The large flat mushrooms are baked and topped with gremolata, which is a mixture of chopped parsley, lemon zest, hazelnuts and garlic. Any leftover gremolata is also delicious on top of salmon, grilled chicken or even lamb chops.

Numerous Jewish recipes include almonds but this focuses on hazelnuts. I have roasted them, which brings out their amazing aroma and flavour.

Method
- Pre-heat the oven to 200°C/400°F/Gas mark 6.
- Place the whole hazelnuts on a baking tray and roast for 10 minutes or until golden. Remove and roughly chop.
- Place the mushrooms on a tray lined with baking parchment, stalk side up.
- Brush mushrooms with olive oil and season with salt and pepper to taste.
- Bake for about 10 minutes or until just cooked through.
- Combine the gremolata ingredients in a medium bowl and season with salt and pepper to taste.
- Spread the gremolata over the mushrooms.
- Return to the oven for 10 minutes to complete cooking.

To serve the stylish way: Sit a Portobello mushroom on top of a bed of rocket salad. Drizzle with some olive oil.

Herb Omelette

PAREV P V DAIRY-FREE GLUTEN-FREE

Info
- Preparation Time: 10 minutes
- Cooking Time: Approximately 15 minutes
- Serves: 6–8

Ingredients
- 2–3 tbsp vegetable oil

✡

- 4 spring onions, finely chopped
- 2 cloves garlic, peeled and finely chopped
- 4 cherry tomatoes, cut into quarters
- 4 tbsp mixed fresh herbs (basil, mint, parsley or thyme), finely chopped
- 8 eggs

✡

- sea salt and freshly ground black pepper

✡

- Garnish: 6 tsp pesto sauce or sundried tomato paste, 5–6 cherry tomatoes, sliced, sprigs of basil

I am always looking for creative ways to introduce vegetables into family cooking, and I think you will find this herb omelette is a brilliant way of coping with fussy eaters. It is made with a variety of chopped herbs and some finely chopped tomatoes and spring onions. It can be eaten hot or cold. When cold, it makes a delicious option to go in a picnic box or packed lunch. Keep for Passover, for breakfast, a light lunch or as a tasty canapé.

A key ingredient is, of course, eggs, which have great symbolic meaning in Judaism. During Passover we use a hard-boiled egg to represent the festival sacrifices that were offered in the Temple. My husband's family take it one stage further by serving up sliced eggs in salt water as a sort of soup. It is to remind us of sorrow, the tears of the Israelites, and also the destruction of the Temple, because an egg is linked to death as it is traditionally served to mourners after a funeral.

Method
- Heat the oil in a large non-stick frying pan. Stir in the spring onions and garlic and cook for 3 minutes. Add the tomatoes and herbs.
- Break the eggs into a bowl, beat lightly with a fork and season with salt and pepper. Raise the heat under the vegetables. After a minute pour in the eggs, mix them with the other ingredients and stop stirring.
- Cook over a moderate heat for 5–6 minutes or until the omelette is puffed and golden brown. Use a palette knife to release the sides and base.
- Take a large plate, place it upside down over the pan and, holding it firmly with oven gloves, turn the pan and the omelette over onto it.

- Slide the omelette back into the pan and continue cooking until golden brown on the other side – 3–4 minutes.
- Remove from the heat and cut into wedges.

To serve the stylish way: Spoon a small amount of pesto on the centre of each wedge and garnish with slices of tomato and sprigs of basil.

Mini Spinach and Pine Nut Pies

D **V**

Info
- Preparation Time: 45 minutes
- Cooking Time: 45 minutes–1 hour
- Serves: 8

Ingredients
For the pastry
- 250g/9 oz plain flour
- pinch of salt
- 1 egg
- 75g/3 oz margarine
- 100g/4 oz Lancashire OR feta cheese

✡

For the filling
- 1 tbsp olive oil

✡

- 750g/1¾ lb frozen spinach, defrosted
- salt and freshly ground black pepper

✡

- 300ml/½ pint single cream
- 3 eggs, lightly whisked

✡

- 100g/4 oz Lancashire cheese
- 100g/4 oz pine nuts

These delicious individual pies are made with crumbly Lancashire cheese, similar in texture to feta but not as salty. The tartlets are ideal for a starter, picnics, packed lunches, as part of a buffet or on the menu for Shavuot. Serve them hot, cold or warm and enjoy with a tomato and olive salad. If you don't have eight mini loose-based pie tins make one large 22cm/9 inch pie and cut it into slices.

By and large the Jewish recipes from London and those from the North of England are very much the same but there is a distinctly Northern tradition of 'cheese buns' at Shavuot. Probably originating from Poland, they are made with sweet yeast dough with a filling of cream or curd cheese inside.

Manchester has an expanding Jewish community with a population of 35,000. In the early nineteenth century many immigrants arrived from Eastern and Central Europe, escaping persecution and poverty and attracted by the developing textile businesses, or simply stopping longer than expected on the long sea journey from Russia to the United States. Congregating in Red Bank and Strangeways, the new migrants worked hard making clothing, furniture and cloth caps and made a major contribution to the local economy.

The Manchester Jewish museum near Strangeways is well worth a visit; it is a former Spanish and Portuguese synagogue and dates back to 1874.

Method
- Place the flour, salt, egg, margarine and Lancashire or feta cheese in a food processor and whiz together to form a dough. Wrap the dough in cling film, slightly flatten and refrigerate for 30 minutes.
- Heat the olive oil in a frying pan. Cook the spinach gently to remove any excess water. It must be as dry as possible.

- Season well with salt and black pepper. Stir in the cream and eggs. Set aside.
- Pre-heat the oven to 200°C/400°F/Gas mark 6.
- Cut the pastry in half. Place on a lightly floured work surface. Roll out and make eight circle templates about 15 cm/6 inches in diameter to fit 11.5 cm/4½ inch individual loose-based tins. Press the pastry into the tins, line with foil and insert baking beans.
- Bake the pastry for 20 minutes. Remove the foil and baking beans.
- Crumble the Lancashire cheese into the base of the cooked pies. Spoon over the creamed spinach mixture and bake for 20 minutes or 40 minutes if you have made a large pie. Take out of the oven, scatter the pine nuts over the pies and cook for a final 5 minutes.

To serve the stylish way: Garnish with some chopped tomatoes and olives. Drizzle over a little extra virgin olive oil.

Lemongrass Fish Cakes with Lime Mayonnaise

PAREV   DAIRY-FREE

Info
- Preparation Time: 35 minutes
- Cooking Time: 15 minutes
- Makes: 36 fish cakes

Ingredients
- 400g/14 oz fresh white bread
- 6 tbsp fresh coriander
- 200g/7 oz/1 cup desiccated coconut

✡

- 2 stalks lemongrass

✡

- 950g/2¼ lb boneless, skinless white fish fillets e.g. cod or haddock
- 1–2 small red chillies, deseeded and finely chopped
- 3 tbsp light soy sauce
- 4 spring onions, roughly chopped
- 5–6 eggs

✡

- 3 tbsp cornflour
- zest of 2 limes
- salt and freshly ground black pepper, to taste
- 4 tbsp plain flour, for dipping
- 8 tbsp vegetable oil, for frying

✡

For the lime mayonnaise (or alternatively use chilli dipping sauce)
- 6 tbsp mayonnaise
- 2 tsp lime juice
- dash of chilli oil (optional)
- 0.5 cm/¼ inch piece of fresh ginger, peeled and finely grated

This recipe for impressive little Thai-flavoured fish cakes is ideal as one of a selection of canapés served before a dinner party.

Method
- Put the bread, coriander and coconut in a food processor and whiz briefly. Set aside.
- Clean the lemongrass by first removing the tough outer casing and finely chop.
- Roughly chop the fish fillets and place in the food processor. Add the chillies, chopped lemongrass, soy sauce, spring onions and 1 of the eggs. Blitz the mixture until you have a smooth paste – about 20 seconds.
- Spoon the fish mixture into a bowl, stir in the cornflour and lime zest and season with salt and pepper. Divide the mixture into 36 evenly sized portions and roll into round flat cakes.
- Dip them into some flour and the remaining 4–5 eggs (beaten) and finally into the coconut, coriander and breadcrumb mix.
- Heat the oil in a large frying pan. Add the fish cakes and cook for 3 minutes on each side until golden and crispy.
- Remove and drain on kitchen paper.
- For the mayonnaise, mix the ingredients together until combined.

To serve the stylish way: Place on a dark plate with the mayonnaise in a small dish and garnish with sprigs of coriander.

Mini Corn Fritters with Guacamole

PAREV Ⓥ CHANUKAH

Info
- Preparation Time: 35 minutes
- Cooking Time: 40 minutes
- Makes: 50

Ingredients
- 1 red pepper, deseeded, and cut in quarters
- 2 tbsp olive oil

✡

- 300g/11 oz/2 cups plain flour
- 100g/4 oz/¼ cup cornmeal (polenta)
- 1 tbsp baking powder
- 1 tbsp sugar
- 1–2 tsp dried chilli powder, or to taste
- 3 tbsp ground coriander
- salt and freshly ground black pepper, to taste

✡

- 3 eggs, lightly beaten
- 450ml/¾ pint milk or soya milk
- 3 tbsp snipped fresh chives
- 500g/1 lb frozen corn kernels, defrosted

✡

- vegetable or rapeseed oil, for frying

✡

- Garnish: sprigs of fresh coriander

This scrumptious recipe for corn fritters is a tasty vegetarian treat and is ideal as part of a Chanukah menu. It is terrific as a starter, snack or part of a finger food party menu. I like to serve it with an avocado dip of guacamole but if you prefer, enjoy with sweet chilli sauce or sour cream.

Corn fritters are typically associated with the American South (Georgia, West Virginia, North and South Carolina, Maryland and Delaware) where they are popular fried comfort foods. In fact, 16 July in America is National Corn Fritters day on which crispy fritters similar to the recipe below are enjoyed at tables across the nation.

South Carolina was the first place in the western world to elect a Jew to public office (in the eighteenth century) and it was also the birthplace of Reform Judaism in America.

In Maryland's Jewish museum visitors can view the historic site of the nation's third-oldest surviving synagogue, the Lloyd Street Synagogue.

Chef's Tip: These fritters freeze well but pack them between layers of baking parchment for ease of separation.

Method
- Pre-heat the grill to its highest setting.
- Brush the red pepper with the olive oil. Place under the grill for approximately 10 minutes or until the pepper is browned. Remove and place in a bowl. Cover immediately with cling film. Leave to cool. Remove the skin and set aside. Roughly chop.
- Place the flour, cornmeal, baking powder, sugar, chilli powder, coriander, salt and pepper in a large mixing bowl.
- Add the eggs, milk, chives, corn and chopped red pepper to the flour mixture and stir to combine. Leave to rest for 30 minutes.

- Pour the oil into a large frying pan so that it is 2 cm/1 inch deep. Heat it over a medium heat. Using a tablespoon, drop 5 to 6 spoonfuls of the batter into the oil. Do not overcrowd the frying pan. Use a slotted spoon to turn the fritters and cook until golden brown on both sides.
- Drain well on kitchen paper.
- Serve with a garnish of coriander sprigs and accompany with the Guacamole on page 16.

Guacamole

PAREV ⓟ DAIRY-FREE GLUTEN-FREE

Info
- Preparation Time: 15 minutes
- Cooking Time: No cooking
- Serves: 6

Ingredients
- 4 ripe tomatoes

✡

- 3 large ripe avocados
- 1 tbsp lemon juice
- 2 spring onions, finely chopped
- 2 tbsp finely chopped fresh coriander
- 1 red chilli, deseeded and finely chopped
- 2 cloves garlic, peeled and finely chopped
- salt and freshly ground black pepper

This is a very quick spicy dip that requires no cooking. This dip is also ideal with an assortment of crudités such as carrot sticks, radishes, peppers, button mushrooms, strips of celery, mangetout, sugar snaps, cucumber or even grilled vegetables.

Method
- Plunge the tomatoes into boiling water for 1–2 minutes or until the skins start to peel away. Peel off the skins and discard, remove the seeds and discard and roughly chop the rest.
- Halve and stone the avocados. Mash the avocado flesh in a bowl with the lemon juice. Stir in the chopped tomatoes, spring onions, coriander, chilli and garlic.
- Season well with salt and pepper and place in a serving bowl. Cover and refrigerate until ready to use.

To serve the stylish way: Put a teaspoon of guacamole on each corn fritter and garnish with a sprig of coriander. Alternatively put the guacamole into a ramekin surrounded by a plate of fritters.

Roasted Beetroot with Goat's Cheese Layers

(V) DAIRY-FREE GLUTEN-FREE

Info
- Preparation Time: 15 minutes
- Cooking Time: 1 hour and 10 minutes
- Serves: 6

Ingredients
- 3–4 raw beetroots, peeled

✡

- 4 tbsp olive oil
- salt and freshly ground black pepper
- 6 pieces of toast

✡

- 3 red onions, peeled and sliced
- 2 tbsp brown sugar
- 3 goat's cheese cylinders, cut 6 thin slices per cheese

✡

- 6 cocktail sticks
- 6 cherry tomatoes
- 200g/7 oz rocket/rucola

This is an easy tasty starter. It looks colourful and the goat's cheese and beetroot combine well. Beetroot is one of those vegetables that most people seem to dislike, often with no reason – when I made this for a cookery class, my students were pleasantly surprised. The circles of roasted beetroot and goat's cheese are stacked up and garnished with caramelised onions. The bottom layer of crispy toast adds texture and substance to this recipe.

Beetroot features in some of the most traditional Ashkenazi Jewish dishes such as Borsht and Chrain (a popular table pickle). In recent years the wider community has revived its use and popularity for two main reasons – its versatility and its healthiness. Beetroots can be steamed, boiled or roasted or even grated and eaten raw, and they are packed with antioxidants, iron, magnesium, potassium and vitamin B. In addition, they are low in fat and calories and help to stabilise blood glucose levels.

Chef's Tip: For a short cut, buy ready-cooked vacuum-packed beetroots with no vinegar.

Method
- Pre-heat the oven to 200°C/400°F/Gas mark 6.
- Using gloves, peel the beetroots and slice into thick rounds. You will need 18 slices.
- Place on a tray lined with baking parchment, drizzle with 2 tbsp of the olive oil and season with salt and pepper.
- Roast for 35–40 minutes, or until soft.
- Using an 7.5 cm/3 inch round cutter, make six round templates out of the toast.
- Heat the remaining olive oil in a frying pan. Sauté the onions with the brown sugar on a low heat with the lid on for 25 minutes so that they are sweet and golden. (Burnt onions taste bitter.)

- Line a baking tray with baking parchment and arrange the toast circles in an even layer.
- To assemble, place a generous spoonful of onions on each toast circle. Add some roasted beetroot and goat's cheese. Insert a cocktail stick in the centre to secure the layers. Sit a cherry tomato at the end of the stick.
- Reheat for 8–10 minutes until warm.

To serve the stylish way: Sit the goat's cheese layer in the centre of the plate and make a circle salad with the rocket. Drizzle over some extra virgin olive oil and serve immediately.

Onion Bhaji

PAREV • **V** • **DAIRY-FREE** • **GLUTEN-FREE**

Info
- Preparation Time: 30 minutes
- Cooking Time: 25 minutes
- Makes: Approximately 18 balls

Ingredients
- 5 large onions: 2 peeled and sliced, 3 peeled and finely chopped
- 2 tbsp coriander seeds, roughly crushed
- 2 tbsp cumin seeds
- 1–2 tsp chilli flakes
- 250g/9 oz gram flour (use plain flour if not available)
- 4 egg whites
- salt and freshly ground black pepper
- 5 tbsp baking powder
- vegetable oil, for deep-frying

A bhaji is a traditional Indian snack food, usually bought in the street and eaten with strong coffee or tea as a very basic versatile comfort food. Broken-up bhajis are used to top curries and other Indian meals. The main vegetables used are potatoes, onions and aubergines.

In the West, however, the onion bhaji is king of the starters in most Indian restaurants. It appears in a ball or cutlet shape served with a selection of chutneys or raita – natural yoghurt mixed with fresh mint, chopped cucumber, dried cumin and fresh coriander; its main function is to counter the heat of the chillies which I suggest you include according to your taste.

You can vary the size of these bhajis – small are ideal served as canapés with drinks.

Chef's Tip: They can be made in advance, stored for 1 day and reheated in the oven at 200°C/400°F/Gas mark 6 for 10 minutes.

Method
- Mix all the ingredients, except the oil, together.
- Divide into 18–20 balls.
- Heat the oil until hot and deep-fry the bhajis in batches until crisp and golden.
- Transfer to a plate lined with kitchen paper.
- Pre-heat the oven to 200°C/400°F/Gas mark 6.
- Place the cooked bhajis on a tray lined with baking parchment. Bake for a final 10 minutes to complete cooking.

To serve the stylish way: Place in a basket or deep bowl. Serve with raita and/or a selection of chutneys.

Soups

The most famous soup in the world has to be 'Jewish chicken soup' also known as 'Jewish Penicillin'. Traditionally made by boiling a chicken carcass and giblets alongside a range of vegetables including carrots, onions, leeks, parsnips, turnips and swedes, this consommé style soup improves the longer it cooks for and is always better the next day. And it's not all grandmothers' myths: researchers from the Nebraska Medical Centre, USA found that chicken soup (even when diluted with water) has anti-inflammatory properties that help soothe cold-ridden stuffy noses and sore throats. And you certainly don't have to be Jewish to make and enjoy chicken soup.

The secret of a good soup is an excellent stock, so either make your own or choose one that is not too salty. Personally if I use a bought stock, I never add salt until the very end as it is far easier to add than take away.

In this section I have included a variety of soups using both familiar and different ingredients – ideal at any time of the year.

Carrot and Apple Soup

Info

- Preparation Time: 20 minutes
- Cooking Time: 30 minutes
- Serves: 8

Ingredients

- 2 tbsp olive oil, for frying

✡

- 1 onion, peeled and roughly chopped
- 2 leeks, peeled and sliced

✡

- 1 kg/2¼ lb carrots (ideally organic), peeled and finely chopped
- 3 apples, peeled, cored and roughly chopped
- 2 litres/3½ pints/8 cups vegetable stock
- salt and freshly ground black pepper

✡

- Garnish: 1 carrot, peeled, 1 red apple, cored and thinly sliced

I love to bring spirituality to the table through recipes that have symbolic references to the relevant festival, either through their names or through their ingredients.

At Rosh Hashanah the focus is on 'simanim' – foods to eat to improve our year to come. So we eat carrots because the name in Yiddish is 'merren' which also means 'to increase' and because they look like gold coins and thus represent prosperity. Leeks also appear on this list – by eating them we are wishing bad luck to our enemies.

Apples are traditionally included in many Rosh Hashanah recipes as they remind us of the beautiful scent of the orchards in the Garden of Eden and are also associated with the giving and receiving of blessings.

Method

- Heat the olive oil in a large deep saucepan.
- Sauté the onion and leeks together until soft but not brown.
- Add the carrots, apples and stock. Bring to the boil, cover and simmer for 25 minutes or until soft.
- Transfer to a liquidiser and purée to a smooth consistency.
- Taste and season with salt and pepper.
- For the garnish, using a paring knife make very thin strips of carrots and apple.

To serve the stylish way: Sprinkle over some carrot 'spaghetti' and strips of apple.

Italian Tomato and Bread Soup   `PAREV` Ⓥ `SUCCOT`

Info
- Preparation Time: 10 minutes
- Cooking Time: 45 minutes
- Serves: 8

Ingredients
- 6 tbsp olive oil
- 175g/6 oz stale bread,
  cut into cubes
- salt and freshly ground black
  pepper

✡

- 2 onions, peeled
  and finely chopped
- 4 cloves garlic, peeled
  and finely chopped
- ½ red chilli, deseeded
  and finely chopped (optional)

✡

- 1 kg/2¼ lb ripe plum tomatoes,
  peeled and chopped or
  3 × 400g cans peeled plum
  tomatoes, chopped
- 1 tsp sugar
- 4 tbsp roughly chopped fresh
  basil
- 2 litres/3½ pints vegetable stock

✡

- Garnish: extra virgin olive oil,
  sprigs of fresh basil, croutons

This is a delicious Italian soup recipe that is made with store cupboard ingredients. Originally it was created to use up stale bread but if you do not have any, fresh bread placed in a low oven for 5 minutes will dry out to become 'stale'. Ripe plum tomatoes when in season provide the best flavour, but as their season fades, you can substitute canned for the fresh. Plum tomatoes are oval-shaped with less liquid and firmer flesh than salad varieties.

Jews have lived in Italy since the time of the Ancient Romans and they have had both good and bad times – depending on whoever ruled the country.

Almost all Italian Jews were deported, or worse, during World War Two. However, in the village of Assisi in central Italy, Father Rufino Niccacci, a Catholic priest, sheltered and protected almost 300 Jews from the Nazis. He hid them in monasteries and convents and taught them to behave as fake nuns and priests. Not a single Jew in Assisi was betrayed by the townsfolk or captured by the Nazis. Today there are over 40,000 Jews in Italy, most of them living in Rome and Milan.

Method
- Pre-heat the oven to 200°C/400°F/Gas mark 6.
- Drizzle 2–3 tbsp of the olive oil over the cubed bread. Season with salt and pepper and bake for 10 minutes. Remove and set aside.
- Heat the remaining oil in a large saucepan and add the onions, garlic, chilli (if using) and cook until they soften. Stir in the tomatoes, bread (leave some for garnish), sugar and basil. Season with salt and pepper to taste.
- Cook over a moderate heat for 15 minutes, stirring occasionally.
- Add the stock to the tomato mixture, bring to the boil, cover and reduce the heat to simmer for 15 minutes.

- Liquidise or purée 3 ladles of the soup and return to the saucepan.
- Taste and adjust the seasoning accordingly.

To serve the stylish way: Swirl a little extra virgin olive oil onto the soup and garnish with some sprigs of fresh basil and the reserved croutons.

Sweet Potato and Chestnut Soup with Garlic Croutons

PAREV V RH
SUCCOT DAIRY-FREE

Info
- Preparation Time: 20 minutes
- Cooking Time: 30 minutes
- Serves: 6–8

Ingredients
- 2 tbsp olive oil

✿

- 1.3 kg/2½ lb sweet potatoes (approximately 5 potatoes), peeled and roughly chopped into small pieces
- 2 red onions, peeled and roughly chopped
- 2 tsp dried cinnamon
- 4 cloves garlic, peeled and finely chopped

✿

- 1.5 litres/2¼ pints/6 cups vegetable or chicken stock
- salt and freshly ground black pepper
- 200g/7 oz/1 cup vacuum-packed chestnuts, roughly chopped

✿

- Garnish: garlic croutons: 3 slices bread, 3 cloves garlic, peeled and crushed, 3 tbsp extra virgin olive oil, salt and pepper, to taste

I first came across sweet potatoes as an exciting new product about 18 years ago when I was weaning my daughter onto solids. Today they are readily available in supermarkets and like all potatoes are extremely versatile.

With the ever-growing interest in health and natural foods, the low-fat high-vitamin sweet potato is quickly finding its place in the family diet. It blends well with herbs, spices and flavourings, producing delicious dishes of all types from main dishes, casseroles and salads to breads and desserts… and soups.

This is a wonderful, warming soup with a great combination of flavours. It is easy to prepare and makes an interesting start to most main courses. It will freeze, so make double and keep one batch for another time. Although roasting chestnuts is a fun way of spending a Sunday afternoon and they taste delicious hot off the pan, for this recipe you can buy them ready-peeled, vacuum-packed or frozen to save time.

Sweet potato and chestnuts is quite an American combination and ideal for those who celebrate Thanksgiving – and America has the second-largest Jewish population in the world (Israel being first of course).

Method
- Heat the olive oil in a large saucepan. Sauté the sweet potatoes, onions, cinnamon and garlic for 5 minutes.
- Add the stock. Bring to the boil and simmer for 20 minutes.
- Pre-heat the oven to 200°C/400°F/Gas mark 6.
- To make the croutons, cut the bread into cubes. Place on a baking sheet lined with baking parchment. Sprinkle over the crushed garlic, oil and seasoning. Combine.
- Bake for 10 minutes or until golden brown. Remove from the oven and set aside.

- Taste the soup and season accordingly. Add the chestnuts.
- Liquidise or purée to a smooth consistency. Return this to the saucepan and reheat when ready to serve.

To serve the stylish way: Serve the hot soup in warmed bowls with the garlic croutons.

Beetroot and Carrot Soup with Coriander Oil

PAREV ⓟ ◆RH

Ⓥ DAIRY-FREE GLUTEN-FREE

Info
- Preparation Time: 15 minutes
- Cooking Time: 1 hour
- Serves: 10
- Will freeze

Ingredients
- 2 tbsp olive oil

✡

- 2 medium-sized onions, peeled and roughly chopped
- 2 tbsp dried coriander
- 2 cloves garlic, peeled and sliced

✡

- 900g/2 lb carrots, peeled and sliced
- 7 raw beetroots (1.3 kg/2½ lb), peeled and roughly chopped
- 650g/1½ lb sweet potatoes, peeled and roughly chopped
- 2 litres/3½ pints/8 cups vegetable stock
- salt and pepper, to taste

✡

- Garnish: coriander oil: 50ml/2 fl oz/¼ cup extra virgin olive oil, 20g/¾ oz fresh coriander

The Jewish celebration of Passover is full of symbolism. One of the items on the Seder plate is the lamb shank bone, which reminds us of the Passover sacrifices. Some communities use chicken bones in place of the shank bone as chickens were never sacrificed, and I know some vegetarians who use beetroot to represent the blood of the Paschal lamb.

This colourful beetroot soup is perfect for family-style eating either at Yom Tov or for those looking for a bit of a change on Friday night. It is easy to cook and can be made in advance, taking some of the pressure off the cook.

Method
- Heat the oil in a deep saucepan. Fry the onions, dried coriander and garlic for about 5 minutes until soft.
- Add the carrots, beetroots, sweet potatoes and stock.
- Bring to the boil and simmer for about 50 minutes or until the vegetables are soft.
- Pour into a blender and whiz until smooth. Return to the saucepan and reheat. Season with salt and pepper to taste.
- For the coriander oil, place the oil and coriander in a food processor and pulse until smooth.

To serve the stylish way: Garnish with a swirl of coriander oil.

Tricolour Minestrone

PAREV SUCCOT V

Info
- Preparation Time: 25 minutes
- Cooking Time: 25 minutes
- Serves: 8

Ingredients
- 3 tbsp olive oil
- 2 red onions, finely chopped
- 3 cloves garlic, peeled
  and finely chopped

✡

- 1 tbsp sun-dried tomato paste
- 450g/1 lb plum tomatoes, cut
  into small pieces
- 2 green courgettes, trimmed and
  roughly chopped
- 1 yellow courgette or use a yellow
  pepper if unavailable, trimmed and
  roughly chopped
- 400g/14 oz can cannellini beans,
  rinsed and drained

✡

- 3 litres/5¼ pints/12 cups
  vegetable stock
- 50g/2 oz/¼ cup small pasta
  e.g. farfalline (small bows) or
  macaroni, cooked
- salt and freshly
  ground black pepper
- 6 tbsp shredded fresh basil
- 75g/3 oz ⅓ cup Parmesan
  cheese, grated

In Italy, minestrone usually means a vegetable soup, although it might also contain chicken or meat broth, so always check this. The vegetables vary from recipe to recipe and region to region and may have pasta, beans or rice added as well. For this soup I have chosen vegetables that are green, red and white, giving a bright-coloured appearance and texture that make the most of the freshness from summer produce.

Of all the amazing cities in Italy, Venice has to be the one I could visit time and time again. On our first anniversary, my husband and I went around the Jewish quarter: five ancient synagogues, a museum, a yeshiva and a kosher restaurant all within a small block of ancient buildings. Gam Gam kosher restaurant in the ghetto is a real must, offering the authentic flavour of Venice with tasty dishes such as fried artichokes, sour sardines (sounds strange but it is truly delicious), and salads like roasted peppers with balsamic vinegar as well as a good bowl of minestrone soup.

We spoke to the Chabad Rebbetzin who runs the restaurant and she told us how the name of the restaurant came about. In Hebrew 'Gam gam' means 'also' and they used the name because they like to bring Jewish tradition and Italian food together.

Method
- Heat the oil in a large saucepan and sauté the onions and garlic and cook gently for 5 minutes.
- Stir in the sun-dried tomato paste, chopped tomatoes, courgettes, yellow pepper (if using) and beans.
- Mix well and cook for a further 5 minutes. Stir from time to time so that the vegetables do not stick to the saucepan.
- Add the stock, bring to the boil and simmer gently for 10 minutes or until the vegetables are just cooked. (Overcooked courgettes lose their colour and texture.)
- Add the cooked pasta and stir. Check the seasoning.

To serve the stylish way: Remove the pan from the heat and stir in the basil and half of the cheese. Taste for seasoning. Serve hot with the remaining cheese.

Roasted Red Pepper and Carrot Soup

PAREV V P

RH DAIRY-FREE GLUTEN-FREE

Info
- Preparation Time: 20 minutes
- Cooking Time: 35 minutes plus 10 minutes for cooling
- Serves: 8

Ingredients
- 6 large red peppers, deseeded and cut into quarters
- 3 tbsp olive oil

✿

- 2 onions, peeled and roughly chopped
- 6 carrots, peeled and roughly chopped
- 4 cloves garlic, peeled and finely chopped
- 2 litres/3½ pints/8 cups vegetable or chicken stock

✿

- large bunch of fresh basil
- salt and freshly ground black pepper

✿

- Garnish: sprigs of basil

Soup is one of the best starters for a Seder meal because it is so easy and quick to serve, especially if you have a large crowd to cater for. This recipe is a delicious, vibrant, tasty soup that can be made in advance and uses readily available low-fat Passover ingredients. Cooked with garlic and basil, it is full of the flavours of the Mediterranean and provides a delightful change from regular carrot soup.

Method
- Pre-heat the grill to its highest setting.
- Place the peppers on an oven tray and brush them with olive oil. Grill skin side up for about 10 minutes, or until the skins have blackened and blistered.
- Meanwhile, heat a large deep saucepan with the remaining olive oil. Sauté the onions, carrots and garlic for about 5 minutes. Add the stock and bring to the boil. Cover and simmer for 15 minutes or until the carrots are soft.
- Remove the peppers from the grill and immediately transfer to a dish and cover with cling film. Leave for 10 minutes to cool.
- Remove the skins from the peppers and roughly chop. Keep one red pepper back for garnish but add the rest to the soup with the basil.
- Simmer the soup for a final 5 minutes.
- Liquidise the soup to produce a vibrant purée consistency. Return to the saucepan. Taste and adjust the seasoning.

To serve the stylish way: Sprinkle the retained chopped red pepper over the soup and garnish with sprigs of fresh basil.

Cinnamon and Pumpkin Soup   PAREV ◆RH◆ Ⓥ DAIRY-FREE

Info
- Preparation Time: 40 minutes
- Cooking Time: 45 minutes
- Serves: 8

Ingredients
- 2 tbsp vegetable oil, for frying

✿

- 2 onions, peeled and finely chopped
- 2 tbsp dried cinnamon
- 1 leek, trimmed and sliced
- 1 kg/2¼ lb pumpkin flesh, peeled and diced
- 2 carrots, peeled and finely chopped
- 2 sticks of celery, sliced

✿

- 75g/3 oz/¼ cup plain flour

✿

- 1.5 litres/2½ pints/6 cups hot vegetable stock
- 250ml/9 fl oz/1 cup orange juice
- bouquet garni made with 2 bay leaves, 2 sprigs of thyme, 2 half sticks of celery
- salt and freshly ground black pepper

✿

For the cinnamon croutons
- 4 slices of bread
- extra virgin olive oil
- 2 tsp dried cinnamon
- salt and freshly ground black pepper

✿

- Garnish: cinnamon croutons

This recipe produces a tasty smooth soup that is ideal for Shabbat and Yom Tov as it makes a large quantity and is quick to prepare. In addition, pumpkin is listed as one of the symbolic foods that we should have on Rosh Hashanah. Pumpkins have thick skins, and so when we eat them or dishes made from them we are expressing the hope that 'as this vegetable has been protected by a thick skin, God will protect us and gird us with strength'.

Pumpkin is an extremely versatile vegetable and not just at Hallowe'en! It is great baked, in risottos, roasted, stuffed, made into pies, or even used to make bread. Its vibrant colour indicates that it is abundant in beta-carotene, an important antioxidant (like carrots).

Method
- Heat the vegetable oil in a large saucepan.
- Sauté the onions, cinnamon, leek, pumpkin, carrots and celery for about 5 minutes until slightly softened.
- Stir in the flour and cook for 1 minute.
- Add the stock and orange juice and bring to the boil.
- Make the bouquet garni (mixed fresh herbs) by tying a piece of string around the bay leaves, thyme and celery sticks and add to the soup. Season with salt and pepper.
- Simmer for 40 minutes. Remove the bouquet garni.
- Pre-heat the oven to 200°C/400°F/Gas mark 6.
- Make the croutons by cutting the bread into small cubes. Drizzle with extra virgin olive oil, sprinkle with cinnamon and season with salt and pepper. Toss together so that they are all evenly coated.
- Bake for 8–10 minutes or until crispy and evenly toasted. Remove and set aside.
- Liquidise the soup until smooth. Return to the saucepan, reheat and adjust the seasoning accordingly.

To serve the stylish way: Serve hot with cinnamon croutons.

Chinese Chicken and Sweetcorn Soup

Info
- Preparation Time: 15 minutes
- Cooking Time: 25 minutes
- Serves: 4

Ingredients
- 1.3 litres/2¼ pints/5 cups chicken stock

✡

- 450g/1 lb canned sweetcorn (drained)
- 3 spring onions, trimmed and finely chopped
- 1 cm/½ inch piece of fresh ginger, peeled and finely chopped
- 1 tbsp dry sherry or Chinese rice wine
- 2–3 tsp soy sauce
- 1 tsp soft brown sugar

✡

- 225g/8 oz cooked chicken, shredded into pieces

✡

- 2 eggs
- 1 tsp sesame oil
- freshly ground black pepper

✡

- Garnish: 2 tbsp roughly chopped fresh coriander

Most Jews just love Chinese food and there are a number of excellent kosher Chinese restaurants in London that I enjoy visiting. Perhaps it is because Chinese food – like Jewish food – is based around tradition, sharing, family meals, symbolic ingredients and special dishes. We also share a love of dumplings, noodles, rice, fried and stuffed foods and sweet, sour and salty flavours.

This particular soup is authentic, delicious and simple to make. It's a real crowd pleaser and will quickly become a family favourite.

There are records of Jews in China from the seventh and eighth centuries. Numbers have always been very small as historically religious pluralism and diversity have never been well tolerated by the Chinese. The Jews of Kaifeng are probably the most famous; however, today only about 400 remain with only a few dozen practising the religion.

Most Jews in China today are tourists, expatriate workers, academics or students and the Chabad centres in both Beijing and Shanghai help to ensure a full Jewish and kosher life can be enjoyed by them all. My own daughter, Abbie, visited them during her recent trip to China.

Method
- Pour the chicken stock into a wok or saucepan and bring to the boil.
- Add the corn, spring onions, ginger, sherry or Chinese rice wine, soy sauce and brown sugar.
- Bring back to the boil, then add the chicken.
- Beat the eggs with the sesame oil and pepper and stir into the soup in a slow steady stream, stirring constantly.
- Taste and season accordingly.

To serve the stylish way: Garnish with chopped coriander and serve immediately.

Udon Noodles with Egg Broth and Ginger

DAIRY-FREE   PAREV   SHABBAT   V

Info
- Preparation Time: 20 minutes
- Cooking Time: 15 minutes
- Serves: 6–8

Ingredients
For the soup
- 2 litres/3½ pints/8 cups water
- 2 cubes vegetable stock or parev chicken stock
- 3 tbsp mirin (Chinese rice wine) or kosher dry sherry
- 4 tbsp soy sauce
- 1 tbsp Chinese 5 spice powder or to taste
- 10 cm/4 inch ginger, peeled and finely grated
- salt and freshly ground black pepper

✡

- 1 nori seaweed roll, finely shredded
- 2 tbsp cornflour
- 300g/11 oz udon noodles or thick egg noodles
- 4 eggs, beaten
- 100g/4 oz/¼ cup mustard and cress
- 8 spring onions, trimmed and finely sliced

✡

- Garnish: soy sauce

I like to make this soup as the starter of a Japanese meal and it is perfect for a cold winter's day as it is filling and uses ginger, an ingredient which is highly valued for its medicinal properties: it is believed to warm the body and help the digestion. This recipe is thickened with cornflour and retains its heat for a long time. Kosher oriental ingredients are increasingly easy to obtain: check your local kosher store and see their new stock. Udon noodles are thick wheat noodles which are eaten all over the world, but if unavailable use broad lokshen as a substitute.

Method
- To make the soup, place the water and the soup ingredients in a deep saucepan and bring to the boil. Taste and adjust the seasoning. Add the seaweed.
- Blend the cornflour with 4 tbsp of water. Add the cornflour to the simmering soup, stirring continuously.
- Cook the noodles according to the packet instructions.
- Mix the eggs, mustard and cress and spring onions in a small bowl. Stir the soup once again to create a whirlpool. Pour the eggs slowly into the soup pan just before serving.
- Drain the noodles, divide between eight bowls and pour over the soup.

To serve the stylish way: Garnish with a swirl of soy sauce.

Wild Mushroom and Leek Soup

GLUTEN-FREE Ⓥ
DAIRY-FREE **PAREV**

Info
- Preparation Time: 15 minutes
- Cooking Time: 35 minutes
- Serves: 8

Ingredients
- 675g/1½ lb fresh assorted mushrooms

✡

- 3 tbsp olive oil
- 4 leeks, trimmed and thinly sliced
- 1 onion, peeled and finely chopped
- bunch of fresh thyme, leaves only
- 4 cloves garlic, peeled and finely chopped

✡

- 2 litres/3¼ pints/8 cups parev chicken or vegetable stock (use 2 stock cubes)
- 150ml/5 fl oz/¾ cup red wine
- salt and freshly ground black pepper

✡

- Garnish: 120ml/4 fl oz/½ cup double or soya cream

I like to serve soup as the starter when I am entertaining for a large family gathering as it is easy to serve, can be made in advance and only takes up one ring on my stove and one saucepan.

For this recipe I have used a combination of mushrooms, which helps to strengthen the true earthy flavour and colour.

To store mushrooms never put them in a plastic bag as they will sweat and rot. Put them in a paper bag (some supermarkets provide these next to the mushroom shelves) and keep them in the vegetable section of the fridge for no more than three days.

Method
- Finely chop the mushrooms and set aside.
- Heat the oil in a large saucepan. Add the leeks, onion, thyme, garlic and mushrooms.
- Sauté for 5 minutes, stirring frequently until softened but not coloured.
- Pour in the stock and red wine. Season well with salt and pepper. Simmer for 30 minutes over a low heat, stirring from time to time.
- Pour about three-quarters of the soup into a blender and process until smooth. Pour this back into the saucepan.
- Check the seasoning and reheat the soup when ready.

To serve the stylish way: Serve the soup hot and garnish with a tablespoon of cream swirled on the top of each bowl.

Turkish Red Lentil and Carrot Soup

V · PAREV · RH · DAIRY-FREE · GLUTEN-FREE

Info
- Preparation Time: 20 minutes
- Cooking Time: 35 minutes
- Serves: 10

Ingredients
- 280g/10 oz red lentils

✡

- 1 tbsp vegetable oil

✡

- 3 onions, peeled and finely chopped
- 3 cloves garlic, peeled and chopped
- ½–1 tbsp smoked paprika
- 1 tbsp sumac
- 6 carrots (approx. 700g/1¾ lb), peeled and roughly chopped
- 200g/7 oz potatoes, peeled and diced

✡

- 2 litres/3½ pints/8 cups vegetable stock
- 2 tbsp tomato purée
- 1 tsp salt (or to taste)
- freshly ground black pepper, to taste

✡

- juice of 1 lemon

✡

- Garnish: 1 lemon, cut into wedges

Red lentil soup can be found on the menu at most Turkish restaurants and as you can imagine, each has their own secret twist of the classic version – in this one it is the smoked paprika and sumac that provide the subtle and exquisite flavours.

When I was in Istanbul recently, I attended a local cookery class and this is a variation of one of the recipes we prepared. I have kept this recipe vegetarian and without butter and love to serve it with sesame bread.

Method
- Place the lentils in a colander and rinse. Set aside.
- Heat the oil in a large deep saucepan.
- Sauté the onions, garlic, smoked paprika, sumac, carrots and potatoes in the oil for 5 minutes.
- Add the lentils, stock and tomato purée.
- Bring to the boil, reduce the heat, cover and simmer for 30 minutes.
- Season with salt and pepper to taste.
- Liquidise the soup. Taste, add the lemon juice and adjust the seasoning accordingly.

To serve the stylish way: Garnish with segments of lemon on the side.

Breads

Since the days of the Old Testament, bread has played a significant role in Jewish life, linking the past with today.

In the wilderness of the Sinai desert, manna was sent by God from heaven every day and was like 'coriander seed, white and tasted like wafers made with honey'. The Israelites had to have faith that the supplies of manna would last; however, on Friday they were allowed to collect twice the amount of manna as it was forbidden to collect on the Sabbath. Today, on a Friday night and all festival evenings we bless and enjoy two loaves of challah (traditional plaited bread) before commencing the meal, as a reminder of those ancient days.

For me homemade bread is as therapeutic to make as it is to eat. It fills my kitchen with a delicious aroma and the anticipation of eating it fresh and warm always makes my mouth water. I have included a variety of breads from fancy tomato and basil to onion. For those wanting a quick bread fix, recipes such as bread sticks and beer bread will satisfy your hunger.

Making homemade bread is easier than you think and a bread maker is not necessarily required: although if you have one, add the ingredients and follow the instructions according to your machine.

There are a few essential rules:

- Yeast needs warm tepid water in order for it to ferment; if it is too hot it will kill the yeast.
- It is quickest and easiest to make bread in a food mixer using a dough hook. Alternatively use a flat beater – a whisk will not work.
- A warm place is required for the dough to rise to double its volume – somewhere like an airing cupboard, near a radiator or on a sunny window sill.
- A second rising (proving) will guarantee a light texture.

Onion Bread

Info

- Preparation Time: 15 minutes plus 1½ hour rising and 25 minutes proving
- Cooking Time: 45 minutes for a loaf or 20 minutes for rolls
- Makes: 1 loaf or approximately 16 small rolls

Ingredients

- 1 sachet dried yeast (7g/¼ oz)
- 250ml/9 fl oz/1 cup warm water

✡

- 1 tbsp olive oil
- 1 onion, peeled and roughly chopped

✡

- 550g/1¼ lb strong white bread flour
- 1 tsp sugar
- 3 tsp salt

✡

- 1–2 egg yolks, for glazing

After Passover, I always like to be creative and write a new bread recipe. It's the smell and texture of fresh bread that I miss most during this festival and this recipe satisfies on both counts.

This tasty savoury bread is great with most soups and makes a delicious combination with cheddar and pickles. You can use red or white onions – just make sure that when you cook the onions you do not burn them as this will make the bread taste bitter.

Method

- Sprinkle the yeast into 100ml/3½ fl oz of the warm water and leave it for 5 minutes to dissolve.
- Heat the olive oil in a small frying pan. Sauté the onion until it is soft but not brown.
- Place the flour, cooked onion, sugar, salt and yeast mixture in the mixer. Gradually add the remaining water as needed until it forms a moist dough.
- Turn the dough out onto a lightly floured work surface. Knead gently for 2 minutes. Place in a bowl greased with some olive oil. Cover with some cling film and leave to rise for 1½ hours in a warm room or until doubled in size.
- Pre-heat the oven to 200°C/400°F/Gas mark 6.
- Knock back the dough and shape into a round loaf, or cut off 55g/2 oz portions of dough to make individual round rolls.
- Place on a baking tray lined with baking parchment. Leave to prove for 25 minutes.
- Glaze with beaten egg yolk.
- Bake for 45 minutes, or 20 minutes for the individual rolls, until golden and hollow-sounding when tapped underneath.
- Cool on a wire rack.

Granary Bread

PAREV **V**

Info
- Preparation Time: 10 minutes plus 2 hours rising and 25 minutes proving
- Cooking Time: 45 minutes for a loaf or 20 minutes for the rolls
- Makes: 1 loaf or approximately 22 small rolls

Ingredients
- 2 x 7g/¼ oz sachet of fast action yeast
- 450ml/15 fl oz/ 2 cups warm water

✡

- 500g/1 lb granary flour
- 2 tsp salt
- 250g/9 oz strong white flour
- 2 tbsp olive oil
- 1 tbsp honey

✡

- 2–3 egg yolks, for glazing

Today, probably more than ever, we are spoilt for choice with the vast variety of breads available in our kosher shops: rye, wholemeal, brown, white, coarse semolina, spelt and, my favourite, granary.

However, home baking is still very satisfying and can produce excellent breads, with that delicious fresh baked taste and smell. This recipe is so simple and well worth the effort.

Method
- Sprinkle the yeast into 100ml/3½ fl oz of the warm water and leave it for 5 minutes to dissolve.
- Using a food mixer, combine the granary flour, salt, strong white flour, olive oil and honey. Add the yeast mixture.
- Gradually add the remaining water as needed until it forms a moist dough.
- Turn the dough out onto a lightly floured work surface. Knead gently for 2 minutes. Place in a bowl greased with olive oil. Cover with cling film and leave to rise for about 2 hours in a warm room or until doubled in size.
- Pre-heat the oven to 200°C/400°F/Gas mark 6.
- Knock back the dough and shape into a loaf or cut off 55g/ 2 oz portions to make individual round rolls.
- Place on a baking tray lined with baking parchment. Leave to prove for 25 minutes.
- Glaze with beaten egg yolk.
- Bake for 45 minutes, or 20 minutes for the individual rolls, until golden and hollow-sounding when tapped underneath.
- Cool on a wire rack.

Sesame Bread

PAREV V

Info
- Preparation Time: 15 minutes plus 1 hour for rising
- Cooking Time: 25–30 minutes
- Makes: 8 rolls

Ingredients
- 1 × 7g/¼ oz sachet dried yeast
- 250ml/9 fl oz warm water
- 1 tsp sugar

✿

- 500g/1 lb strong white flour
- 1 tbsp salt

✿

- 2–3 egg yolks, for glazing
- 4 tbsp sesame seeds

This tasty round bread is delicious with soup, stews, tagines and dips or as a snack with your favourite spread. Instead of sesame seeds you can use cumin seeds, poppy seeds or black sesame seeds. The puffy round loaves freeze well; make double the quantity and keep the extra for another time.

Sesame bread is very much on the menu for most Mizrachi Jews – those who come from Syria, Iraq, Lebanon, Yemen, Iran (Persia), Afghanistan, Uzbekistan, Egypt, Kurdistan and Georgia. Their cuisine makes liberal use of cumin, pepper, saffron and sesame seeds, and many recipes are influenced by the hot climate and feature salads, stuffed vegetables, lentils, dried fruits, herbs, chickpeas and nuts. Sesame bread is used as a dipping bread to soak up the juices of popular dishes like tebit (chicken and rice) and ingriyi (sweet-and-sour meat topped with aubergines) as well as all the meze dishes like hummus, moutabel and tabbouleh.

Method
- Dilute the yeast in 100ml/3½ fl oz of the warm water. Stir in the sugar and leave for 5 minutes.
- Place the flour and salt in a food mixer. Add the diluted yeast and mix the dough adding the remaining warm water so that it forms a round ball. Add more flour if it is too sticky to handle.
- Divide the dough into eight equal parts and shape into rounds.
- Line an oven tray with baking parchment. Place the rolls on the baking tray and cover. Leave to rise for 1 hour.
- Glaze with beaten egg yolk and sprinkle with sesame seeds.
- Pre-heat the oven to 200°C/400°F/Gas mark 6.
- Bake for 25–30 minutes or until golden.

Tomato and Basil Bread

Info

- Preparation Time: 20 minutes plus 1 hour 30 minutes for rising
- Cooking Time: 30 minutes
- Makes: 3 loaves

Ingredients

- 100g/4 oz ripe tomatoes

✡

- 2 × 7g/¼ oz sachets dried yeast
- approx. 400ml/14 fl oz warm water

✡

- 800g/2 lb strong white flour
- 2 tsp salt
- 1 tsp sun-dried tomato paste
- 2 tbsp roughly chopped fresh basil
- 1 tsp dried chilli pepper flakes or ½ tsp fresh chilli, finely chopped (optional)

✡

- 1 tbsp olive oil, to grease bowl

✡

- To glaze: 2–3 egg yolks

I love everything about this bread: the taste, colour and texture.
  Some tomatoes are juicier than others. Because of this you may have to vary the amount of additional water in this recipe. You are aiming for a smooth, workable dough.

Method

- Skin the tomatoes by immersing them in boiling water for 1 minute. Score the skin with a knife and peel away. Discard the cores and remove the seeds using a teaspoon. Roughly chop the remaining flesh and use this flesh only.
- Dissolve the yeast in 100ml/3½ fl oz of the warm water and leave for 5 minutes.
- Mix the flour and salt together. Add the yeast mixture, chopped tomatoes, tomato paste, basil and chilli (if using).
- Knead the dough either in a food mixer or by hand. Add the remaining warm water slowly so that the dough is smooth and not too wet. Add extra flour if it becomes too sticky.
- Grease a large bowl with a little olive oil. Transfer the dough, cover with cling film and leave in a warm place for 1 hour or until doubled in size.
- Line a tray with non-stick baking parchment.
- Knock back the dough and divide into three pieces.
- Lightly knead and shape into round loaves. Leave to rise again for 30 minutes. Glaze with beaten egg yolk.
- Pre-heat the oven to 200°C/400°F/Gas mark 6.
- Bake for 30 minutes or until golden and hollow-sounding when tapped underneath.
- Cool on a wire rack.

To serve the stylish way: Cut into slices and serve with a dipping bowl of extra virgin olive oil and balsamic vinegar.

Cheese and Beer Bread

Info
- Preparation Time: 15 minutes
- Cooking Time: 45 minutes
- Makes: 1 loaf

Ingredients
- 1 tbsp vegetable oil, to grease the tin

✡

- 675g/1½ lb plain flour
- 1 tbsp sugar
- 1 tsp salt
- 1 tsp baking powder
- 2 tbsp grated Cheddar cheese
- 1 tsp mustard

✡

- 370ml/13 fl oz beer or lager

✡

- To glaze: 1 egg yolk

One of the main excuses people give for not making their own bread is that it is too time-consuming. Another popular one is that they don't understand the rules of yeast. Well I have solved both of these culinary challenges with this amazing beer bread. Simply by using beer to make bread you bypass all the rising and proving stages (which are the time-consuming elements). And you don't have to manage the yeast as beer already contains yeast.

Using very few ingredients, this bread is both quick and delicious. The stronger the beer, the heavier the bread will be. Serve as part of a ploughman's lunch or enjoy with soup.

For a parev version omit the cheese and mustard and substitute 2 tbsp chopped sun-dried tomatoes and 1 tbsp chopped fresh basil.

Method
- Line and grease a 900g/2 lb loaf tin with baking parchment.
- Pre-heat the oven to 180°C/350°F/Gas mark 4.
- Combine the flour, sugar, salt, baking powder, cheese and mustard in a food processor.
- Slowly add the beer and mix until well combined.
- Spread into the loaf tin so it is evenly distributed.
- Make diagonal knife slashes about 1 cm/½ inch deep.
- Glaze with egg yolk.
- Bake for 45 minutes or until golden brown and when a skewer inserted in the centre comes out clean.
- Leave in the tin for 10 minutes before removing.

Serve warm or at room temperature.

Herb Pitta Bread Sticks

Info
- Preparation Time: 10 minutes
- Cooking Time: 10 minutes
- Serves: 6

Ingredients
- 6 pitta bread, cut into 2 cm/1 inch wide strips
- 2 tbsp extra virgin olive oil

✡

- salt and freshly ground black pepper
- 2 tbsp dried herbs, zaatar or dried garlic herb mix

Pitta bread is widely available and extremely versatile. Turning fresh or slightly stale pitta bread into these tasty and very more-ish bread sticks is simple and useful. Serve as part of a meze starter, with your soup, or with a dip – the choice is yours. Whilst devising this recipe I also discovered that the sticks are delicious eaten on their own.

Chef's Tip: Can be made up to 3 days in advance and stored in a sealed bag or frozen.

Method
- Pre-heat the oven to 200°C/400°F/Gas mark 6.
- Place the pitta strips on a baking tray.
- Drizzle over the oil, coating the strips evenly.
- Season with salt, pepper and the dried herbs.
- Bake for 10 minutes or until golden. Serve immediately or when required.

To serve the stylish way: Serve in a wine glass.

Chapter 2

Fresh and Crunchy

—

Salads

Fresh and Crunchy

Salads have had a complete transformation over the last decade. Thirty years ago, a salad consisted of cos lettuce, tomatoes, grated carrots, cucumber and possibly peppers. We now have readily available in the supermarkets an explosion of new ingredients – a vast array of seeds, leaves, oils and fresh herbs. With the enormous possible combinations you can have a completely new salad experience every day. They can be hot, cold or warm (tiede), themed with a Thai or Chinese flavour and served as a starter, main course or side dish.

A salad a day keeps the doctor away. With vegetables at their core, salads are a great source of vitamin C, the leafiest amongst them supply plenty of fibre and the more colourful they are, the more vitamins they include. I feel that you can never have too many salad recipes especially as on Shabbat and Yom Tov cold meals are popular. My recipes include salads that have ingredients ideal for these occasions as well as for quick lunches, side dishes or starters for dinner parties.

A good chef tip is if you buy bags of salads or herbs, take them out of their wrapping. Wash, dry and transfer to a plastic container and cover with damp kitchen paper. You will be amazed how much longer they will last.

Salads
- Sweet potato, pomegranate and pumpkin seed salad
- Crunchy papaya salad
- Gravadlax and green lentil salad
- Red and green summer salad
- Vegetarian sushi salad
- Sicilian baby aubergine salad
- Crispy noodle salad
- Mozzarella salad with pear and cranberries
- Cherry and chicken salad
- Pomegranate kasha salad with honey dressing
- Italian matza salad
- Lancashire cheese with honey roasted beetroot salad

Sweet Potato, Pomegranate and Pumpkin Seed Salad

Info
- Preparation Time: 20 minutes
- Cooking Time: 25 minutes
- Serves: 6

Ingredients
- 900g/2 lb (about 2 large) sweet potatoes, peeled and cut into cubes
- 1 tbsp olive oil
- salt and freshly ground black pepper

✡

For the dressing
- 5 tbsp extra virgin olive oil
- 1 tbsp balsamic vinegar
- 1 tsp sugar, or to taste
- 2 tsp mustard, of any variety
- 1 tsp lemon juice
- salt and freshly ground black pepper

✡

For the salad
- 175g/6 oz rocket (rucola) leaves
- 1 large pomegranate, halved and deseeded
- 200g/7 oz goat's cheese, crumbled
- 75g/3 oz/⅓ cup pumpkin seeds

This salad makes a lovely refreshing Rosh Hashanah starter before a dairy main course. I have mixed an unusual selection of vegetables to create a dish strong with vibrant colour and full of varied interesting textures and flavours.

On one of my recent trips to Israel I was walking on the outskirts of Jerusalem where the hills were full of ripe pomegranate trees. Their beautifully formed crowns with vibrant red fruit explain why they are one of the most photographed fruit images in Israel. Pomegranates are recognised as symbols of fertility, frequently mentioned in the Torah and are also one of the 'seven species of Israel'. However, be aware if you are buying fresh pomegranate juice from the street vendors: it may be sharper than you expected.

On a health note, pomegranates provide a substantial amount of potassium and antioxidants, are high in fibre, and contain vitamin C and niacin.

When pomegranates are not available, substitute the seeds of passion fruit to make this salad.

Method
- Pre-heat the oven to 200°C/400°F/Gas mark 6.
- Put the sweet potatoes in a roasting tin, drizzle with the olive oil and season with salt and pepper.
- Roast for 20–25 minutes, turning once during cooking.
- To make the dressing, mix all the ingredients together and season to taste.
- Put the sweet potato in a bowl with the rocket, pomegranate seeds and goat's cheese.

To serve the stylish way: Drizzle over the dressing and sprinkle with the pumpkin seeds.

Crunchy Papaya Salad

DAIRY-FREE   PAREV   V
DIABETIC FRIENDLY

Info
- Preparation Time: 30 minutes
- Cooking Time: None
- Serves: 4

Ingredients
For the dressing
- zest and juice of 1 lime
- 1 tbsp clear honey
- 3 tbsp olive oil
- 1–2 tbsp soy sauce, to taste
- 1 clove garlic, finely chopped
- freshly ground black pepper

✡

For the salad
- 2 papayas

✡

- 100g/4 oz cherry/grape tomatoes, sliced
- 3 spring onions, sliced into matchsticks
- 1 red chilli, deseeded, very finely chopped
- 100g/4 oz bean sprouts
- 50g/2 oz/4 tbsp fresh basil, roughly chopped

✡

- 100g/4 oz honey-roasted peanuts

✡

- To serve: 4 large Chinese cabbage leaves, basil, roughly chopped

This Thai papaya salad, known as 'Som Tam', is popular in most areas of Thailand, and when you taste it you will know why. Traditionally it is made with unripe green papaya, which combines well with the spice of the chilli and sweetness of the honey dressing. Crunchy papaya salad is beautifully unique in its flavour and makes a great nutritious starter.

There have been Jews in Thailand since the seventeenth century, when the families of traders from Baghdad arrived at one of the main stopping points on the Spice Route from China. The current community of about 1,000 is served by synagogues and they are mainly Ashkenazi – descendants of Russian immigrants. Getting kosher food there can be organised online in advance which makes travelling the kosher way a bit easier, but for a more communal experience there are two main Chabad centres in Thailand: Bangkok and Phuket. In Bangkok the Friday night dinner is served in the Rabbi's house above the synagogue.

Method
- Prepare the dressing by combining all the ingredients. Taste and set aside.
- Peel the papayas, slice in half and remove all the seeds. Using a sharp knife cut into thin slices. Transfer to a bowl.
- Add the tomatoes, spring onions, chilli, bean sprouts and most of the basil and combine.
- Add the peanuts and stir in the dressing.
- Serve immediately.

To serve the stylish way: Place a Chinese leaf on each plate. Fill with salad and garnish with chopped basil.

Gravadlax and Green Lentil Salad

PAREV SHABBAT ◆ YT
DIABETIC FRIENDLY DAIRY-FREE

Info
- Preparation Time: 15 minutes
- Cooking Time: 30 minutes
- Serves: 6

Ingredients
- 200g/7 oz puy lentils
- 1 red onion, peeled and finely chopped

✡

For the dressing
- 1 tbsp white wine vinegar
- 2 tbsp mustard and dill sauce (or substitute 2 tsp mustard and 2 tbsp mayonnaise)
- 2 tbsp extra virgin olive oil
- salt and freshly ground black pepper

✡

For the salad
- 6 cherry/grape tomatoes, cut in half
- 2 tbsp finely chopped fresh flat-leaf parsley finely chopped
- 2 tbsp finely chopped fresh dill
- 1 ready-cooked beetroot bulb, not in vinegar, sliced

✡

- 300g/11 oz cured gravadlax
- 35g/1 oz baby spinach

✡

- Garnish: 1 lemon, cut into wedges, freshly ground black pepper

This salad makes a little luxury ingredient go a long way as you mix the delicious cured salmon with some nutty green lentils. It is ideal as a tasty starter or used as part of a buffet.

Gravadlax originated as a method of food preservation during the Middle Ages when the fishermen salted the salmon and lightly fermented it by burying it in the sand above the high-tide line. The word comes from the Scandinavian word 'grav' which literally means 'grave' or 'hole in the ground', and 'lax' which means salmon, thus gravadlax means 'salmon dug into the ground'. Today the salmon is 'buried' in a dry marinade of salt, sugar and dill for a few days. As the salmon cures by the action of osmosis, the moisture turns the dry cure into a highly concentrated brine.

A couple of years ago I went on a tour of Europe, giving demonstration cookery classes in about ten cities, including the delightful capital of Denmark, Copenhagen. After my session at the Chabad house before a large audience, the Rabbi was kind enough to drive me around and show me the Jewish landmarks including the Great Synagogue, cemetery and museum. The Jews of Denmark are very Danish in their way and this is reflected in their cooking style, which includes lots of open sandwiches using rugbod bread (a multi-grain dark brown bread) and layered apple crumble topped with whipped cream.

Method
- Put the lentils and onion in a pan with 750ml/1¼ pints water. Bring to the boil and simmer for 25 minutes or until tender but not mushy.
- In a bowl, mix the vinegar, mustard sauce and olive oil and season with salt and pepper. Drain the lentils and onion. Rinse in cold water and drain again.
- Add the dressing and lightly toss. Stir in the tomatoes, herbs and beetroot.

- Arrange the salmon slices on each plate and top with the lentil mixture and baby spinach.

To serve the stylish way: Dust the plate with a sprinkling of black pepper and garnish with lemon wedges.

Red and Green Summer Salad

DAIRY-FREE PAREV V

DIABETIC FRIENDLY

Info
- Preparation Time: 15 minutes
- Cooking Time: No cooking
- Serves: 6

Ingredients
For the dressing
- 60ml/2½ fl oz/¼ cup olive oil
- 1 tbsp wholegrain mustard
- zest and juice of 1 lemon
- 1 tbsp clear honey
- salt and freshly ground black pepper

✡

For the salad
- 1 bulb of fennel, trimmed, core removed and roughly chopped
- 2 avocados, peeled, stoned and cut in strips
- 225g/8 oz fresh baby spinach or rocket
- 300g/11 oz strawberries, trimmed and cut in half
- 2 red peppers, deseeded and roughly chopped

I love to combine fresh summer strawberries with salad ingredients, both for colour and taste. This unusual salad tastes great with cold meats, fish or even crumbled goat's cheese. Ideal as part of a BBQ, buffet side dish — or just enjoy it as it is.

Strawberries were first grown in Italy, where they grew wild. The ancient Romans loved them, but after the fall of Rome their popularity declined. Not until the Middle Ages did strawberries regain their popularity, this time across all of Europe. The Europeans saw the strawberry not so much as a delicious treat but as a food that could help with depression, fainting, inflammation, fevers, throat infections, kidney stones and many other sicknesses. Its leaves and roots were used for gout. Over the years strawberries were used for skin rashes, sunburn, discolouration of teeth and digestive disorders. There is also a legend that says if you find a double strawberry you should break it in half and share it with a member of the opposite sex. You will then soon fall in love with each other. I have my doubts.

There is even a Jewish connection with strawberries. They are a popular fruit in Israel, grown mainly for the export market, and the late Prime Minister Golda Meir indicated their importance to the economy with her famous statement 'We do not rejoice in victories. We rejoice when strawberries bloom in Israel.'

This salad is extremely nutritious with its avocados that provide nearly twenty essential nutrients, including fibre, potassium, vitamins E and B and folic acid, and strawberries that help the heart and lower the risk of some cancers and blood pressure. Spinach and peppers are equally beneficial and are also on the 'superfood' healthy-eating list.

Method

- Make the dressing by whisking together all the ingredients. Taste and adjust seasoning according to taste.
- Combine the fennel, avocados, spinach or rocket, strawberries and peppers.
- Pour the dressing over the salad.

To serve the stylish way: Serve on a white plate, stacked in a mound.

Vegetarian Sushi Salad

DAIRY-FREE PAREV Ⓥ

Info
- Preparation Time: 15 minutes
- Cooking Time: 15 minutes plus 10 minutes cooling
- Serves: 4

Ingredients
- 225g/8 oz sushi rice
- 500ml/1 pint water
- 1 tsp salt
- 1 tbsp sugar
- 1 tbsp rice vinegar or dry sherry

✿

For the dressing
- zest of 1 lemon
- 2 tsp lemon juice
- 2 tbsp sugar
- 2 tbsp soy sauce
- juice of 1 orange
- 1 tbsp mirin
- ½ tsp wasabi

✿

For the salad
- 200g/7 oz/1 cup frozen soya beans

✿

- 1 sheet of nori seaweed, cut into small strips
- 2 avocados, peeled and sliced into wedges
- 100g/4 oz rocket (rucola) leaves
- 2 tbsp pickled ginger, drained

✿

- Garnish: 2 tbsp sesame seeds, 2 tbsp black sesame seeds

The idea for this salad came about one day when I had finished a series of sushi cookery classes and was left with some very tasty ingredients.

All too often specialist ingredients only come in large quantities with relatively short sell-by dates so be creative, don't wait for them to go off, and enjoy this unusual salad.

Keeping kosher in Japan if you are not Japanese is extremely difficult because of the language barriers. However, the local Chabad website has a list of the kosher foods translated, and with the right amount of pointing and hand gestures I am sure you can get by.

Method
- Cook the rice in the water with the salt, according to the packet instructions. When cooked transfer to a dish to cool.
- Stir the sugar and rice vinegar or sherry into the rice.
- Place the dressing ingredients in a small saucepan. Bring to the boil and simmer until the sugar has dissolved. Remove and leave to cool.
- Cook the soya beans in a saucepan of boiling water for about 3 minutes or until cooked. Drain and set aside.
- Roast the sesame seeds in a dry frying pan over a medium heat until just golden. Remove and leave to cool.
- Prepare the salad ingredients, divide between 4 plates and drizzle over some dressing.

To serve the stylish way: Garnish with roasted sesame seeds and black sesame seeds.

Sicilian Baby Aubergine Salad

Info
- Preparation Time: 5 minutes
- Cooking Time: 15 minutes
- Serves: 4–6 as a side salad

Ingredients
- 12 baby aubergines, halved lengthways
- 200ml/7 fl oz/1 cup extra virgin olive oil

✿

- 25g/1 oz pine nuts

✿

- juice of 1 lemon
- 2 tbsp balsamic vinegar
- 2–3 cloves garlic, peeled and crushed
- 2 tbsp granulated sugar
- 2 tbsp raisins
- salt and freshly ground black pepper

✿

- Garnish: large bunch of fresh basil

This is just the perfect salad for Shabbat and Yom Tov as it needs to be made in advance for the flavours to infuse and develop. Aubergines are particularly popular in southern Italy; in this recipe the basil, extra virgin olive oil, lemon and garlic marinate them so that they are succulent and tender.

This is quick to prepare and can be served with meat, fish or a dairy meal. It is a tasty salad for a buffet table and does not spoil with time.

You can use regular-sized aubergines if you cannot find the baby variety; just slice thickly and cut in half.

Jewish influence in Sicily can be traced back to the fifteenth century. In 1492 the King of Spain, a country where there was a large Jewish community, issued an edict that outlawed all forms of Jewish practice. Although a great number of Jews converted to Catholicism many fled across the sea to Sicily. Few traces of Sicilian Jewish heritage remain today beyond a handful of inscriptions and small structures scattered around the island, and Sicilian Jewish cuisine is closely related to Arab cooking – with both sharing an absence of pork in their recipes. According to some historians, the Sicilian pizza 'sfincione', topped with tomatoes, onions and anchovies, was invented by the Sicilian Jews.

Method
- Pre-heat the grill/broiler to its highest setting.
- Brush the cut side of the aubergines with a little of the oil and place under the grill, oiled side up.
- Grill for approximately 10–15 minutes until slightly blackened, turning over half way through cooking and checking frequently.
- Pre-heat the oven to 200ºC/400ºF/Gas mark 6.
- To toast the pine nuts, place on an oven tray in the pre-heated oven for about 5 minutes, or until golden. Remove from the tray and set aside.

- To make the marinade, put the remaining oil, lemon juice, vinegar, garlic, sugar, toasted pine nuts, raisins and salt and pepper in a jug and mix.
- Place the hot aubergines in a dish and pour over the marinade. Leave to cool, turning the aubergines once or twice before serving.

To serve the stylish way: Garnish with sprigs of basil

Crispy Noodle Salad

SHABBAT   PAREV   Ⓥ   DAIRY-FREE

Info
- Preparation Time: 25 minutes
- Cooking Time: 10 minutes
- Serves: 6–8

Ingredients
- 350g/12 oz red cabbage, shredded
- 4 carrots, peeled and shredded

✡

- 250g/9 oz fresh bean sprouts
- 12 radishes, sliced
- 12 spring onions, trimmed and chopped
- 2 orange peppers, deseeded and chopped

✡

- 500ml/1 pint groundnut or sunflower oil, for frying
- 100g/4 oz stir fry noodles

✡

For the dressing
- 6 tbsp kosher duck sauce or chicken sauce
- 2 tbsp rice wine vinegar (cider or white vinegar may be substituted)
- 2 tbsp vegetable or sesame oil
- salt and freshly ground black pepper

✡

- Garnish: 6 tbsp sesame seeds

I created this recipe whilst planning dishes for an oriental buffet. No Jewish buffet is complete without coleslaw or a similar dressed shredded salad. This is the oriental variation – using an Eastern dressing instead of mayonnaise and with a delicious crunchy topping. Garnish at the last minute to maintain the crispness of the noodles. Quick and easy to make with a very impressive end result.

You will need to find a jar of kosher 'duck sauce' or 'chicken sauce', which is widely available in kosher shops and some large supermarkets.

Method
- Mix together the red cabbage and carrots. Stir in the bean sprouts, radishes, spring onions and orange peppers.
- Heat the oil in a deep frying pan or wok. When the oil is hot, add the noodles in small batches. Remove the fried noodles as they cook, using a slotted spoon, and drain on kitchen paper. When cool, crush them slightly and set aside.
- Toast the sesame seeds in a dry frying pan. This takes about 1–2 minutes and they will burn quickly so keep an eye on them. Remove from the pan and transfer to a dish. Set aside.
- Mix together all the dressing ingredients.
- Dress the salad and toss with salt and pepper to taste.
- Just before serving add the crispy noodles.

To serve the stylish way: Garnish with the toasted sesame seeds.

Mozzarella Salad with Pear and Cranberries

GLUTEN-FREE Ⓓ Ⓥ

Info
- Preparation Time: 10 minutes
- Cooking Time: 10 minutes
- Serves: 6

Ingredients
For the dressing
- 6 tbsp extra virgin olive oil
- 1 tbsp red wine vinegar
- 1–2 tsp honey, to taste
- 2 tsp wholegrain mustard
- salt and freshly ground black pepper

✡

For the salad
- 30g/1 oz unsalted butter or margarine
- 2 tbsp golden caster sugar or brown sugar
- 3 pears, peeled, cored and halved

✡

- 2 tbsp Poire eau-de-vie or other fruit liqueur

✡

- 3 x 125g/4½ oz buffalo mozzarella balls

✡

- 200g/7 oz mixed salad leaves
- 50g/2 oz dried cranberries

✡

- Garnish: bunch of fresh mint, roughly chopped

Look at the cheese counter in any kosher deli and you will be amazed at the range of different cheeses now on offer to the kosher cook. Two of the most popular mozzarellas are buffalo and smoked. Smoked mozzarella has a golden brown colour and an interesting smoky flavour. Fresh mozzarella is so versatile – raw in salads, especially with tomato, avocado and basil (the traditional Tricolore) and baked in lasagne or on top of pizza.

The finest mozzarella is made in and around Naples, using water buffalo's milk. It has a moist, springy texture and a delicious milky flavour. The cheese is made using the layering method where the curds are cut into strips, then covered with boiling water. As they rise to the surface they are torn into shreds and scrunched into egg-shaped balls weighing 200g/7 oz each. These are placed in light brine for 12 hours, then packed in their own whey inside a bag to keep them fresh.

Opened mozzarella can be kept for a brief time in a covered bowl containing the whey from the bag – but ideally consume once opened.

This mozzarella salad is simple to make and provides a delicious starter or light lunch. Use your best extra virgin olive oil to dress the salad.

Today the main synagogue in Naples is near the Palazzo Sessa and dates back to 1864, when it was built with financial help from Baron Rothschild. Prior to World War Two there were almost 10,000 Jews in the city; now the total is under 2,000.

Method
- Make the dressing by whisking together all the ingredients.
- Place the butter or margarine and sugar into a pan over a medium heat and stir until the sugar has dissolved. When the butter starts to foam, toss in the pears and cook, stirring for 5 minutes.

- Add the eau-de-vie and cook for 2–3 minutes until the pears are coated in a rich syrup and are just tender. Set aside to cool slightly.
- Cut the mozzarella cheese into slices.
- Toss the salad leaves in the dressing. Arrange the salad leaves and pears on a plate. Scatter over the cranberries and mozzarella slices. Serve immediately.

To serve the stylish way: Garnish with mint.

Cherry and Chicken Salad

Info
- Preparation Time: 20 minutes
- Cooking Time: 30 minutes
- Serves: 6

Ingredients
- 6 boneless, skinless chicken breasts
- 100ml/3½ fl oz/¼ cup white wine

✡

- 450g/1 lb fresh cherries
- 250g/9 oz mixed bag of lettuce
- bunch of spring onions, trimmed and cut on a diagonal

✡

For the dressing
- 1–2 tbsp mild curry powder
- 1 tsp clear honey
- 1 tbsp lemon juice
- bunch of fresh mint, stalks removed
- 4 tbsp mayonnaise
- 4 tbsp mint jelly
- salt and freshly ground black pepper

✡

- Garnish: sprigs of mint

Ever since I was a little girl, I have always loved cherries. In fact my parents bought me a gold necklace with a charm in the shape of a bunch of cherries. So this salad is my idea of heaven; all the flavours of summer packed into a delicious fresh dish.

Cherries have a magical history; the Romans discovered sweet cherries in Asia Minor in about 70 BCE and introduced them to Britain in the first century. Although the fruit has always been popular for dessert and culinary purposes, cherries were used during the fifteenth and sixteenth centuries for their medicinal properties. Hot cherry stones were once used in bed-warming pans and Shakespeare's *A Midsummer Night's Dream* associates cherries with love and romance.

The most famous Hungarian Jewish dish is cold sour cherry soup. This dairy delight containing sour cream, chives and sugar is served at Shavuot to coincide with the prolific Hungarian cherry harvest. For most palates it is too sweet to start a meal with, but it does make a refreshing and unusual dessert.

Chef's Tip: If cherries are too expensive use large black seedless grapes instead.

Method
- Place the chicken breasts in a large pan in one layer. Cover completely with cold water, season with salt and pepper and add the wine.
- Bring to the boil and turn down to simmer.
- Partially cover with a lid and simmer for 15 minutes.
- Turn off the heat, fully cover and leave for 10–15 minutes.
- Check that the chicken is cooked through before leaving to cool and shred later.

- Stone the cherries. Do this by cutting the cherries in half using a sharp knife and easing out the stones (or use a cherry stoner if you have one!)
- Mix all the dressing ingredients in a food processor until the dressing is fairly smooth, but with flecks of mint, rather than a purée. Store in the refrigerator until ready to use.
- Tear the cooled chicken into bite-sized pieces.
- Spread the salad leaves over a platter, scatter over the chicken pieces, followed by the cherries and spring onions.
- Just before serving drizzle the dressing in thin lines over the prepared salad platter.

To serve the stylish way: Garnish with sprigs of mint.

Pomegranate Kasha Salad with Honey Dressing

PAREV RH V

DAIRY-FREE GLUTEN-FREE

Info
- Preparation Time: 20 minutes
- Cooking Time: 15 minutes
- Serves: 6

Ingredients
- 300g/11 oz/2 cups coarse bulgur wheat
- 450ml/¾ pint vegetable stock

✡

For the honey dressing
- juice of 1 pomegranate
- 1 clove garlic, peeled and crushed
- 2 tsp honey
- salt and freshly ground pepper
- 6 tbsp extra virgin olive oil

✡

For the salad
- seeds of 1 pomegranate
- 100g/4 oz walnuts, roughly chopped
- 1½ tbsp finely chopped flat-leaf parsley
- 2 tbsp finely chopped fresh mint
- 150g/5 oz/¼ cup celery, finely sliced at a slight angle
- salt and freshly ground pepper

✡

- Garnish: sprigs of parsley

This salad is made with roasted bulgur wheat (kasha) and a delicious mix of fresh herbs, celery and, of course, pomegranate seeds. Bulgur wheat can be purchased fine, medium and coarse. For a proper kasha experience, use the coarse variety. It can be served hot, cold or warm so is perfect for Shabbat and Rosh Hashanah. At New Year we all wish for the forthcoming year to be a healthy one, and pomegranates are rich in antioxidants. Regular consumption of pomegranate juice has been associated with benefits against cancer, and maintaining a healthy heart.

Kasha is an old-fashioned Ashkenazi ingredient and is often served with onions, bow pasta (farfalle) and gravy in a recipe called Kasha Varnishkes. It is also a popular filling for knishes and is sometimes used to make kneidlach (matza balls).

Method
- Toast the bulgur wheat in a large frying pan for about 5 minutes or until the grains start to turn golden. Add the stock and stir vigorously to incorporate the liquid.
- Cook for about 5 minutes until the liquid has been absorbed and the kasha is soft. Remove from the pan and transfer to a serving dish to cool.
- Combine all the dressing ingredients and pour over the kasha.
- Add the pomegranate seeds, walnuts, parsley, mint and celery and mix well.
- Taste and seasoning accordingly.

To **serve the stylish way:** Garnish with sprigs of parsley.

Italian Matza Salad

P D V

Info

- Preparation Time: 10 minutes
- No cooking, but minimum 15 minutes standing time
- Serves: 6

Ingredients

For the dressing

- 100ml/3½ fl oz extra virgin olive oil
- 2 tbsp red wine vinegar
- 3–4 cloves garlic, peeled and finely chopped
- 1 tbsp sugar
- salt and freshly ground black pepper

✡

For the salad

- 20 tea matzas or 20 matza crackers, crumbled

✡

- 675g/1½ lb cherry tomatoes, red, yellow, plum, organic, on the vine, or a mixture, cut in half
- 150g/5 oz/½ cup black olives, pitted
- 200g/7 oz/1 cup feta or mozzarella cheese, cut into cubes
- large bunch of fresh basil

✡

- To serve: salad leaves

Use a variety of tomatoes to get the best flavours for this crunchy Italian salad. It is a twist on the Tuscan bread recipe panzanella but here I am using broken pieces of matza tossed in chopped garlic and extra virgin olive oil. It makes a delicious accompaniment to fish and is perfect to make for a Shabbat or Yom Tov as you need to make it in advance.

Matza, unleavened bread, is the well-known symbolic food eaten primarily during the eight days of Passover. It is recognised both as 'poor man's bread', because it was all the poor could afford, and it is also called the 'bread of affliction', eaten by the Jews during their time as slaves under the rule of the Pharaohs. But it is also associated with the Jews' speedy exodus from Egypt in Biblical times. As the Jews left in haste, 'in the blink of an eye', they did not have time to bake regular bread, so this unleavened bread was all that they had to take with them.

Method

- Put the olive oil, vinegar, garlic, sugar, salt and plenty of pepper in your serving bowl.
- Add the crumbled matzas and mix.
- Add all the remaining ingredients.
- Toss to combine well, taking care not to break up the feta or mozzarella cheese.
- Let the salad stand at room temperature for a minimum of 15 minutes or overnight in a fridge to allow the matza pieces to soak up some of the dressing.

To serve the stylish way: Serve with a green salad that includes rocket or baby spinach.

Lancashire Cheese with Honey Roasted Beetroot Salad

Info
- Preparation Time: 20 minutes
- Cooking Time: 1 hour
- Serves: 6

Ingredients
- 900g/2 lb small raw beetroots (beets), peeled and roughly chopped
- 3 cloves garlic, peeled and roughly chopped
- 1 tbsp coriander seeds, lightly crushed
- 6 tbsp olive oil
- 100ml/3½ fl oz/½ cup medium-bodied red wine
- 2 tbsp clear honey
- salt and freshly ground black pepper

✡

- 150g/5 oz puy lentils

✡

- 150g/5 oz Lancashire cheese, crumbled

✡

- Garnish: extra virgin olive oil, 2 tbsp fresh coriander, roughly chopped

Dairy foods and Shavuot are synonymous and here I have created an unusual salad combination to celebrate this joyous festival.

Beetroot takes on a completely new flavour once it has been roasted and mixed with Lancashire cheese. Lancashire cheese has a delightful crumbly consistency, which blends beautifully into this salad.

It is delicious hot, cold or warm and can be enjoyed as a healthy lunch, starter or part of a buffet selection.

I have added the cheese at the end but if you prefer the topping to have a slightly gratin effect, open up the beetroot parcels 5 minutes before the end of cooking and sprinkle over the cheese evenly. Leave the parcels open so the cheese can cook a little over the beetroot.

Chef's Tip: Wear rubber gloves to peel the beetroot so it does not stain your fingers.

Method
- Pre-heat the oven to 200°C/400°F/Gas mark 6.
- Place the beetroots, garlic and coriander in a bowl with the olive oil, wine and honey. Season with salt and pepper and toss well to coat.
- Place a large square of foil on a baking tray, top with a similar-sized piece of greaseproof paper, then add the beetroot mixture. Cover with another square of greaseproof paper and foil. Fold all the edges well to seal.
- Roast for 1 hour, shaking the tray once to move the beetroot a little. You will notice that the foil has puffed up, a good sign as it shows there is enough steam in the parcel to cook the vegetables, which should be tender and caramelised when ready.

- Cook the lentils for about 15 minutes or until soft. Drain and set aside.
- Stir the lentils into the cooked beetroot and sprinkle with the Lancashire cheese.

To serve the stylish way: Drizzle over a little extra virgin olive oil and garnish with chopped coriander.

Chapter 3

Eat Out, Eat In

—

Fine Dining and Quick Fixes

Eat Out, Eat In

In this section I have created recipes that reflect many characteristics of the Jewish people.

Throughout history Jews have travelled to and from every corner of the world. Often this has been because they were fleeing persecution or seeking escape from oppression. But in times of peace their natural interest in the world around them has made visiting other places a passion. And when you visit you have to eat.

In Eat Out, Eat In, I have tried to capture the essence of worldwide dining and bring it to your table. The eating-out experience – whether in a fine restaurant or as a takeaway – has come home. By following my clear guidelines, you can now replicate those much-loved meals in your own kitchen.

The recipes in the Fine Dining section will take you a little longer and use more luxurious ingredients. Your results will be worth the effort as your guests appreciate truly 'fine dining' without the need to make reservations.

The Quick Fix section does exactly what it says. It is fast, tasty, popular, family-orientated and reflects the takeaway culture that we are part of, adapted for the kosher table.

On the one hand, Jews are naturally curious; they like to experiment and create. On the other, Jews are traditional; they don't stray too far from their (culinary) roots and have a strong sense of history and continuity. In my recipes I have combined new ingredients and substitutes for the familiar to create a balance of both.

Fine Dining

- Oriental sea bass en papillotte
- Griddled tuna on a bed of red lentils with crunchy beetroot slaw
- Plaice fillets with mushrooms
- Sea bream with saffron and coriander
- Salmon teriyaki
- Sole kebabs with parsley couscous
- Lamb and apricot tagine
- Roast rib of beef spiked with horseradish sauce
- Chicken paella
- Hazelnut-stuffed turkey with brandy sauce
- Italian chicken spirals
- Honey-glazed lamb with minted mash
- Middle Eastern lamb with dill, olives and spring onion mash

- Tender beef and crispy sweet potato pie
- Veal chops with mushroom sauce
- Golden glazed cinnamon chicken with red rice

Quick Fixes

- Chicken livers with golden rice
- Jamaican lime chicken
- Tandoori chicken with tomato, cucumber and coriander salad
- Rigatoni with spiced meatballs and red wine sauce
- Schnitzel noodle stir fry
- Crispy shredded chilli beef
- Thai chicken cakes
- Hot and sour duck
- Salmon crumble
- Crusted cod with salsa
- Sesame fish with udon noodles
- Mediterranean tuna stacks

Oriental Sea Bass En Papillotte

`PAREV` `DAIRY-FREE`

`GLUTEN-FREE`

Info
- Preparation Time: 25 minutes
- Cooking Time: 30 minutes
- Serves: 4

Ingredients
- 4 x 170–200g/6–7 oz sea bass fillets, skin on

✡

- 6 tbsp sesame oil
- 6 cm/3 inch piece of fresh ginger, peeled and finely chopped
- 6 tbsp soy sauce
- 2 tsp sugar
- juice of 1 lemon
- 4 cloves garlic, peeled and finely chopped

✡

For the shredded vegetables
- For a short cut, you can buy a packet of stir fry ready-washed and chopped vegetables but you can't beat making your own
- 4 tbsp roasted sesame oil
- 3 cloves garlic
- ½ red chilli, deseeded and very finely chopped
- 3 carrots, peeled and finely cut into thin strips or use a peeler to make the strips

✡

- 200g/7 oz mangetout, finely sliced
- ½ green Savoy or Chinese cabbage, finely chopped

✡

- Garnish: sprigs of fresh coriander (cilantro)

This is a delightful oriental dish; the fused flavours of garlic, ginger, chilli and lemon produce the most delicious recipe. It is cooked wrapped in paper in the oven and makes a most impressive main course for any occasion. I like to serve it on a bed of shredded vegetables using carrots, cabbage, fennel and mangetout.

Method
- Pre-heat the oven to 200°C/400°F/Gas mark 6.
- Cut four pieces of kitchen foil and four pieces of non-stick parchment paper large enough to wrap each fish.
- Combine the sesame oil, ginger, soy sauce, sugar, lemon juice and garlic in a jug.
- Prepare four double foil and parchment layers with the foil on the outside. Sit one fillet in the centre of one square of baking parchment. Pour the sauce ingredients equally over each fish and wrap up like a loose parcel. Place the fish parcels on a baking tray. Pour 100ml/3½ fl oz of water onto the base of the tray so that it slightly steams the fish.
- Bake for 20 minutes.
- Heat the sesame oil in a wok or large frying pan. Add the garlic, chilli and carrots. Cook for about 4 minutes or until they just begin to soften.
- Add the mangetout and cabbage and cook for a final 2 minutes.

To serve the stylish way: Place the shredded vegetables on a large platter. Pour any excess juices from the fish over the vegetables. Sit the cooked sea bass on top and garnish with sprigs of coriander.

Griddled Tuna on a Bed of Red Lentils with Crunchy Beetroot Slaw

PAREV **DAIRY-FREE**

GLUTEN-FREE

Info
- Preparation Time: 25 minutes
- Cooking Time: 20 minutes
- Serves: 4

Ingredients
- 4 x 150–170g/5–6 oz tuna steaks
- 2 tbsp olive oil
- salt and freshly
  ground black pepper

✡

For the lentils
- 200g/7 oz red lentils
- 600ml/1 pint/2½ cups vegetable
  stock

✡

For the beetroot slaw
- 1 red eating apple, peeled, cored
  and grated
- 2 raw beetroots, peeled and grated
- 150g/5 oz shredded cabbage
- 50g/2 oz toasted
  split almonds
- 1 tbsp balsamic vinegar
- 2 tbsp extra virgin olive oil

✡

- Garnish: slices of lemon

This is a very healthy recipe using several 'superfoods' – tuna, olive oil, apple, beetroot, lentils and almonds. Even the cooking method, griddling, is healthy. For a change use skinless, boneless chicken breasts instead of tuna but ensure these are cooked through before serving.

Jewish people love coleslaw of all descriptions and you will find it on many menus at home as well as at popular kosher restaurants. The word 'coleslaw' is a corruption of the Dutch word *koolsla*, a shortened version of *koolsalade*, meaning cabbage salad.

Method
- Rub the tuna steaks with a little olive oil and season with salt and pepper. Set aside on a covered plate.
- Place the lentils in a medium-sized saucepan. Add the stock, season with salt and pepper, bring to the boil and simmer covered for 15 minutes or until the lentils are soft.
- Heat a griddle pan until hot and cook the tuna for approximately 3 minutes or until seared and then turn over for a final 2 minutes. Tuna should be served slightly undercooked.
- Mix the apple with the beetroots. Stir in the cabbage, almonds, vinegar, extra virgin olive oil and season.
- Drain, taste and season the lentils.

To serve the stylish way: Spoon a large serving of hot lentils onto a warm plate, top with the tuna steak and some beetroot slaw alongside. Complete with a dusting of black pepper and a slice of lemon.

Plaice Fillets with Mushrooms

PAREV

Info

- Preparation Time: 25 minutes
- Cooking Time: 20 minutes
- Serves: 4

Ingredients

For the stuffing

- 2 tbsp roughly chopped parsley
- 3 spring onions, finely chopped
- zest of 1 lemon
- 2 cloves garlic, peeled
- 75g/3 oz brown breadcrumbs (approx. 2 slices of bread)
- salt and freshly ground black pepper

✡

- 8 plaice fillets, skinned

✡

For the mushroom sauce

- 2 tbsp olive oil
- 2 cloves garlic, peeled and finely chopped
- 2 onions, peeled and finely chopped
- 250g/9 oz brown-cap mushrooms or your favourite variety, sliced
- 2 tbsp dried mushrooms/ceps

✡

- 50ml/2 fl oz/¼ cup white wine
- salt and pepper, to taste
- 2 tbsp cornflour

✡

- Garnish: lemon wedges and sprigs of parsley

I have transformed plain plaice fillets into a low-fat and creative recipe with a mushroom sauce. The use of dried ceps (wild mushrooms) gives the most aromatic flavour that fuses into the delicate fish. I like to serve it with mashed potato and peas for a truly winter-warming comfort meal. Plaice is not generally perceived as haute cuisine but this humble fish is delicious as well as being a good source of iodine and protein. The fish is fresh when the orange spots on the skin are bright and the eyes are protruding.

Ceps are one of the most famous foods in France. These wild mushrooms grow all over the countryside but you should only pick them if you can correctly identify them. If you are unsure, pharmacies in France will confirm identification for you.

Jews have lived in France since Roman times. Despite a history of anti-Semitic incidents, France has the fourth-largest Jewish community in the world with about 600,000 Jews, 375,000 of whom live in Paris. The Belleville area to the north-east of Paris, Place d'Italie in the south and the Marais in the centre are the main Jewish neighbourhoods and have numerous synagogues, restaurants and sites of Jewish interest.

The community is predominantly Sephardi originating from North Africa, Morocco and Tunisia but there is also a significant Ashkenazi community. The Jews of France have made French food their own, just as their culinary traditions have seeped into the food of the country. Historically French Jews have worked as chocolate-makers, food merchants and chefs and essentially enjoyed the food of the region – without the pork, of course.

Method

- Make the stuffing by placing all the ingredients in a food processor. Whiz briefly so that you have a chunky filling.
- Pat dry the plaice fillets. Lay the fillets skin side up on a chopping board. Spread the stuffing along the centre and roll up tightly.
- For the sauce, heat the olive oil in a large frying pan. Sauté the garlic, onions and sliced, fresh mushrooms together for about 5 minutes. Add 150ml/¼ pint boiling water to the dried mushrooms and add to the pan.
- Stir in the wine and season with salt and pepper.
- Using 3 tbsp of hot water make a paste with the cornflour. Add to the sauce and stir continuously until it thickens.
- Sit the plaice fillets on top of the sauce, cover with a lid and cook for 10 minutes until the fish is cooked.

To serve the stylish way: Spoon the sauce onto a hot plate. Sit the fish on top and garnish with lemon wedges and sprigs of parsley.

Sea Bream with Saffron and Coriander

PAREV

Info
- Preparation Time: 25 minutes
- Cooking Time: 35 minutes
- Serves: 6

Ingredients
- 2 tsp coriander seeds

✡

- 1 hot red chilli

✡

- 5 cloves garlic, peeled
- 3 cm/1¼ inch piece of fresh ginger, peeled
- 3 tbsp sunflower oil, plus oil for frying
- 1 tsp turmeric
- 12 strands of saffron, infused in 2 tsp of hot water
- 4 tbsp white wine
- 1 tbsp sugar

✡

- 300g/11 oz fresh tomatoes, peeled, deseeded and chopped, or 1 x 400g can chopped tomatoes
- 300ml/½ pint/1¼ cups vegetable stock

✡

- 6 x 175g/6 oz sea bream fillets
- salt and freshly ground black pepper

✡

- 225g/8 oz couscous
- 600ml/1 pint hot vegetable stock

✡

I wrote this recipe with thoughts of creating a stylish fusion combination dish. Sea bream is plentiful along the Spanish/Portuguese coastline so it has a Mediterranean influence but combined with saffron and coriander it is then transformed into a Moroccan experience. The sea bream sits on a bed of couscous that successfully soaks up all the delicious colourful sauce. When frying the sea bream, I have kept the skin on as it gives it a golden crispy coating and also prevents it from falling apart. You can make the sauce in advance and reheat just before serving.

Method
- Crush the coriander seeds with the base of a rolling pin or in a pestle and mortar.
- Remove the stem and seeds from the chilli.
- Put the crushed coriander, chilli, garlic and ginger in a food processor; whiz together so that they form a paste.
- Heat the 3 tbsp oil in a large frying pan over a low heat. Stir in the spice paste from the food processor and cook gently for 3 minutes.
- Add the turmeric, and saffron with its liquid. Stir in the wine and sugar and cook for a further 3 minutes.
- Add the fresh or canned tomatoes and the 300ml/½ pint vegetable stock to the sauce, increase the heat, bring to the boil and simmer for 8 minutes.
- Heat a heavy frying pan until very hot. Brush the fish fillets on both sides with some sunflower or vegetable oil. Season with salt and pepper and lay them skin side down in the pan.
- Cook undisturbed for 3–4 minutes, or until the skin has a good dark colour. Continue to cook for a final 3 minutes or until the fish is completely cooked.

- 55g/2 oz/4 tbsp cold unsalted butter/non-dairy margarine cut into cubes

  ✡

- Garnish: bunch of fresh coriander (cilantro)

- Pour the 600ml/1 pint hot stock over the couscous, cover with cling film and leave for 5 minutes.
- Whilst the fish is cooking, whisk the butter or margarine pieces into the sauce.

To serve the stylish way: Add the coriander leaves to the sauce. Immediately spoon the sauce onto the plate. Spoon some couscous on top of the sauce and finish with a fillet of sea bream – skin side up. Sprinkle some more coriander leaves over the complete dish.

Salmon Teriyaki

PAREV **DAIRY-FREE** **GLUTEN-FREE**

Info
- Preparation Time: 15 minutes plus 10 minutes to cool and 30 minutes to marinate
- Cooking Time: 10 minutes
- Serves: 4

Ingredients
For the teriyaki sauce
- 4 tbsp soy sauce
- 3 tbsp sake
- 3 tbsp mirin (Japanese rice wine) or kosher dry sherry
- 1 tbsp sugar (plus two extra tsp later)

✡

- 4 x 150g/5 oz salmon fillets, skinned

✡

- 150g/5 oz carrots, peeled and cut into thin strips
- 150g/5 oz mangetout
- 100g/4 oz bean sprouts, washed
- salt and pepper to taste

This Japanese salmon dish uses a sweet and shiny sauce for marinating as well as for glazing. It is a tasty, low-fat main course that is delicious with sushi rice. The teriyaki sauce is also perfect with tuna, steak or chicken. I like to serve it with mangetout and bean sprouts; enjoy with chopsticks for the genuine experience. Kosher mirin wine (Chinese rice wine) is now available in the kosher supermarkets or you can use kosher dry sherry.

Method
- Mix all the ingredients for the teriyaki sauce in a pan. Heat to dissolve the sugar. Remove and cool for 10 minutes.
- Place the salmon fillet in a shallow dish and pour over the teriyaki sauce. Leave to marinate for 30 minutes.
- Pre-heat the grill to medium. Take the salmon fillet out of the marinade and pat dry with kitchen paper. Reserve the marinade. Lightly oil a grill pan.
- Grill the salmon for about 10–12 minutes.
- Pour the sauce into the original pan. Add the extra 2 tsp sugar and heat until dissolved. Remove from the heat.
- Brush the salmon with the sauce, then grill until the surface of the fish bubbles.
- Meanwhile, boil the carrots in lightly salted water. After 5 minutes drain the water away. Add the mangetout and bean sprouts and mix well. Remove the pan from the heat after 1 minute. Serve immediately.

To serve the stylish way: Heap the vegetables onto a serving plate. Place the salmon on top and spoon over the rest of the sauce.

Sole Kebabs with Parsley Couscous

PAREV

Info
- Preparation Time: 15 minutes plus 30 minutes to marinate
- Cooking Time: 25 minutes
- Serves: 4

Ingredients
- 4 tbsp extra virgin olive oil
- 4 cloves garlic, peeled and crushed
- zest and juice of 1 lemon
- salt and freshly ground black pepper

✡

- 4 lemon sole fillets, cut in half lengthways
- 2 red peppers, halved, deseeded and cut into 2.5 cm/1 inch pieces
- 400g/14 oz button mushrooms, stalks removed

✡

- 250g/9 oz Israeli couscous
- 500ml/1 pint vegetable stock (mushroom is good)

✡

- 2 large courgettes (zucchini), coarsely grated
- large bunch of fresh parsley, roughly chopped

✡

- Garnish: 1 lemon, cut into wedges

Delicate fish like sole is best served as simply as possible without fussy creamy sauces. This recipe is pleasantly seasoned with lemon and garlic and makes a lavish piece of fish go a long way. The fish can be prepared in advance and cooked just before your guests arrive, making it a hostess's delight.

I like to serve this with Israeli couscous – a type of toasted pasta – which provides the perfect texture to accompany the fish. It is extremely versatile and is delicious hot, cold or warm. Due to its round nature, my family call it 'bubbles'.

Israel is the only place in the world where Jews are not in the minority. Ever since the state was established in 1948, Jews from all over the world have moved to live in Israel; in particular Holocaust survivors and Jews fleeing Arab lands. In more recent times there has been a large influx from Ethiopia, Russia, Latin America and Western Europe. This mix of nations has greatly influenced 'Israeli' cuisine and foods like falafel, hummus, shakshouka and couscous often represent a delicious merger of both Mediterranean and Middle Eastern ingredients and styles.

Method
- Mix together the olive oil, garlic, lemon zest and juice, salt and pepper.
- Pour this marinade over the sole fillets and leave covered for 30 minutes in the refrigerator.
- Roll up each sole fillet like a Swiss roll and carefully thread onto the kebab skewers alternately with the pepper pieces and mushrooms.
- Brush each threaded kebab with a little of the lemon and oil marinade.
- Arrange the kebab skewers on a grill tray and cook under a moderately hot grill for about 8 minutes, carefully turning the

kebabs once or twice during cooking and brushing them with the remaining marinade if required.

- Whilst the kebabs are cooking, cook the Israeli couscous. Pour hot stock over it and bring to the boil.
- Cook for 10 minutes or until soft. Stir in the courgettes and cook for a further 3 minutes. Taste and adjust seasoning accordingly. Add the parsley.

To serve the stylish way: Spoon a generous helping of couscous onto a hot plate. Top with the kebabs. Garnish with lemon wedges and a drizzle of extra virgin olive oil.

Lamb and Apricot Tagine

Info
- Preparation Time: 25 minutes
- Cooking Time: 1 hour 45 minutes
- Serves: 6–8

Ingredients
- 2 tbsp olive oil
- 6 threads of saffron
- 1 tsp ground turmeric
- 1 tsp ground black pepper
- 2 cm/1 inch piece of ginger root, peeled and grated
- 1 tsp cayenne pepper
- 2 red onions, peeled and sliced

✡

- 1.3 kg/3 lb boned shoulder of lamb, cut into large cubes
- 300g/11 oz/1¼ cups dried apricots
- 450g/1 lb butternut squash, lpeeled, seeded and cut into 5 cm/2 inch pieces
- 6 tbsp honey
- 3 tbsp orange blossom or rosewater (or zest and juice of 1 orange)
- 2 x 2.5 cm/1 inch stick of cinnamon

✡

For the lemon couscous
- 500g/1 lb couscous
- 1 litre/1¾ pints/4 cups vegetable stock

✡

- zest of 1 lemon
- 2 tbsp roughly chopped parsley
- 2 tbsp roughly chopped coriander
- 2 pomegranates, halved and deseeded
- Garnish: 2 tbsp toasted almonds, sprigs of flat-leaf parsley

Tagine is the Moroccan word for both a glazed earthenware cooking vessel with a conical lid and the stew cooked and served in it. This tasty aromatic recipe demonstrates Sephardi cooking at its best, with its abundant use of spices: saffron, turmeric, cinnamon, cayenne, ginger and rosewater. The spice market in Marrakesh is an amazing, colourful experience with labyrinths of souks all around the main Medina square. When I last went I purchased all my favourite spices as they are far more pungent than any supermarket equivalent and take up very little space in the suitcase.

Most of the original Moroccan Jews have now moved to Israel, France, Canada, Spain and Venezuela. However, there is still an active community today and a well-preserved synagogue and cemetery in Marrakesh.

Moroccan Jews enjoy 'henna' parties, which usually take place a week before a wedding, and sometimes before a bar mitzvah or bat mitzvah. The oldest member of the family, normally the grandmother, smudges henna in the palm of the bride and groom to bless the new couple with good health, fertility, wisdom and security. It is believed that the henna acts as a protection against demons. The henna dye often lasts for up to 2 weeks and in Morocco the tradition is for the bride to be exempt from housework duties until it has completely faded.

Method
- In a large bowl, mix together the oil, saffron, turmeric, pepper, ginger, cayenne and onions until well blended. Add the meat and toss to coat.
- Heat a large saucepan over a moderately high heat, then add the meat and sear on all sides.
- Add enough water to just cover the meat, bring to the boil, then reduce the heat, cover and simmer for 1 hour 30 minutes or until the meat is very tender.

- Add the apricots, butternut squash, honey, orange blossom or rosewater and cinnamon sticks and mix well. Cook for a final 15 minutes.
- Place the couscous in a large bowl, pour over the vegetable stock, stir in the lemon zest and fresh herbs and season well. Cover with cling film and leave until the stock is absorbed. Fluff up with a fork just before serving and stir in the pomegranate seeds.

To serve the stylish way: Sprinkle with the toasted almonds and sprigs of parsley and serve hot with the couscous.

Roast Rib of Beef spiked with Horseradish Sauce

M RH

Info
- Preparation Time: 5 minutes
- Cooking Time: 2 hours
- Serves: 8

Ingredients
- 1.8kg/4 lb rib of beef
- 1 tbsp olive oil
- 1 onion, peeled and cut in quarters

✡

- 2 tbsp horseradish sauce

✡

- 150ml/¼ pint red wine
- 150ml/¼ pint beef stock

✡

For the gravy
- 1 tbsp plain flour
- 1 tbsp red wine/hot water
- salt and pepper

✡

- Garnish: sprigs of fresh thyme

Cooked with red wine and beef stock, this rib of beef will just melt in the mouth. The general rule for cooking times is 20 minutes per 450g/1 lb for rare, add 10 minutes per pound for medium-cooked and a further 20–30 minutes for well done. For perfect succulent meat cook covered and baste the meat with the stock and red wine every 30 minutes. To check if the beef is cooked, insert a skewer into the thickest part and press out some of the juices: the red, pink or clear colour will indicate how much the beef is cooked.

Roast beef is the national signature dish of Britain and cooking it with the horseradish sauce gives all the flavour without the heat.

The Jews of London's East End came mainly from Russia at the beginning of the nineteenth century. Aldgate, Mile End, Whitechapel, Stepney, Spitalfields and Brick Lane were some of the main Jewish areas at this time but living conditions were poor and community life was very insular. Most people only spoke Yiddish and the local shops sold bagels, salted herrings and pickled cucumbers. My great-grandmother Golda and great-grandfather Samuel were part of this community. They had a kosher butcher's shop at 70 Old Bethnal Green Road called 'Ziff's Butcher' and they produced their own schmaltz, pickled beef and tongue and gribines (rendered chicken fat with onions and seasoning).

It was in the 1930s and '40s that the Jews moved to the more prosperous areas of London, in the suburbs, and now there are few Jews living in the old East End although there are still plenty of Jewish landmark buildings and streets.

Chef's Tip: Check that the horseradish sauce is dairy-free as many contain double cream.

Method

- Pre-heat the oven to 240°C/475°F/Gas mark 9.
- Coat the meat in the olive oil. Place the onion on the base of a large roasting tin and position the meat on top.
- Cook for an initial 20 minutes. Remove and spread a layer of horseradish sauce over the top of the meat.
- Carefully pour in the red wine and beef stock. Cover with foil and return to the oven.
- Reduce the oven temperature to 180°C/350°F/Gas mark 4 and cook for approximately 1½ hours, according to how well done you like your meat.
- Baste the juices over the meat every 30 minutes.
- Once cooked, remove and leave covered for 30 minutes before carving.
- For the gravy, transfer the roasting tin to the hob. Remove any excess fat and discard the pieces of onion.
- Stir in the flour and cook for 2 minutes, scraping up all the sticky caramelised meat and onion sediment as you go.
- Pour in a little red wine or hot water until you have the pouring consistency you like. Bring to the boil and simmer for 5 minutes or until thickened. Season with salt and pepper to taste.
- Strain the gravy into a clean pan. Bring to the boil again before serving.

To serve the stylish way: Carve the meat into thin slices, garnish with sprigs of thyme and serve with the gravy.

Chicken Paella

M **DAIRY-FREE** **GLUTEN-FREE**

Info
- Preparation Time: 25 minutes
- Cooking Time: 40 minutes
- Serves: 6

Ingredients
- 6 chicken breasts, skinned
- 2 tbsp smoked paprika
- 2 tbsp olive oil

✡

- 1 red onion, peeled and sliced
- 3 cloves garlic, peeled and roughly chopped
- 2 red peppers, deseeded and roughly chopped
- 1 red chilli, deseeded and finely chopped

✡

- 100ml/3½ fl oz white wine
- 200ml/7 fl oz chicken stock
- 6 mini kabanos (smoked sausage), sliced
- 300g/10 oz paella rice

✡

- 450g/1 lb salad tomatoes, skinned, quartered and deseeded
- 1 lemon, sliced
- salt and freshly ground black pepper, to taste

✡

- Garnish: 1 lemon, cut into wedges

The combination of the smoked paprika and the spicy chorizo sausage gives this Spanish chicken recipe its distinctive flavour and rich colour. In Spain paprika is known as pimentón and has a smoky flavour and aroma as it is dried by smoking, typically using oak wood. Pimentón is a key ingredient in several Spanish sausage products such as chorizo, as well as this dish.

I like to serve this with plain rice garnished with sprigs of parsley and lemon wedges.

The Jewish community today in Spain are mainly of Sephardi descent hailing from North Africa, along with some Ashkenazi Jews from Argentina who fled the military Junta in the 1970s. Murcia in south-eastern Spain has a flourishing Jewish community and it is here that kosher olives are produced and exported all over the world.

Method
- Dust the chicken breasts with the smoked paprika so that they are evenly coated.
- Heat the olive oil in a large frying pan. Sauté the chicken breasts for about 4 minutes on each side until they are golden. Remove and set aside.
- Add the onion, garlic, peppers and chilli to the pan and cook for 2 minutes until just softened.
- Return the chicken to the frying pan. Add the wine, stock and sausage.
- Cook rice according to packet instructions.
- Bring to the boil, reduce the heat, cover and simmer for 15 minutes. Add the tomatoes and lemon and cook for a final 10 minutes. Season with salt and pepper.

To serve the stylish way: Dust the plate with smoked paprika, spoon on the cooked rice and ladle the Spanish chicken on top. Garnish with lemon wedges.

Hazelnut-stuffed Turkey with Brandy Sauce

M SHABBAT YT

DAIRY-FREE GLUTEN-FREE

Info
- Preparation Time: 20 minutes
- Cooking Time: 2–3 hours depending on weight after stuffing (see introduction for directions)
- Serves: 10–12

Ingredients
- 1 turkey weighing 3.5–5kg/ 8–11 lb

✡

- 1 tsp salt
- 1 tsp freshly ground black pepper
- 1 tsp sweet or smoked paprika
- 2 eating apples
- 200g/7 oz chopped hazelnuts
- 150g/5 oz can chestnut purée
- 100g/4 oz marzipan, finely chopped
- 1 tsp cinnamon

✡

- 250ml/9 fl oz/1 cup hot chicken stock
- 125ml/4 fl oz/½ cup white wine

✡

For the brandy sauce
- 2 tbsp cornflour
- 3 tbsp brandy
- salt and pepper, to taste
- 1 tsp cinnamon

✡

- To serve: dried cranberries, roast potatoes

Turkey is a special occasion meal and this is a perfect festive recipe. I love the hazelnut, apple and marzipan stuffing which cooks gently inside the turkey neck cavity. Allow about 450g/1 lb turkey per person.

The cooking time is an estimate; weigh the stuffed bird before roasting. As a general guide, if the turkey weighs under 4 kg/9 lb, allow 20 minutes per kg/2½ lb plus 70 minutes cooking time, and if it is over 4 kg/9 lb allow 20 minutes per kg plus 90 minutes cooking time. Remember that fan-assisted ovens cook quicker than conventional ovens so adjust your timings accordingly.

Many American Jews celebrate Thanksgiving and turkey would certainly be part of the festive menu. Numerous Rabbis have commented on this tradition and concluded that since it is not a religious festival, partaking of this American holiday is permitted.

Method
- Pre-heat the oven to 200°C/400°F/Gas mark 6.
- Wash and dry the turkey and rub well inside with the salt, pepper and paprika.
- Peel and quarter the apples then core and chop them. Combine the apples with the nuts, chestnut purée, marzipan and cinnamon.
- Stuff the neck cavity with this mixture. Using household string tie the turkey together to prevent the stuffing from coming out.
- Pour the chicken stock and wine into the roasting tin. Roast the turkey breast side down covered with aluminium foil for 1 hour
- Turn the turkey over and continue to roast covered according to its weight (see above).
- Switch off the oven and leave the bird in there to stand for 15 minutes. To make the brandy sauce, strain the cooking juices into a small saucepan. Mix the cornflour with 2 tbsp of the

Bread selection including: onion bread, granary bread, tomato & basil bread and herb pitta bread sticks.
(Pages 36, 37, 39, 41)

Crispy shredded chilli beef. (Page 98)

Crunchy papaya salad. (Page 46)

Italian chicken spirals with basil dressing. (Page 82)

Jerusalem kugel. (Page 118)

Lemongrass fish cakes with lime mayonnaise. (Page 13)

ABOVE Crispy noodle salad. (Page 54)
BELOW Molotov pudding. (Page 172)

Moroccan vegetable tagine. (Page 153)

reserved cooking juices. Stir in the brandy, salt, pepper and cinnamon. Bring to the boil and simmer for 3 minutes or until thickened.

- Slice the turkey breast with a sharp knife or an electric knife.
- Serve accompanied by dried cranberries and roast potatoes and pour the sauce over the sliced turkey.

Italian Chicken Spirals

M · SHABBAT · YT · SUCCOT

Info
- Preparation Time: 25 minutes
- Cooking Time: 45 minutes
- Serves: 4

Ingredients
- 1 aubergine, cut lengthways into 4 thin slices
- 6 tbsp olive oil

✿

- 2 red peppers, cut in half and deseeded

✿

- 4 chicken breasts, skinned

✿

- 4 tsp sun-dried tomato paste or tomato purée
- 8 basil leaves
- salt and freshly ground black pepper
- 2 cloves garlic, peeled and crushed

✿

- 1 egg, for coating
- 8 tbsp breadcrumbs or medium matza meal

✿

For the basil dressing
- 75g/3 oz pine nuts
- large bunch of fresh basil, at least 30g/1 oz/2 tbsp
- 2 cloves garlic, peeled and roughly chopped

✿

- 100ml/3½ fl oz olive oil

✿

- Garnish: 4 cherry tomatoes, sliced, sprigs of basil

This recipe transforms a simple chicken breast into a delicious wrap of aubergine, peppers, basil and tomatoes: the flavours of Italy. It can be prepared in advance and cooked at a later stage. To continue the Italian theme serve with a basil dressing.

Method
- Pre-heat the grill to its highest setting.
- Place the aubergine slices on a baking tray. Drizzle over 3 tbsp of the olive oil and grill for 5 minutes on each side or until golden.
- Place the red peppers on a tray. Drizzle over 1 tbsp of the olive oil. Grill until blackened. This will take 5–8 minutes. Remove and transfer to a dish and cover with cling film. Leave for 10 minutes and then remove the skin.
- Place the chicken breasts between two pieces of non-stick baking parchment. Flatten them by gently bashing with a rolling pin until they are evenly 2 cm/1 inch thick.
- Pre-heat the oven to 200°C/400°F/Gas mark 6.
- Spread each chicken breast with sun-dried tomato paste, then an aubergine slice, then half a red pepper, top with a few basil leaves and a sprinkling of salt, pepper and crushed garlic.
- Roll up firmly and secure with a cocktail stick. Brush with a little beaten egg and sprinkle with breadcrumbs or matza meal.
- Heat the remaining 2 tbsp of olive oil. Sauté the chicken breasts for about 3 minutes on each side or until golden.
- Place the spirals on a baking tray.
- Cook for 25–30 minutes or until thoroughly cooked.
- To make the dressing, roast the pine nuts in a dry frying pan for 2–3 minutes. They will cook fast so keep an eye on them. Remove immediately and transfer to another dish.

- Place the pine nuts, basil and garlic in a food processor. Blitz together into a paste. Gradually add the olive oil and season with salt and pepper to taste.

To serve the stylish way: Place the chicken spirals on a warmed plate. Remove the cocktail sticks. Drizzle over some basil dressing and garnish with sliced cherry tomatoes and sprigs of basil.

Honey-glazed Lamb with Minted Mash

M SHABBAT ◆RH◆

Info
- Preparation Time: 15 minutes
- Cooking Time: 40 minutes
- Serves: 4

Ingredients
- 2 tbsp olive oil
- 2 eggs, beaten

✿

- 8 large lamb cutlets
- 8–10 tbsp breadcrumbs or medium matza meal, seasoned with salt and pepper

✿

For the sauce
- 2 tbsp soy sauce
- 1 tsp mustard
- 3 tbsp red wine vinegar
- 4 tbsp brown sugar
- 4 tbsp honey
- 150ml/¼ pint/5 fl oz tomato ketchup
- salt and freshly ground black pepper

Tender, lean lamb cutlets are delicious glazed with a honey sauce. This recipe is particularly good for a dinner party, impressive as well as straightforward to serve. I like to prepare the cutlets and mashed potato in advance so that very little time is required in the kitchen when my guests arrive. Mint is traditionally the accompaniment for lamb – in my stylish twist I have added it to the potato.

Health Hint: The lamb in this dish serves up excellent amounts of vitamin B12, which is needed to make red blood cells and build nerve fibres; particularly good if you are anaemic.

Method
- Pre-heat the oven to 200ºC/400ºF/Gas mark 6.
- Mix together the oil and beaten eggs. Brush each cutlet lightly with this mixture. Coat each cutlet on both sides with the breadcrumbs or matza meal. Place on a tray lined with baking parchment.
- Bake uncovered for 20 minutes.
- Make the sauce by combining all the ingredients. Taste and season accordingly. Remove the cutlets from the oven and brush with the sauce mixture.
- Reduce the oven temperature to 180ºC/350ºF/Gas mark 4.
- Return the cutlets to the oven for a further 20 minutes.
- Serve with minted mash (see facing page).

Minted Mash

Info
- Preparation Time: 10 minutes
- Cooking Time: 20 minutes
- Serves: 4–6

Ingredients
- 900g/2 lb white potatoes, peeled and roughly chopped

✡

- 110g/4 oz margarine
- 2 tbsp olive oil
- 1 tbsp mint jelly
- pinch of nutmeg
- 4 tbsp roughly chopped fresh mint
- salt and freshly ground black pepper

Mashed potato at any time of the year is most welcome in my household and combining it with fresh mint is a special treat. It is quick and easy to make and will easily reheat in the microwave should you wish to make it in advance. My chef's secret is to use a ricer to avoid undesirable lumps. Adding margarine, olive oil and seasoning well with salt and freshly ground black pepper or a pinch of nutmeg help to maximise the flavour.

Method
- Cook the potatoes in a large saucepan of boiling water until soft – about 20 minutes. Drain well.
- Mash the potato using a masher or fork or ricer. Return the mashed potato to the saucepan.
- Stir in the margarine, olive oil and mint jelly whilst the potato is still hot.
- Add the nutmeg and mint and season well with salt and pepper.

Middle Eastern Lamb with Dill, Olives and Spring Onion Mash

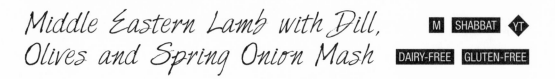

Info

- Preparation Time: 15 minutes
- Cooking Time: 2 hours 15 minutes
- Serves: 6

✡

Ingredients

- 2 tbsp olive oil
- 1 kg/2¼ lb shoulder of lamb, cubed
- 2 onions, peeled and finely chopped

✡

- 2 tsp turmeric
- freshly ground black pepper, to taste
- 1 tsp salt
- 600ml/1 pint beef stock
- juice of 2 lemons
- 4 sticks of celery, finely chopped
- 8 spring onions, finely chopped

✡

- 300g/10 oz/2 cups green olives, pitted and rinsed
- 300g/10 oz/1 cup frozen or fresh peas

✡

- 225g/8 oz spinach, roughly chopped
- 2 tbsp finely chopped fresh dill

✡

- Garnish: 1 lemon, sliced, sprigs of fresh dill

This recipe is Sephardi: the flavours of turmeric and lemon amongst its ingredients reflect its Syrian origin. Low wages and large numbers of mouths to feed made these dishes popular – they used cheaper cuts of meat and by adding the peas and olives, small amounts of meat went a long way. The slow gentle cooking transforms the meat into succulent tender pieces and the visual impact of the yellow and green ingredients make it most impressive. Enjoy it with pitta bread to mop up the tasty juices.

Other typical Jewish Syrian foods include dishes like mjaddrah (lentils, vermicelli and fried onions), sweet and sour chicken with apricots, pastilles (savoury meat pies) and cheese dumplings.

Method

- Heat the oil in a large pan. Brown the lamb cubes and onions.
- Add the turmeric, pepper and salt. Pour over the stock and lemon juice. Add the celery and spring onions. Bring to the boil, cover and simmer for 2 hours.
- Add the olives and peas and cook for a further 3 minutes.
- Taste and adjust the seasoning accordingly. Stir in the spinach and dill.
- Serve with spring onion mash (see facing page) and garnish with slices of lemon and sprigs of fresh dill.

Spring Onion Mash

PAREV ● P ● V ● DAIRY-FREE ● GLUTEN-FREE

Info
- Preparation Time: 15 minutes
- Cooking Time: 25 minutes
- Serves: 6 people
- Can be made in advance

Ingredients
- 1.8 kg/4 lb white potatoes, peeled and roughly chopped

✡

- 2 tbsp olive oil
- 2 bunches of spring onions, trimmed and roughly chopped
- 4 cloves garlic, peeled and finely chopped

✡

- 150g/5 oz margarine
- salt and freshly ground black pepper

Method
- Cook the potatoes in boiling salted water until tender – about 20 minutes.
- While the potatoes are cooking, heat the olive oil in a frying pan and sauté the spring onions and garlic until softened.
- Drain the potatoes, then mash. Add the fried spring onions and margarine.
- Season with salt and pepper to taste.

Tender Beef and Crispy Sweet Potato Pie

M | SHABBAT | CHANUKAH | YT

Info
- Preparation Time: 35 minutes
- Cooking Time: 2 hours 10 minutes
- Serves: 6

Ingredients
- 900g/2 lb cubed beef steak or cubed shoulder of lamb
- ½–1 tbsp cinnamon
- 3 tbsp plain flour

✡

- 6 tbsp extra virgin olive oil or rapeseed oil
- 2 onions, peeled and sliced
- 3 cloves garlic, finely chopped

✡

- 300g/11 oz chestnut mushrooms, cut into quarters
- 300g/11 oz butternut squash, peeled and cubed
- 2 orange peppers, cut in half, deseeded and roughly chopped
- 2 carrots, peeled and coarsely chopped
- 300ml/½ pint/1¼ cups red wine
- 2 tbsp beef or mushroom stock powder
- salt and freshly ground black pepper, to taste

✡

- 2–3 sweet potatoes, peeled and finely sliced

✡

- To serve: green vegetables

This is a tasty winter warming beef stew made with a selection of seasonal vegetables. My favourite part is the crispy topping of sweet potatoes.

When buying sweet potatoes they should be firm, without bruises and without a smell. Ideally they should be stored unwrapped in a cool, well-ventilated, dark, dry place.

Chef's Tip: This recipe can be frozen once cooled. When reheating, defrost and allow an hour on 170ºC/325ºF/Gas mark 3 to warm up.

Method
- Pre-heat the oven to 170ºC/325ºF/Gas mark 3.
- Dust the beef with the cinnamon and flour.
- Heat 3 tbsp of the olive oil or rapeseed oil in a large saucepan and brown the beef in batches, followed by the onions and garlic together.
- Add the mushrooms, butternut squash, peppers and carrots to the beef mixture, followed by the wine, beef or mushroom stock powder, salt and pepper.
- Cover with a lid, bring to the boil and simmer for 1½ hours.
- Transfer to an ovenware dish and fan the sliced sweet potatoes on top. Drizzle the remaining oil over the potatoes, season with salt and pepper. Cook for a final 40–50 minutes in the oven or until the potato is cooked and crispy.
- Serve with green vegetables.

Veal Chops with Mushroom Sauce

Info
- Preparation Time: 20 minutes
- Cooking Time: 30 minutes
- Serves: 4

Ingredients
- 2 tbsp olive oil

✡

- 4 veal chops, trimmed of any excess fat
- salt and freshly ground black pepper
- 1 large onion, peeled and sliced
- 3 cloves garlic, peeled and finely chopped
- 300g/11 oz brown cap mushrooms, thinly sliced
- 15g/½ oz/1 tbsp dried mushrooms, ideally porcini, soaked in 200ml/7 fl oz hot water
- 100ml/3½ fl oz mushroom or vegetable stock
- 100ml/3½ fl oz dry white wine
- 1 tbsp fresh thyme

✡

- 400g/14 oz fettuccine, tagliatelle or pappardelle pasta

✡

- Garnish: sprigs of fresh thyme

Veal is the meat produced from very young cattle – mainly male calves from dairy herds. It is regarded as something of a delicacy and rarely features in the kosher cook's repertoire. However, things are changing. Kosher veal, produced according to strict humane laws, is now readily available in the UK and comes from France.

At my local butcher's you can buy veal chops, veal osso bucco, veal mince, rolled breast and cutlets. This is a tasty recipe and makes a special treat for the whole family. I like to serve it with long pasta such as fettuccine, tagliatelle or pappardelle.

Method
- Heat the olive oil in a large frying pan.
- Season the veal with salt and pepper. Pan fry for 2–3 minutes on each side to give a little colour. Remove and set aside.
- Sauté the onion, garlic and brown cap mushrooms until soft. Add the veal, dried mushrooms with mushroom liquid, mushroom or vegetable stock, wine and thyme. Bring to the boil and simmer for 15 minutes.
- Cook the pasta according to the packet instructions. Drain and transfer to individual dishes.
- Place a veal chop on each dish and spoon on the sauce.

To serve the stylish way: Garnish with sprigs of fresh thyme and a dusting of black pepper.

Golden Glazed Cinnamon Chicken with Red Rice

M **DAIRY-FREE** **GLUTEN-FREE** **RH**

Info

- Preparation Time: 25 minutes plus overnight marinating
- Cooking Time: 50 minutes
- Serves: 8

Ingredients

- 1 tsp salt
- 100g/4 oz brown muscovado sugar

✡

- 2 red onions, peeled and finely chopped
- 4 cloves garlic, peeled and finely chopped
- 1 large tbsp dried cinnamon
- zest and juice of 2 oranges

✡

- 8 chicken leg portions or chicken breasts
- 500g/1 lb red rice, rinsed
- 1 litre/1¾ pints/4 cups vegetable or chicken stock

✡

- Garnish: 1 orange, sliced

This is an ideal recipe for Rosh Hashanah – family-friendly, easy to make and serve and fantastic served with red rice.

Red rice originates from the Camargue, Southern France. It has a unique nutty taste and a firmer texture than most other rice and subsequently may need additional cooking water. Its wonderful red colour enhances this tasty chicken dish.

Method

- For the chicken marinade, mix the salt, sugar, 100ml/3½ fl oz cold water in a small saucepan. Gently heat to dissolve the sugar.
- Stir in the onions, garlic, cinnamon and orange zest and juice and cook for 5 minutes. Remove and set aside.
- Using a sharp knife make several incisions in the chicken flesh before adding the marinade. Using your hands, rub the marinade into the chicken, turning to ensure that it is well coated. Cover with cling film and leave at the bottom of the fridge overnight.
- Pre-heat the oven to 200°C/400°F/Gas mark 6.
- Transfer the chicken to an ovenproof dish and pour over the marinade. Cover with foil and roast for 35 minutes or until cooked and golden.
- Cook the rice in the stock according to the packet instructions.

To serve the stylish way: Sit the golden glazed chicken on top of the warmed red rice and garnish with slices of orange.

Chicken Livers with Golden Rice

M · CHANUKAH

DAIRY-FREE · GLUTEN-FREE

Info
- Preparation Time: 15 minutes
- Cooking Time: 20 minutes
- Serves: 4

Ingredients
- 2–3 tbsp rapeseed or sunflower oil
- 2 onions, peeled and sliced
- 4 cloves garlic, peeled and finely chopped
- 1 tbsp brown sugar

✡

- 50g/2 oz/¼ cup dried apricots, roughly chopped
- 1 tsp turmeric
- 340g/12 oz basmati rice
- 850ml/1½ pints/3½ cups chicken stock

✡

- 4 tbsp chopped flat-leaf parsley

✡

- 340g/12 oz chicken livers, ready-koshered and sliced
- 2 tbsp red wine
- salt and freshly ground black pepper, to taste

✡

- Garnish: 50g/2 oz/¼ cup roasted flaked almonds, sprigs of fresh parsley

This recipe is typical of Persian Jewish cooking – basmati rice is a staple of Persian cuisine and when combined with the chicken livers it makes a very quick and tasty nutritious meal. Coloured and flavoured with turmeric and stock, the golden rice has a great aroma and appearance. The addition of brown sugar helps to caramelise the onions and bring all the delicious tastes together.

Chef's Tip: Koshered chicken liver is readily available at the kosher butcher's.

Method
- Heat the rapeseed or sunflower oil in a large frying pan. Sauté the onions, garlic and sugar until the onions are soft and golden. Set aside.
- Place the apricots, turmeric, rice and stock in a saucepan. Cover, bring to the boil and simmer until cooked – about 20 minutes. Stir in the parsley.
- Add the chicken livers to the onions with the wine and cook for a final 5 minutes until hot and cooked through. Season with salt and pepper.

To serve the stylish way: Spoon a generous circle of rice onto a warmed plate. Add the cooked chicken livers to the middle and top with toasted almonds and sprigs of parsley.

Jamaican Lime Chicken

M DAIRY-FREE

GLUTEN-FREE   SHABBAT   YT

Info

- Preparation Time: 10 minutes, plus 8 hours marinating
- Cooking Time: 30 minutes
- Serves: 6

Ingredients

For the marinade

- 4 spring onions, finely chopped
- ½ green chilli, deseeded and finely chopped
- 4 tbsp orange juice
- 1 tbsp finely chopped fresh ginger
- juice of 1 lime
- 2 tbsp soy sauce
- 2 cloves garlic, peeled and finely chopped
- 1 tsp allspice
- 1 tsp cinnamon
- pinch of ground cloves
- 6 chicken breasts, skinned

✿

- Garnish: ground cinnamon, 1 lime, sliced

This is an easy recipe made with a Jamaican jerk sauce of soy sauce, lime, orange juice and numerous spices. It makes a mouth-watering marinade that is also delicious on other poultry such as turkey and duck. I like to serve it with coconut rice and peas, the true Caribbean way.

Jamaica has a history of hosting Jews dating back to Columbus' times, when Sephardi Jews fled the Spanish Inquisition. In 1882, the synagogue in Kingston was destroyed by fire and today there is just one other remaining synagogue. The floor is covered in sand, which is a Marrano tradition to conceal any noise made during prayer. Various Jewish voluntary organisations are active there and since Jamaican Independence in 1962, Israel and Jamaica have developed and maintain full diplomatic relations.

Method

- Make the marinade by combining the spring onions, chilli, orange juice, ginger, lime juice, soy sauce, garlic, allspice, cinnamon and cloves. Add the chicken and marinate for 8 hours or overnight.
- Pre-heat the oven to 200°C/400°F/Gas mark 6.
- Transfer the chicken to an ovenproof dish and pour over the marinade juices.
- Cook covered for 30 minutes or until cooked.

To serve the stylish way: Dust the plate with ground cinnamon and serve on a bed of coconut rice with peas. Garnish with slices of lime.

Tandoori Chicken With Tomato, Cucumber and Coriander Salad

M GLUTEN-FREE
DAIRY-FREE

Info
- Preparation Time: 20 minutes plus 6 hours marinating
- Cooking Time: 30 minutes
- Serves: 4

Ingredients
- 4 large chicken breasts, boneless and skinless, cut in half lengthways

✡

- 4 tbsp soya yoghurt
- 2 tbsp tandoori curry paste
- 2 cm/1 inch piece of fresh ginger root, peeled and grated
- 1 tsp paprika
- ½ tsp salt
- 2 tsp lemon juice
- 2 cloves garlic, peeled and finely chopped
- 2 tbsp tomato paste
- 1–2 green chillies, deseeded and finely chopped
- 1 tsp turmeric

✡

For the salad
- 6 salad tomatoes, deseeded and chopped
- 1 small cucumber, diced
- 1 red onion, peeled and finely chopped
- 3 tbsp fresh coriander, roughly chopped
- salt and freshly ground black pepper

✡

- Garnish: 1 lemon cut into wedges

With the use of soya yoghurt and soya creams, recipes like tandoori chicken can now be made kosher. This is an extremely likeable dish and looks as good as it tastes. Like most tandoori recipes, it requires at least 6 hours' marinating time; plan it well and you will be delighted with the end result; pieces of succulent chicken with a delicious curry flavour. Tandoori paste is now available from most kosher supermarkets.

Tandoori comes from the Punjab region of India and is made by tenderising the meat in a yoghurt and spice marinade. It is traditionally cooked in a tandoor, a clay oven that fires up to a really high temperature but a grill or very hot oven will achieve similar results when you are cooking at home.

I like to serve this with a selection of chutneys and naan bread and a soothing dip of freshly made raita, a soya yoghurt dip made with finely chopped cucumber, chopped coriander, salt and pepper and a pinch of sugar.

Method
- Make three deep slashes in each chicken fillet and put them in a non-metallic shallow dish.
- Mix the yoghurt with the curry paste, ginger, paprika, salt, lemon juice, garlic, tomato paste, chillies and turmeric.
- Pour the marinade over the chicken and leave for 6–8 hours or overnight.
- Pre-heat the oven to 240°C/475°F/Gas mark 9.
- Lift the chicken out of the marinade and put on a rack in a roasting tin. Cook in the oven for 20 minutes.
- Pre-heat the grill to high. Pour the marinade over the chicken and grill for 10 minutes turning once until golden and cooked through.

- For the salad, mix together all the ingredients and season just before serving.

To serve the stylish way: Garnish with lemon wedges and serve with the salad.

Rigatoni with Spiced Meatballs and Red Wine Sauce M SHABBAT YT RH

Info
- Preparation Time: 25 minutes
- Cooking Time: 40 minutes
- Serves: 4

Ingredients
For the meatballs
- 450g/1 lb minced beef
- 1 onion, peeled and finely chopped
- 50g/2 oz/¼ cup black olives, stoned and roughly chopped
- 50g/2 oz/¼ cup medium matza meal
- 1 egg
- 1 tbsp smoked paprika
- 1 red chilli, deseeded and finely chopped
- 2–3 tbsp finely chopped fresh parsley
- salt and pepper, to taste

✿

For the red wine sauce
- 250ml/9 fl oz/1 cup red wine
- 2 x 400g/14 oz cans chopped tomatoes
- 2 tsp sugar
- large bunch of fresh basil, roughly chopped
- salt and pepper

✿

- 400g/14 oz rigatoni pasta

✿

- Garnish: smoked paprika and sprigs of basil

You can never have too many pasta or meatball recipes and this one should certainly be added to your repertoire. Family-friendly, it can be made in advance: what more could you ask for on a cold winter's night? I have used rigatoni pasta, which is shaped like a tube and can vary in length and diameter. Its name comes from the Italian word meaning 'ridges'. The sauce gets trapped in the tubes and ridges. It is most common in southern and central Italy.

In my opinion there is no such thing as cooking wine – the better the wine, the better the sauce – however, if you already have a bottle of wine that has been opened and it is unlikely to be drunk, use it for cooking.

Method
- Heat the oven to 200°C/400°F/Gas mark 6.
- To make the meatballs combine all the ingredients.
- With wet hands, divide the mixture into small balls about the size of a walnut.
- Place the meatballs on a tray lined with baking parchment and bake for 15 minutes.
- Place the red wine sauce ingredients in a saucepan. Mix together, bring to the boil and simmer for 20 minutes until reduced and thickened.
- Remove the meatballs from the oven tray and transfer to the red wine sauce.
- Cook the pasta according to the packet instructions.
- Drain the pasta, return to the saucepan and pour over the meatballs and sauce. Mix well.

To serve the stylish way: Dust the plate with smoked paprika and garnish with sprigs of basil.

Schnitzel Noodle Stir Fry

M CHANUKAH YT

Info
- Preparation Time: 30 minutes
- Cooking Time: 25 minutes
- Serves: 6

Ingredients
- 6 chicken breasts, skinned and boneless

✡

- salt and freshly ground black pepper
- 4 eggs, slightly beaten
- 100g/4 oz fine matza meal
- 200g/7 oz breadcrumbs

✡

- 6 tbsp rapeseed oil or other quality frying oil

✡

For the dressing
- 2 tbsp soy sauce
- 3 tbsp rapeseed/extra virgin olive oil
- 1 tsp honey
- 1 tbsp sesame oil
- juice of 1 lime

✡

For the noodle stir fry
- 3 cloves garlic, peeled and finely chopped
- 6 spring onions, trimmed and chopped
- 2 cm/1 inch fresh ginger, peeled and finely chopped
- 3 red peppers, deseeded and sliced in cubes

I am always looking for an easy meal that will be nutritious and filling with whole family appeal. Usefully, this recipe can be made in several stages; first the chicken breasts need to be coated and fried and then the vegetables and noodles cooked.

Cooking the schnitzel in cold pressed rapeseed oil means that the frying pan does not need to be cleaned half way during cooking as the oil has a high resistance to heat. Other oils tend to burn the crumb remains by the time you have cooked a second batch of schnitzels. If you cannot get the rapeseed oil any quality frying oil will be fine.

The secret of a good stir fry is to have all the ingredients ready chopped in advance.

Method
- Slice the chicken breasts into goujon-size strips. Season with salt and pepper.
- Dip the chicken in the beaten egg then in the matza meal. Coat once more with the egg and finally dip into the breadcrumbs.
- Heat 4 tbsp of the rapeseed oil in a large frying pan.
- Fry the chicken until golden, then transfer to a plate lined with kitchen paper. Set aside.
- Make the dressing by combining all the ingredients.
- Heat the remaining 2 tbsp rapeseed oil in a large wok or deep frying pan.
- Add the garlic, spring onions, ginger and peppers and cook for 3 minutes.
- Cook the egg noodles according to the packet instructions, drain and set aside.
- Pour in the dressing, schnitzel, mangetout and bean sprouts and cook for a final 2–3 minutes, or until the vegetables are al dente and the noodles and the meat hot.

- 200g/7 oz mangetout, trimmed
- 200g/7 oz bean sprouts

  ✡

- 375g/13 oz thick egg noodles

  ✡

- Garnish: sprigs of coriander,
  2 limes, cut into wedges

- Transfer to a large serving dish and serve immediately.

To serve the stylish way: Garnish with sprigs of coriander and wedges of lime.

Crispy Shredded Chilli Beef

DAIRY-FREE GLUTEN-FREE
M CHANUKAH SUCCOT

Info
- Preparation Time: 20 minutes
- Cooking Time: 15 minutes
- Serves: 3–4

Ingredients
- 2 eggs, beaten
- 1 tsp salt
- 4 tbsp cornflour

✡

- 800g/2 lb (approx. 200g/7 oz per person) large pieces of prime bola steak, cut into strips
- Oil, for frying

✡

- 3 spring onions, shredded
- 1–2 red chillies, deseeded and shredded
- 3 carrots, peeled and finely shredded

✡

For the sauce
- 1 tbsp brown sugar
- 1 clove garlic, peeled and finely chopped
- 2 tbsp white rice vinegar
- 4 tbsp sweet chilli dipping sauce
- 1 tbsp soy sauce

✡

- Garnish: sprigs of coriander and chopped spring onions

This is an all-time Chinese favourite – but kosher of course. Getting the beef really crispy is the secret of its success and can only be achieved by frying it in very hot oil and cutting the meat very fine. Like all Chinese dishes, preparing the ingredients in advance, ready for the pan, will make the process easier. The best way to shred the carrots is to use a mandolin or food processor.

I like to serve this with either egg noodles or plain rice.

In Beijing there is a very active Jewish community, mostly made up of expats and there is a Chabad centre with a kosher restaurant and mikveh. Ingredients can be found in Western-style grocery stores, but because they come from all over the world, working out whether they are kosher or not can be tricky. The following are some of the main symbols used by Beth Din around the world to indicate that a product is kosher.

Ⓤ ⓀKSAⓀ ✩ ⒸⓄⓇ cRc

Method
- Combine the eggs, salt and cornflour and coat the beef strips.
- Heat the oil to 180°C/350°F/Gas mark 4 in a deep wok or frying pan. Fry the beef strips taking care to add them to the pan one by one. Don't stir for approximately 10 seconds, then stir to ensure the pieces don't stick together (use a chopstick to separate). Cook for approximately 6–7 minutes until brown and crispy. Remove and drain on a plate covered with kitchen paper.
- Using some of the oil from your wok in a separate pan, stir fry the spring onions, chillies and carrots.

• For the sauce, mix together the sugar, garlic, vinegar, chilli dipping sauce and soy sauce. Stir into the vegetable pan and cook gently for 2 minutes. Finally add the cooked beef and toss together.

To serve the stylish way: Garnish with sprigs of coriander and chopped spring onions.

Thai Chicken Cakes

M · SHABBAT · YT

Info

- Preparation Time: 20 minutes
- Cooking Time: 15 minutes
- Serves: 6
- Suitable for freezing

Ingredients

- 3 cloves garlic, peeled and roughly chopped
- small piece of ginger, peeled and finely chopped
- 3 tbsp fresh coriander
- 1 red chilli, deseeded and finely chopped
- 5 spring onions, trimmed
- 1 slice of white bread
- 3 tbsp shredded coconut
- salt and freshly ground black pepper

✡

- 900g/2 lb minced chicken

✡

- vegetable oil, for frying

✡

- Garnish: sprigs of fresh coriander, wedges of lime
- Serve with: shredded Chinese leaves, rocket leaves, bean sprouts and sweet chilli sauce

This quick and versatile new way of spicing up chicken breasts was a great success at my cookery class 'Something different with chicken'. Use it for a mid-week family supper with salad (the kids will love it), dress it up for a dinner party starter, or make mini chicken cakes for a picnic or packed lunch.

The oriental flavours of coconut, ginger, chilli and garlic come through in every mouthful. Serve the chicken cakes with noodles or rice for a complete oriental feast.

As this recipe freezes easily I like to make double quantity so I can use some and freeze the second batch.

Method

- Place the garlic, ginger, coriander, chilli, spring onions, bread, coconut, and salt and pepper in a food processor.
- Whiz together until the ingredients are finely chopped. Remove from the food processor and stir in the minced chicken.
- With wet hands shape into 12 small cakes.
- Heat the oil in a frying pan. Cook the chicken cakes for 6–8 minutes, turning once. Alternatively cook them in a deep fat fryer.
- Garnish with sprigs of fresh coriander and lime wedges.

To serve the stylish way: Serve hot on a bed of shredded Chinese leaves, rocket and bean sprouts and sweet chilli sauce.

Hot and Sour Duck

M **DAIRY-FREE** **GLUTEN-FREE** **SHABBAT** ◆RH▶

Info
- Preparation Time: 20 minutes plus 20 minutes to debone duck if you are doing this yourself
- Cooking Time: 20 minutes
- Serves: 6

Ingredients
- 1 large duck

✡

- 4 tbsp tamarind pulp
- 6 shallots, peeled
- 3 cloves garlic, peeled
- 2.5 cm/1 inch piece of fresh ginger
- 1 tsp dried coriander
- 2 tbsp soy sauce
- 1 tbsp ground cinnamon
- 1 large red chilli, cut in half, deseeded and vein removed
- 1 tsp turmeric
- 100g/4 oz blanched almonds

✡

- 225g/8 oz bamboo shoots
- 5 salad tomatoes, cut in quarters
- 2–3 tbsp vegetable oil

✡

- salt and pepper, to taste

✡

- Garnish: sprigs of coriander (cilantro)

Thai cuisine includes a wonderful range of different strong flavours; turmeric, ginger, cinnamon, tamarind and soya sauce are particular favourites. This duck recipe is a tasty aromatic dish that makes one duck go a long way. I like to serve it with plain rice and a stir fry of pak choy.

You may not have come across tamarind but it is now available in most kosher supermarkets. The tamarind fruit is used as a flavouring ingredient especially in Latin American and Asian cuisine and pre-packaged snacks. Tamarind is purchased as a pulp and has to be soaked in hot water to soften and then you need to press it through a sieve to release the juice, which is the part you need. It is slightly sour but is perfect in dishes like this hot and sour recipe.

Method
- Remove the duck meat from the bones into bite-size pieces, or ask your butcher to do this for you.
- Place the tamarind pulp in a small bowl, pour over 4 tbsp of hot water and leave for 3 minutes to soften. Press the mixture through a sieve to produce about 2 tbsp of smooth juice.
- Place the tamarind juice in a food processor with the shallots, garlic, ginger, coriander, soy sauce, cinnamon, chilli, turmeric and almonds.
- Blend until smooth, adding a little more water if necessary. Set aside.
- Heat the oil in a wok or large frying pan and stir fry the duck in batches for about 3 minutes or until just coloured.
- Add the paste and stir fry for 5 minutes.
- Add the bamboo shoots and tomatoes and stir fry for 2 minutes.
- Taste and adjust seasoning accordingly.

To serve the stylish way: Transfer to a large dish, garnish with sprigs of coriander and serve with plain rice.

Salmon Crumble

Ⓓ

Info

- Preparation Time: 20 minutes
- Cooking Time: 45 minutes
- Serves: 6 as a starter or
  4 for a main course
- For starter portions, place in small ramekins and reduce cooking time to 20 minutes

Ingredients

- 450g/1 lb salmon, skinned and cut into cubes
- 330ml/11 fl oz/1½ cups milk

✡

- 2 tbsp olive oil
- 1 onion, peeled and finely chopped

✡

- 30g/1 oz unsalted butter
- 30g/1 oz plain flour

✡

- 1 tbsp tomato purée
- freshly ground black pepper, to taste
- 2 tbsp anchovy essence or 1 small can anchovy fillets, drained and roughly chopped
- 2 tbsp roughly chopped fresh parsley

✡

For the topping
- 2 thick slices of wholemeal bread
- 2 tbsp parsley
- 1–2 tbsp extra virgin olive oil

This is a delicious unusual way of making a little piece of salmon go a long way. Topped with herb breadcrumbs drizzled with olive oil, salmon crumble makes a wonderful alternative to the popular sweet crumble varieties. It is a great family recipe that can be doubled in quantity.

Scottish salmon is internationally recognised and the number one choice for high quality fish. Salmon is popular amongst Jews all over the world, particularly for Shabbat.

One reason for this popularity is that fish do not have any eyelids and thus never close their eyes. Our sages felt that they were a metaphor for God, whose eyes and gaze are always on us. In addition, there is a tradition that each letter in the Hebrew alphabet has a numerical value. The letters of the Hebrew word for fish, *dag*, add up to seven. The seventh day of the Jewish week is Shabbat. Therefore, eating fish is an auspicious and spiritual way of honouring Shabbat.

Serve with a green salad or a selection of seasonal green vegetables.

Chef's Tip: Use the seasoning of salt sparingly as the anchovy essence/fillets are already salty.

Method

- Pre-heat the oven to 190°C/375°F/Gas mark 5.
- Cook the salmon in the milk for about 15 minutes. Drain, retaining the milk to make the white sauce later.
- Heat the olive oil in a medium-sized saucepan. Sauté the onion until soft. Remove and set aside.
- Add the butter to the pan, melt and stir in the flour. Cook for 2 minutes, then gradually add the retained milk, stirring well.
- Return the onion to the pan of white sauce and stir in the tomato purée, pepper and anchovy essence or fillets and parsley.

- Stir the salmon and fold into the milk mixture.
- Transfer to an ovenproof dish.
- Place the bread and parsley in a food processor and whiz to form herb breadcrumbs.
- Sprinkle the breadcrumbs over the top. Drizzle over the extra virgin olive oil.
- Bake for 35 minutes or until brown and crunchy. Serve immediately.

Crusted Cod with Salsa

`PAREV`

Info
- Preparation Time: 20 minutes
- Cooking Time: 35 minutes
- Serves: 6

Ingredients
- 570 ml/1 pint/2½ cups vegetable stock
- 350g/12 oz couscous

✡

For the basil dressing
- 75g/3 oz tbsp pine nuts

✡

- large bunch of fresh basil, at least 30g/1 oz
- 2 cloves garlic, peeled and roughly chopped

✡

- 100ml/3½ fl oz olive oil
- salt and freshly ground black pepper

✡

- 6 x 170g/6 oz cod fillets

✡

For the salsa
- 170g/6 oz cherry tomatoes, cut in quarters
- 1 bulb of fennel, finely chopped
- 1 tbsp lemon juice
- 2 tbsp finely chopped fresh coriander
- 2 tbsp finely chopped fresh basil
- 2 tbsp extra virgin olive oil
- 2 spring onions, trimmed and finely chopped
- 1 tsp caster sugar
- salt and freshly ground black pepper

Cod can be quite bland, but coating it with couscous adds both texture and flavour. Served with a tomato salsa, this dish is healthy, colourful and tasty and an easy supper main course.

Cod is the most commonly caught fish in the world, and we in the UK can choose from either Atlantic or Pacific cod. It is very low in fat and is great grilled, fried or baked.

Serve with basil mashed potato which is simply boiled and seasoned potato, creamed with margarine or butter to taste with a generous helping of finely chopped fresh basil mixed through.

Method
- Pre-heat the oven to 180°C/350°F/Gas mark 4.
- Heat the vegetable stock and pour over the couscous. Cover with cling film and set aside for 10 minutes.
- To make the dressing, roast the pine nuts in a dry frying pan for 2–3 minutes. They will cook fast so keep an eye on them. Remove immediately and transfer to another dish.
- Place the pine nuts, basil and garlic in a food processor. Blitz together into a paste. Gradually add the olive oil and season with salt and pepper to taste.
- Make 2 slits diagonally across each cod fillet. Spread the basil dressing inside the slits and over the cod fillets and then coat with cooked couscous.
- Bake for approximately 30 minutes.
- Mix together all the salsa ingredients and season to taste.

To serve the stylish way: Serve the cod on a warmed plate garnished with the tomato and basil salsa. Complete the meal with basil mashed potato.

Sesame Fish with Udon Noodles

PAREV

Info
- Preparation Time: 10 minutes
- Cooking Time: 15 minutes
- Serves: 4

Ingredients
For the dressing
- 1 tbsp soy sauce
- 1 tsp sesame oil
- 1 tbsp mirin (rice wine)
- 1 tsp lemon juice
- 1 tbsp caster sugar
- ½ red chilli, deseeded and finely chopped (optional)
- 4 spring onions, trimmed and sliced

✡

- 2 tbsp extra virgin olive or rapeseed oil

✡

- 4 x 150g/5 oz skinless pollock fillets

✡

- 200g/7 oz udon or rice noodles 300g/11 oz/1 cup soya beans (found in the frozen vegetable section of the supermarket)

✡

- Garnish: sprigs of fresh coriander, 2tbsp toasted sesame seeds

For this new fish dish, I have used a fish which may be new to you too. Pollock makes a delicious alternative to cod or haddock. It can be poached, baked, pan fried, grilled or put into chowders. In recent years pollock has become more widely available and it can now be found in most supermarkets as fresh fillets. This recipe makes a tasty low-fat mid-week supper. If you like oriental flavours you will like this.

Method
- Mix together the soy sauce, sesame oil, mirin, lemon juice, sugar, chilli (if using) and spring onions.
- Heat the olive or rapeseed oil in a large frying pan. Add the fish and cook for 3 minutes covered and then turn over.
- Pour over the prepared dressing and continue cooking for a final 3 minutes.
- Cook the noodles and soya beans in salted water according to the noodle packet instructions.

To serve the stylish way: Transfer the noodles to individual bowls. Top with the fish and pour over any remaining dressing. Garnish with sprigs of fresh coriander and toasted sesame seeds.

Mediterranean Tuna Stacks

Ⓓ

Info
- Preparation Time: 10 minutes
- Cooking Time: 10 minutes
- Serves: 4

Ingredients
For the tapenade
- 75g/3 oz pitted black olives
- 2 cloves garlic, peeled and roughly chopped
- 1 tbsp balsamic vinegar
- 1 large bunch of basil
- 5 tbsp olive oil
- 1 tsp sugar

✡

- 4 x 170g/6 oz tuna steaks

✡

- 4 slices of thick granary bread

✡

- 100g/4 oz ricotta cheese
- 100g/4 oz baby spinach leaves
- sea salt and freshly ground black pepper, to taste

✡

- Garnish: 1 lemon, cut into slices

This tasty tuna 'gourmet sandwich' is perfect for a summer's evening when you want a quick healthy meal. BBQ, griddle or grill the fresh tuna steaks and enjoy with a glass of chilled white wine. A tomato or green salad is all that is needed to accompany this delicious combination of Mediterranean ingredients.

The secret of perfectly cooked tuna is to undercook it – this will produce a succulent fish steak that just melts in the mouth.

For a vegetarian option substitute thick slices of aubergine for the tuna.

Method
- Heat the griddle pan, BBQ or grill.
- To make the tapenade, place the olives, garlic, vinegar, basil and 3 tbsp of the oil in a food processor and blend to a purée. Taste and add about 1 tsp of sugar or to taste.
- Brush the tuna with the remaining 2 tbsp of oil and then cook in the hot griddle pan, BBQ or grill for 2–3 minutes on each side, or according to personal taste. Cut in half.
- Toast the bread, and spread the ricotta cheese on top. Cut in half to produce a triangle shape. Add a generous helping of spinach and layer with the basil sauce and tuna steaks to produce a stack. Season with salt and pepper.
- Serve with lemon slices.

Chapter 4

Modern Classics

Modern Classics

Here you will find many of the dishes you would expect in a kosher cookbook. From blintzes to borsht and kugel to Challah, these are the recipes of Jewish heritage passed down through the generations, primarily via the matriarch of the family. No two families' recipes are the same, as they were never written down and each cook used their own 'secret' ingredients. Measurements were vague and often included 'using a little bit of this and a little bit of that'.

I have taken the food that we like to eat, particularly at festivals and on Shabbat and, whilst remaining loyal to the classic versions, I have added modern ingredients and techniques to reflect changing food fashions.

It is so important to teach your children to cook so that these family heirlooms do not disappear. The family that cooks and eats together stays together and, for Jewish families around the world, this is still a very important aspect of our culture.

Modern Classics

- Hot or cold borsht
- Purim challah
- Matza granola
- Tzimmes chicken
- Shredded roast lamb and rosemary salad
- Stuffed brisket
- Jerusalem kugel
- Whisky chicken
- Passover beef lasagne
- Chicken goujons with BBQ sauce
- Classic cheese blintzes
- Chicken tagine with citrus couscous
- Lebanese tabbouleh
- Tropical fruit filo pie
- Rye bread
- Duet of fish balls – boiled fish balls/salmon fried fish balls
- Cheese and onion pie

Hot or Cold Borsht

(V) GLUTEN-FREE

Info
- Preparation Time: 30 minutes
- Cooking Time: 50 minutes, if serving cold, add 4 hours cooling time
- Serves: 6

Ingredients
- 500g/1 lb raw beetroot, peeled

✡

- 2 tbsp olive oil
- 200g/7 oz red cabbage, finely shredded
- 1 red onion, peeled and roughly chopped
- 2 cloves garlic, peeled and finely chopped

✡

- 2 potatoes, peeled and roughly chopped
- 4 carrots, peeled and roughly chopped
- 6 salad tomatoes, peeled and deseeded
- 1 litre/1¾ pints/4 cups vegetable stock
- juice of 1 lemon

✡

- 2 tbsp brown sugar
- salt and freshly ground black pepper, to taste

✡

- Garnish: 250ml/9 fl oz/1 cup sour cream, sprigs of fresh dill

Borsht is a favourite Ashkenazi soup, and as with chicken soup every family has its own version. My uncle tells great stories about how my great-grandparents, who lived in the East End of London, used to make borsht with the leaves and stalks cut up, and during the summer it was served with cream but in the winter it was left outside the kitchen door to chill.

I suggest that you use fresh beetroots for the sweetest results although vacuum-packed non-vinegar beetroots will also do.

Beetroot is considered a 'super food'; it contains betaine, a substance that relaxes the mind, and tryptophan, which is also found in chocolate and contributes to a sense of wellbeing. So enjoy the special qualities of this burgundy coloured hot or cold soup topped with some sour cream.

Method
- Grate the beetroot in a food processor. Be careful as the juices do stain.
- Heat the oil in a large pan and sauté the beetroot, cabbage, onion, and garlic for about 10 minutes to soften.
- Add the potatoes, carrots, tomatoes, stock and lemon juice. Bring to the boil and simmer for 40 minutes or until the vegetables are all soft.
- Purée in a liquidiser until smooth.
- Add the sugar and check seasoning.
- Serve straight away *or* leave to cool for a minimum of 4 hours or refrigerate overnight and serve cold.

To serve the stylish way: Ladle the soup into deep bowls and garnish with a generous spoonful of sour cream and a sprinkling of fresh dill.

Purim Challah

PAREV V

Info
- Preparation Time: 10 minutes plus 2 hours to rise, plus 20 minutes for proving
- Cooking Time: 20 minutes
- Makes: 2 large loaves

Ingredients
- 2 × 7g/¼ oz packets dried yeast
- 2 tsp salt
- 250ml/9 fl oz/1 cup warm water (100ml/3½ fl oz, followed by the rest)

✡

- 675g/1½ lb strong white bread flour
- 2 tbsp clear honey
- 100ml/3½ fl oz vegetable oil
- ½ tsp cinnamon
- 50g/2 oz/¼ cup raisins
- 2 eggs

✡

To glaze
- 2 eggs yolks, ½ tsp water

✡

- To decorate: 2 tbsp honey mixed with 1 tbsp boiling water, 2–3 tbsp colourful sprinkles

For Purim there are many festival recipes which relate to the story of Esther and her Uncle Mordechai – Purim challah is one of them. It is known as 'keylitsh' (Kulich) in Russian and this particular style of challah tends to be over-sized and extensively plaited. The plaits/braids are said to remind us of the rope used to hang the evil Haman. On a lighter note, I like to include raisins in the dough and to decorate it with colourful sprinkles.

Chef's Tip: All bread can be frozen.

Method
- Mix together the yeast, salt and 100ml/3½ fl oz of the warm water and leave for 5 minutes.
- Add the yeast mixture to the flour.
- Mix together slowly, either by hand or in the mixer using a dough hook if available.
- Add the honey, oil, cinnamon, raisins, eggs and the remaining warm water to the flour mixture.
- Continue to knead the mixture until it is smooth and shiny (you may need a little extra warm water depending on the size of the eggs.)
- Transfer to an oiled bowl, cover and leave to rise for 2 hours in a warm place.
- Knock back the dough (collapse the air out of the risen dough using your knuckles).
- Divide the dough in half and then separate each one into four equal pieces.
- Knead the dough gently before rolling out each piece to form a thin sausage.
- Divide the dough into four equal parts. Knead each part into a smooth ball and roll each ball into a rope-like strand. Lay the strands side by side and pinch together at the top.

- Grasp the leftmost strand and pass it to the right, under the two strands adjacent to it, and then back toward the left, over one strand (the one closest to it now).
- Grasp the rightmost strand and pass it to the left, under the two strands adjacent to it (which have already been braided), and then back to the right, over one strand.
- Alternately repeat the last two steps.
- When the plaiting is complete, pinch the ends of the strands together.

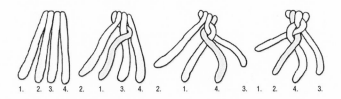

- Line a baking tray with baking parchment.
- Place the challahs on the tray. Glaze with the egg glaze.
- Pre-heat the oven to 200°C/400°F/Gas mark 6.
- Leave to prove for 20 minutes. (Proving is the second rising of the dough.)
- Bake for 20 minutes or until golden brown and hollow-sounding when tapped on the base.
- Cool on a wire rack.
- Brush the cooked challah with a little honey glaze and decorate with colourful sprinkles.

Matza Granola

Info
- Preparation Time: 10 minutes
- Cooking Time: 20 minutes
- Makes: 15–20 servings

Ingredients
- 1 large box matza (300g/11 oz), broken up into small pieces

✿

- 300g/11 oz pecan pieces
- 200g/7 oz/1 cup desiccated flaked coconut
- 200g/7 oz/1 cup slivered almonds

✿

- 200ml/7 fl oz/1 cup honey
- 175ml/6 fl oz vegetable oil
- 1 tsp ground cinnamon
- ½ tsp salt

✿

- 100g/4 oz/¼ cup raisins

It can be a challenge at Pesach to provide the family with satisfying breakfasts, because so many of our regular foods such as cereals are not allowed But now you can relax because I have created this nutritious matza cereal and it will certainly help to delay the onset of hunger pangs until at least 11 a.m.

It is delicious with milk or used as a topping for crumble or fruit pies, but it is also super-portable for when you're rushing out the door to visit family or doing activities with your kids. Just bag it up and go.

For those with nut allergies substitute more dried fruit for the nuts: for example dried apricots, sultanas and apples.

Matza can also be used as the base for other popular dishes, especially during Pesach when regular flour options are prohibited. So matza balls are widely used to accompany soups; Sephardim soak the matza and use it to make lasagne and pastry and make pies known as scacchi (Italian) or mina (Turkish).

Chef's Tip: Store in an airtight container at room temperature or in the refrigerator. It will keep for several weeks.

Method
- Pre-heat the oven to 180°C/350°F/Gas mark 4.
- Line two baking trays with non-stick baking parchment.
- Combine the matza pieces, pecans, coconut and almonds in a large bowl.
- Stir the honey, oil, cinnamon and salt in a medium-sized saucepan. Heat over a medium heat until boiling.
- Pour this over the matza mixture and toss until evenly coated.
- Spread the mixture evenly on the prepared baking trays.
- Bake for 15–20 minutes, tossing occasionally, so that the mixture browns evenly.
- Toss the matza mixture with raisins and allow to cool completely.

Tzimmes Chicken

M | DAIRY-FREE | GLUTEN-FREE | SHABBAT | RH | SUCCOT

Info
- Preparation Time: 15 minutes
- Cooking Time: 1 hour 45 minutes
- Serves: 6–8

Ingredients
- 1 large chicken (2.3 kg/5 lb)

✡

- 4 sweet potatoes, peeled and sliced
- 3 cooking apples, sliced but unpeeled
- 450g/1 lb carrots, peeled and sliced into discs
- 250g/9 oz/1 cup pitted prunes, cut in half

✡

- 300ml/½ pint/1¼ cups chicken stock
- 150ml/5 fl oz red wine
- zest and juice of 1 orange
- 2 tbsp honey
- 2 tbsp light brown sugar
- 2 tsp ground cinnamon
- 2 cm/1 inch piece of fresh ginger, peeled and finely chopped
- salt and freshly ground black pepper

✡

- Garnish: 2 oranges, sliced

At Rosh Hashanah there are frequently extra guests for dinner and I am always looking for a tasty family meal that everyone will enjoy. This recipe is my personal take on classic Tzimmes, a traditional Russian recipe of honeyed carrots baked in the oven. Combining it with chicken makes it a complete and easy to cook main course.

Tzimmes recipes vary considerably but all of them are sweet and contain the essential ingredient of carrots. On Rosh Hashanah carrots are even more popular than normal and appear in many recipes because when they are sliced they look like golden coins and so symbolise our hope that we have a prosperous new year and that our pockets should never be empty in the year to come.

The Jews of Russia historically have had a terrible existence. Anti-Jewish riots (pogroms) occurred frequently in the early nineteenth century and were followed by anti-religious laws aimed primarily against the Jews. Many fled to Poland and from there on to the United States and the UK, including some of my own ancestors.

State oppression of the Jews continued after World War Two. Ironically, these restrictions led to a resurgent interest in Jewish living and many started to look towards the newly created state of Israel as a possible homeland. However, despite protests from the West, emigration to Israel was severely restricted until President Gorbachev came into power in 1988 when there was a general relaxation of the rules on religious practice.

Today there are active communities in all of the main cities of Russia with many Jewish day schools, yeshivas and community centres. Despite a strong government stand against anti-Semitism most Jews continue to prefer to keep a low profile and identify more with their ethnic background than religious practice.

Method
- Pre-heat the oven to 180°C/350°F/Gas mark 4.
- Place the chicken in a large ovenproof dish.
- Mix together the potatoes, apples, carrots and prunes and place round the chicken.
- Combine the stock, wine, orange zest and juice, honey, sugar, cinnamon and ginger. Pour over the chicken.
- Season with salt and freshly ground black pepper.
- Cover with aluminium foil and roast for 1 hour 45 minutes.
- Remove from the oven and leave to rest for 10 minutes. Carve the chicken as desired.

To serve the stylish way: Dust each plate with a sprinkling of ground cinnamon and garnish with sliced oranges.

Shredded Roast Lamb and Rosemary Salad

M **DAIRY-FREE** **GLUTEN-FREE** **RH**

Info
- Preparation Time: 20 minutes
- Cooking Time: 3 hours plus 30 minutes resting time
- Serves: 6–8

Ingredients
- 2.7 kg/6 lb shoulder of lamb on the bone
- 10 sprigs of rosemary
- 200ml/7 fl oz/1 cup red wine
- 1 garlic bulb
- 2 red peppers, cut in quarters and deseeded
- 2 yellow peppers, cut in quarters and deseeded
- 2 tbsp extra virgin olive oil
- sea salt and freshly ground black pepper, to taste

✿

- 250g/9 oz baby spinach, washed
- 200g/7 oz/1 cup frozen soya beans, defrosted

✿

- Garnish: sprigs of fresh rosemary

This is a substantial main course salad that is perfect for a Yom Tov meal, either lunch or dinner. The lamb is roasted with garlic and peppers and is then shredded once cooked. The beauty of this is that it can be served hot or warm and can be left in the oven to keep warm. It can also be made and prepared in advance. Slices of challah are great to mop up the juices.

The only time that there is a restriction on serving roast lamb is at the first night Passover Seder meal. Jewish law says an entire lamb may not be roasted as it resembles the Passover sacrifices and so it is not put on the menu as it would be too similar.

Chef's Tip: Serve this with Date Quinoa on page 164 from the Free From section.

Method
- Pre-heat the oven to 170°C/325°F/Gas mark 3.
- Place the lamb in a roasting tin with the rosemary, wine, garlic cloves, peppers and olive oil. Season well with salt and pepper, cover with foil and roast for 2 hours or until very tender.
- Remove the foil and roast uncovered for 30 minutes.
- Leave the lamb to rest for 30 minutes. Take out the peppers and discard the skins. Remove the rosemary sprigs. Slice the meat into thick strips and shred into bite-size pieces.
- Squeeze the garlic cloves into the cooking juices, (discard the skins of the garlic) and mash with a fork.
- Place the shredded lamb, peppers, spinach, soya beans and cooking juices in a deep covered serving dish and cook in the hot oven for a final 15 minutes.
- Remove and serve immediately or reduce the heat to 150°C/300°F/Gas mark 2 to keep warm, or leave on a hot plate.

To serve the stylish way: Garnish with sprigs of rosemary.

Stuffed Brisket

M | SHABBAT | RH | SUCCOT

Info
- Preparation Time: 40 minutes
- Cooking Time: 3 hours 35 minutes
- Serves 8–10

Ingredients
For the stuffing
- 2 tbsp olive oil

✡

- 2 onions, peeled and chopped
- 4 cloves garlic, finely chopped
- 3 tbsp chopped fresh parsley

✡

- 2 slices of stale bread, roughly torn into pieces
- 1 large egg, beaten
- salt and freshly ground black pepper

✡

For the brisket
- 1.8 kg/4 lb flat-cut fresh brisket

✡

- 4 onions, peeled and thinly sliced
- 600ml/1 pint chicken stock
- 100ml/3½ fl oz red wine
- 3 large carrots, peeled and cut into cubes
- 3 sticks of celery, sliced
- 5 cloves garlic, peeled and roughly chopped
- 2–3 bay leaves

Roast brisket features highly on the Jewish menu as it is one of the dishes that works well if prepared in advance – a common requirement for the Sabbath and festivals when no new cooking can be done. For your convenience, this recipe can be cooked, cooled and refrigerated. Simply remove any excess fat from the surface of the stew, slice thinly using a very sharp knife or an electric knife and then reheat. It will never dry out as the gravy keeps it moist and tender and the slow cooking prevents the meat shrinking.

Method
- To make the stuffing: Heat the oil in a large frying pan over a medium heat.
- Add the onions, garlic and parsley and sauté until the onions soften – about 5 minutes.
- Mix in the bread, egg and season with salt and pepper.
- Transfer to a food processor and whiz together to produce a thick paste.
- To make the brisket: Pre-heat the oven to 180°C/350°F/Gas mark 4.
- Cut a deep pocket in 1 side of the brisket, leaving a 2 cm/1 inch border of meat uncut on the remaining 3 sides.
- Fill the pocket with stuffing. Skewer or sew the pocket closed. Sprinkle salt and pepper all over the brisket.
- Arrange half the onions in the bottom of a large oven tray. Place the brisket, fat side up, on onions.
- Top the brisket with the remaining onions. Pour 3 tbsp of the chicken stock and all the red wine into the oven tray.
- Bake the brisket uncovered until the meat and onions begin to brown, about 1 hour.
- Add the carrots, celery, garlic and bay leaves to the pan around the brisket. Pour over the remaining chicken stock.

- Cover with foil, reduce the oven temperature to 150°C/300°F/ Gas mark 2 and bake the brisket until tender – about 2½ hours or longer.
- Remove from the oven. Uncover the pan and allow the brisket to stand for 30 minutes, or cool and refrigerate. Thinly slice the brisket across the grain.

To serve the stylish way: Overlap the brisket slices on a platter. Surround with the vegetables from the pan and serve the brisket with the pan juices.

Jerusalem Kugel

`PAREV` Ⓥ

Info
- Preparation Time: 15 minutes
- Cooking Time: 45 minutes
- Serves: 6–8

Ingredients
- 1 tbsp vegetable or sunflower oil, to grease the tin

✡

- 225g/8 oz thin lokshen or vermicelli

✡

- 30ml/2 tbsp vegetable oil
- 100ml/3½ fl oz granulated sugar
- pinch of salt
- 1½ tsp black pepper
- 1 tsp dried cinnamon

✡

- 3 eggs, lightly beaten

✡

- Garnish: dill pickled cucumbers, sliced, sprigs of dill

Having recently returned from a trip to Jerusalem I was fascinated by the warm Yerushalayim spicy kugel. It is made by caramelising sugar with oil and then combining this with lokshen vermicelli. If you have never tasted it before it is quite different from classic savoury or sweet kugels. It is often served for Kiddush or at the beginning of the Shabbat lunch with a slice of pickled dill cucumber. The spice comes from a good pinch of black pepper and the tradition comes from the Eastern Hasidic Jews of the eighteenth century. I like to mellow the flavours with a touch of aromatic cinnamon purchased from the Jerusalem market.

Once cooked it can be left on a hot plate overnight.

The Old City of Jerusalem is a fascinating area of living history. You can wander around enjoying the colourful food market with an abundance of hummus, falafel, breads and pâtisseries sold on every street corner. Za'atar, the Middle Eastern dried spice made from thyme, oregano and wild marjoram is widely available and used on bread, salads and as a dip with olive oil and pitta bread. And for Jews, the focal point is the Western Wall, the only remaining section of the Temple built by King Herod in the first century.

However, it is in Mea Shearim, meaning 'A Hundred Gates' that this dish is most popular today. The area is the ultra-religious part of Jerusalem and the streets retain the 'flavour' of Eastern Europe shtetl lifestyle with strict adherence to Jewish learning, modest dress and segregation amongst men and women. And over Shabbat it becomes a car-free zone to maintain religious observance.

Method
- Pre-heat the oven to 180°C/350°F/Gas mark 4.
- Grease and line a 1 kg/2¼ lb loaf tin.
- Cook the lokshen according to the packet instructions. Drain well and set aside.

- In a medium saucepan, heat the oil then add the sugar. Cook over a low heat stirring constantly until the sugar starts to darken to a caramel colour – about 5 minutes.
- Immediately add the lokshen, salt, pepper and cinnamon and stir well.
- Leave to cool slightly and then stir in the beaten eggs. Pour into the prepared loaf tin.
- Bake uncovered until golden brown – about 35 minutes.
- Remove from the oven and invert. It will look like a cake with a golden crust.

To serve the stylish way: Decorate with sliced dill pickled cucumbers, sprigs of dill and a dusting of black pepper.

Whisky Chicken

M DAIRY-FREE SHABBAT RH SUCCOT

Info
- Preparation Time: 15 minutes
- Cooking Time: 45 minutes
- Serves: 6

Ingredients
- 3 tbsp vegetable oil
- 6 breasts of skinless, boneless chicken or 1 whole large chicken (approx. 2.3 kg/5 lb), cut into 6

✿

- 2 onions, peeled and roughly chopped
- 450g/1 lb shiitake or brown cap mushrooms, washed and sliced
- 4 cloves garlic, peeled and finely chopped

✿

- 250g/9 oz/1 cup dried apricots, ready soaked and roughly sliced, or fresh, de-stoned and sliced
- 300ml/½ pint/1¼ cups whisky
- salt and freshly ground black pepper

✿

- 450g/1 lb potatoes, peeled and cut into large pieces
- 450g/1 lb swede, peeled and cut into large pieces
- 450g/1 lb parsnips, peeled and cut into large pieces

✿

- 3 tbsp plain flour

✿

- 2 tbsp chopped parsley
- olive oil, for drizzling
- Garnish: sprigs of fresh parsley

Jews love whisky, it is always served as a 'l'chaim' at family celebrations and at Kiddush on Shabbat in synagogues worldwide.

This recipe makes liberal use of whisky, mushrooms and apricots and I recommend varying the type of mushrooms dependent on the season. I have used ready-soaked dried apricots, which provide an excellent colour and do not fall apart in cooking. They also absorb all the flavours of the whisky and chicken juices, but fresh apricots, if in season, are even better.

This is an easy meal to make that captures the theme of the Highlands, so for any Scottish cooks who celebrate Burns' Night this is perfect alternative to the 'traditional' Haggis with neeps and tatties as part of their celebration. I serve it with roasted swedes, parsnips and potatoes to honour the occasion.

There is even a 'Jewish tartan'. It was designed in 2008 for the Chabad Rabbi Mendel Jacobs of Glasgow and features blue, white, silver, red and gold. These colours represent both Scotland and the colours of the Israeli flag with the central gold line symbolising the Biblical Tabernacle, the Ark and ceremonial vessels.

Chef's Tip: As a variation, liquidise half of the sauce for a smoother consistency.

Method
- Pre-heat the oven to 180°C/350°F/Gas mark 4.
- Heat the vegetable oil in a large frying pan. Brown the chicken pieces or breasts on both sides, remove and place in a large ovenproof dish with a lid.
- Sauté the onions, mushrooms and garlic for 3 minutes in the original pan.
- Add this to the ovenproof dish together with the apricots and whisky.

- Season with salt and freshly ground black pepper. Cover and cook for about 40 minutes.
- Meanwhile, cook the potatoes, swedes and parsnips for 5 minutes in boiling water.
- Drain and dust the vegetables with some seasoned flour and chopped parsley, drizzle with some olive oil and more salt and pepper. Place on a baking tray and roast for 30 minutes. Serve immediately.

To serve the stylish way: Place a selection of the cooked vegetables on each warm serving plate. Sit a cooked chicken piece on top and pour over the apricot and mushroom sauce and garnish with a sprig of parsley. Complete the dish with a dusting of freshly ground black pepper.

Passover Beef Lasagne

Ⓜ Ⓟ

Info
- Preparation Time: 20 minutes
- Cooking Time: 1 hour 30 minutes
- Serves: 6

Ingredients
For the tomato sauce
- 2 tbsp olive oil
- 3 cloves garlic, peeled and chopped
- 2 carrots, peeled and finely chopped
- 2 onions, peeled and chopped
- 1 x 400g/14 oz can tomatoes
- 1 tsp sugar
- 3 tbsp Kosher for Passover red wine
- salt and freshly ground black pepper

✿

- 450g/1 lb minced beef

✿

For the lasagne
- 2 red peppers, quartered, deseeded and roughly chopped
- 1–2 tbsp olive oil

✿

- 6 large square matzas
- 3 eggs, lightly beaten
- large bunch of basil

✿

- Topping: 2 tbsp olive oil

I always find that if I can prepare a few ready-made meals for Passover, a little less time is spent in the kitchen, otherwise with a big family and guests, as soon as one meal is finished, I am busy preparing the next. This lasagne is a delicious combination of red peppers, tomato sauce and minced beef layered with matza. Seasoned with plenty of fresh basil it is a tasty treat. In addition, for those who have nut allergies this is nut-free.

Serve it hot with a green salad or cold cut into squares and taken for packed lunch. It is quicker and easier to use the large square matza (not egg variety) for the filling. Also for a further short cut, buy ready-prepared tomato pasta sauce if available.

This is a 'multi task' recipe so you can cook the sauce and the peppers at the same time if you choose.

Method
- For the tomato sauce, heat the olive oil in a large saucepan. Add the garlic, carrots and onions and sauté until just golden. Lower the heat and stir in the tomatoes, sugar and wine and season with salt and pepper. Add the beef and stir from time to time.
- Simmer covered for 35 minutes.
- Transfer the mixture to a food processor or mixer and whiz briefly to combine.
- Pre-heat the oven to 200°C/400°F/Gas mark 6.
- Place the peppers on a tray lined with non-stick baking parchment. Drizzle with some olive oil and season with salt and pepper. Roast for 15 minutes.
- Reduce the oven temperature to 180°C/350°F/Gas mark 4.
- Run the matzas under water, turning to rinse both sides. Do not soak the matza, just dampen.
- Lightly coat both sides of the matzas with the beaten egg.

- Place ⅓ of the meat mixture on the base of a rectangular ovenproof dish measuring approximately 23 x 23cm (9 x 9 inches).
- Sprinkle over ⅓ of the red peppers, roughly chopped basil and cover with 2 square sheets of matza.
- Repeat the layers twice more.
- Pour any remaining egg mixture and the topping oil over the top layer of matza.
- Bake for 40 minutes or until golden.

Chicken Goujons with BBQ Sauce

Info
- Preparation Time: 10 minutes plus 10 minutes marinating
- Cooking Time: 30 minutes
- Serves: 6–8

Ingredients

For the sauce
- 3 cloves garlic, peeled and chopped
- 2 tbsp red wine vinegar
- 3 tbsp brown sugar
- 60g/2½ oz/¼ cup honey
- 150ml/5 fl oz tomato ketchup
- 60ml/2½ fl oz/¼ cup soy sauce
- 60ml/2½ fl oz/¼ cup sesame oil
- 2 tbsp sweet chilli sauce

✡

For the chicken
- 6 chicken breasts, cut into strips
- juice of 1 lemon

✡

For the coating
- 100g/4 oz breadcrumbs
- 2 tbsp medium matza meal
- zest of 2 lemons
- salt and freshly ground black pepper

✡

- 2 eggs, lightly beaten

✡

- 100ml rapeseed oil, for frying

Goujons or chicken pieces are always a family favourite and these are no exception. Serve at a drinks party, use as part of a buffet selection or make for the children for supper. Serve them with different sauces – tomato ketchup, sweet chilli sauce, lemon mayonnaise. For this recipe I have made my special BBQ sauce.

Every chef has his or her own ingredients for a BBQ sauce and I like to include some sesame oil, which gives it a slight oriental flavour. Keep the sauce for use over turkey, burgers or even duck.

BBQ style cooking is extremely popular amongst South African Jews because of their reliable climate. In the UK we tend to wait for 'the good weather' and still take a risk.

The Jewish population of South Africa started to increase in the nineteenth century with German and Dutch immigrants coming to Cape Town. Some Jews moved into farming, others developed the wine, clothing and steel industries. However, it was the discovery of diamonds that spurred significant growth. Between 1880 and 1910, over 35,000 Yiddish-speaking Jews arrived from Lithuania alone. These new immigrants brought their Eastern European influence to the existing Jewish cuisine: for example perogen, kitke (chollah) herring and gefilte fish. In 1930 a strong Jewish lobby restricted some anti-Semitic legislation and assisted many Jews to escape from persecution in Eastern Europe until 1937 when militant Nazi influences in South Africa restricted further immigration.

Much later, the tensions caused by the anti-Apartheid movement led to the departure of many of the more prosperous Jews, with most going to the UK, the USA and Israel. Within my own community we have several families who moved here in the 1990s. However, there are still over 70,000 Jews in South Africa mainly in Jo'burg and Cape Town.

Boerwors sausages are a South African speciality made from minced beef or lamb and flavoured with toasted coriander, black pepper, nutmeg, cloves and allspice. Traditional Boerwors is formed in a continuous spiral. Another great South African favourite is biltong which is a kind of cured meat made from raw fillets cut into strips or flat pieces sliced across the grain very similar to beef jerky. Kosher butchers in the United Kingdom now sell Biltong and Boerwors and kosher supermarkets stock specific South African items to cater for the immigrant community.

Method

- Combine all the sauce ingredients in a food processor. Pulse it a few times and then blend on high until it has thoroughly combined into a smooth sauce.
- Marinate the chicken pieces in the lemon juice for 10 minutes.
- Mix together the breadcrumbs, matza meal, lemon zest and salt and pepper.
- Dip the chicken pieces into the beaten egg followed by the breadcrumb mixture. Repeat the process twice so they are well coated.
- Heat the oil in a frying pan until it is hot.
- Shallow fry the chicken for 3–4 minutes on each side until crispy.
- Pre-heat the oven to 180°C/350°F/Gas mark 4.
- Line a baking tray with baking parchment. Place the crispy chicken on the oven tray and bake for 10 minutes.
- Heat the sauce either in the microwave or in a small saucepan.

To serve the stylish way: Place in a fancy dish, stack the goujons in layers and serve the sauce separately. Dust with a sprinkling of black pepper.

Classic Cheese Blintzes

D **SHAVUOT** **V**

Info
- Preparation Time: 20 minutes
- Cooking Time: 20 minutes
- Makes: 8 blintzes
- Will freeze

Ingredients
For the batter mixture
- 110g/4 oz self-raising flour
- 1 egg
- pinch of salt
- 300ml/½ pint/1¼ cups milk

✡

- sunflower or vegetable oil,
  for frying

✡

For the cheese filling
- 225g/8 oz cream cheese
- 1 egg
- zest of 1 lemon
- 1 tbsp sugar

✡

- Garnish: granulated sugar,
  zest of 1 lemon, 150ml/¼ pint/
  5 fl oz sour cream

They may be called crepes in France; the Polish call them nalesniki, the Hungarians palascinta, the Lithuanians have naliesnikai, the Ukrainians call them nalysnyky or they are blinis in Russian, but the real Jewish version is a blintze. These are crepe-like thin pancakes filled with cream cheese or cottage cheese and sometimes fruit.

The Polish like to dip their pancakes once filled and rolled in beaten egg and breadcrumbs and either bake or pan fry.

This is my mum's recipe, which she used to cook with her mother. The family version measures the ingredients in spoons, cups and pinches. I have brought it into the twenty-first century by standardising the random quantities. Many traditional Jewish recipes have been passed down through the generations and my cheese blintzes are part of this tradition.

Method
- Make the batter by mixing the flour, egg, salt and milk in a food mixer or blender until smooth.
- Heat a little oil in a 20 cm/8 inch pancake pan. When the oil is hot pour in three-quarters of a soup ladle of batter. Swirl around so the mixture covers the pan in a thin layer.
- When the batter has set and the edges of the pancake begin to lift, gently loosen the edges and flip the pancake over onto the other side for a few seconds. Using a palette knife remove and gently place on some non-stick baking paper. Continue with the remaining batter to make about eight pancakes.
- Mix together all the ingredients for the filling. Place about 1 tbsp of the cheese mixture in the centre of each pancake. Fold in the top and bottom of the pancake over the filling, then fold over one side and roll up carefully to enclose the filling completely.

- To finish the blintzes, heat the pan again with a little oil. Put the pancakes in the pan and fry until slightly golden brown. Turn over for a second so that it is hot on both sides.

To serve the stylish way: Serve hot. Dust with a little sugar, lemon zest and sour cream.

Chicken Tagine with Citrus Couscous

M **SHABBAT** **RH** **YT**

Info
- Preparation Time: 20 minutes
- Cooking Time: 1½ hours
- Serves: 6

Ingredients
- 3 tbsp olive oil
- 6 chicken breasts

✡

- 1 large red onion, peeled and roughly chopped
- 4 cloves garlic, peeled and roughly chopped
- 2 tsp cinnamon
- 2 tsp coriander, ground

✡

- 150g/5 oz/¼ cup dates, stoned
- 1 lemon, sliced
- 8 strands of saffron
- 150ml/¼ pint chicken stock
- 300ml/½ pint/1¼ cups red wine
- 225g/8 oz/1 cup raisins

✡

- salt and freshly ground black pepper

✡

For the citrus couscous
- 570ml/1 pint/2½ cups hot vegetable or chicken stock
- 300g/11 oz/1 cup couscous

✡

- zest and juice of 2 lemons
- salt and freshly ground black pepper

This recipe for me is a modern classic – it captures all the ingredients of a perfect Rosh Hashanah or Shabbat meal and is something that you will want to make time and time again. It does not need any additional vegetables, which makes serving for a dinner party very straightforward. For stunning presentation, use an individual pudding basin or a greased ramekin or an ice cream scoop to portion out the cooked couscous on to each plate. Decorate with pomegranate seeds and dust the edge of the plate with a sprinkling of ground cinnamon.

Chef's Tip: The best way to reheat couscous is to cover it with cling film and place in the microwave.

Method
- Pre-heat the oven to 200°C/400°F/Gas mark 6.
- Heat the olive oil in a frying pan. Sauté the chicken breasts in batches until brown.
- Remove the chicken from the pan and place in a deep oven-proof dish.
- Sauté the onion, garlic, cinnamon and coriander for 2 minutes in the saucepan and mix with the chicken.
- Add the dates, lemon, saffron, stock, wine and raisins to the chicken.
- Season well with salt and pepper before covering the dish and cooking in the oven for 1¼ hours.
- Pour the hot stock over the couscous. Cover immediately with cling film and leave for 10 minutes. Remove the cling film and fluff up the couscous with a fork. Stir in the lemon zest and juice and season with salt and pepper.

- Garnish: bunch of parsley, preferably flat-leaf, 1 large pomegranate, deseeded, 150g/5 oz/¼ cup blanched almonds, toasted

To serve the stylish way: Place a generous helping of couscous on a warmed plate adjacent to a ladleful of chicken tagine. Complete with sprigs of parsley, pomegranate seeds and toasted almonds.

Lebanese Tabbouleh

Info
- Preparation Time: 15 minutes
- Cooking Time: 10 minutes
- Serves: 6

Ingredients
- 110g/4 oz bulgur wheat

✡

- 500g/1 lb tomatoes: chop half and thinly slice the rest
- 3 spring onions, peeled and finely chopped
- 20g/¾ oz mint, finely chopped
- 100g/4 oz parsley, finely chopped
- 1 tbsp sumac

✡

- sea salt and black pepper, to taste

✡

For the dressing
- zest and juice of 1 lemon
- 4 tbsp extra virgin olive oil
- 1–2 cloves garlic, peeled and finely chopped

✡

- Garnish: 12 baby gem lettuce leaves, olives, chopped

Tabbouleh is a traditional Lebanese salad made with bulgur wheat. It is said to have originated as a way of using up the random pickings of whatever was in the kitchen garden. This dish is a standard part of a cold Middle Eastern meze starter. I like to use a ratio of 5:1 parsley to mint for the perfect flavour. Use the baby gem lettuces to scoop the salad into manageable serving portions.

Almost all of what was once a thriving Mizrachi Jewish community in Lebanon has emigrated to the USA, Canada, France, Israel, Argentina, Brazil and Australia. The remaining few Lebanese Jews today live in and around Beirut and tend to keep a low profile.

Method
- Put the bulgur wheat in a pan of boiling water. Cover and simmer for 8–10 minutes or until just soft. Drain and cool.
- Add the tomatoes, spring onions, mint, parsley and sumac and season well.
- Combine the dressing ingredients and pour over just before serving.
- Keep chilled until ready to serve.

To serve the stylish way: Place a circle of baby gem lettuce leaves around the tabbouleh. Garnish with chopped olives.

Tropical Fruit Filo Pie

PAREV SUCCOT SHABBAT RH YT

Info
- Preparation Time: 35 minutes
- Cooking Time: 35 minutes
- Serves: 6

Ingredients
- 75g/3 oz/¼ cup desiccated coconut
- 50g/2 oz/¼ cup split almonds

✡

- 2 ripe mangoes, peeled and stoned
- 1 ripe papaya, peeled and deseeded

✡

- zest of 2 limes

✡

- 250g/9 oz butter or non-dairy margarine
- 5 filo pastry sheets

✡

- 2 tbsp apricot jam

✡

- 250ml/9 oz mascarpone cheese or parev whipping cream
- 3 tbsp icing sugar

✡

- Garnish: toasted coconut, zest of 1 lime

When you think of filo pastry desserts, apple strudel tends to come to mind. This, however, is a layered filo pastry pie topped with tropical fruits of mango and papaya flavoured with roasted desiccated coconut and zest of lime. When buying a mango, make sure it has a tropical fruity aroma; unripe mangoes have no scent. A fresh mango will give slightly to the touch, but avoid very soft or bruised fruit.

This dessert can be parev and made in advance, served hot, cold or warm with mango sorbet or coconut ice cream. I like to keep the same flavours together to enhance the whole dessert.

Strudel originates from Austria; mainly from Vienna. The word 'strudel' means whirlpool, symbolising the way it is rolled. The Jews of Austria adjusted this pastry so that it was non-dairy, making it suitable to enjoy after a meat meal.

Method
- Pre-heat the oven to 200°C/400°F/Gas mark 6.
- Roast the desiccated coconut by placing on a lined baking tray in a single layer. On a separate tray roast the split almonds.
- Bake for about 8–10 minutes or until golden. Remove and set aside.
- Chop the mangoes and papaya into small cubes.
- Stir in the coconut and lime zest. Set aside.
- Melt the butter or margarine. Brush the base and sides of a round 23cm/9 inch loose-based flan tin, 3 cm/1½ inches in depth. Take one sheet of pastry and brush with melted butter/margarine and insert inside the tin. Sprinkle over some toasted almonds and cover with another 3 overlapping sheets, brushing with melted butter/margarine so that the whole tin is covered. Repeat with the final sheet of pastry.
- Use scissors to trim the edges but leave a 3 cm/1½ inch edge.
- Blind bake by covering with foil and insert baking beans.

- Bake for 20 minutes.
- Remove the foil and baking beans and whilst hot gently ease the sides of the pie tin to remove the pastry base and transfer to your serving plate.
- Put the apricot jam in a small glass container. Cover with cling film and place in the microwave on high for 1 minute. Brush the base of the pastry with the melted jam.
- Place the mascarpone cheese in a small bowl. Stir and mix in the icing sugar. If using the parev whipping cream, whip until thick and do not add the sugar.
- When you are ready to serve the dessert, spoon the mascarpone mixture on the base of the pie and add the prepared fruit. Top with toasted coconut.

To serve the stylish way: Garnish with lime zest.

Rye Bread

Info

- Preparation Time: 10 minutes plus 2 hours rising and proving time
- Cooking Time: 25–30 minutes
- Makes: 2 loaves

Ingredients

- 350ml/12 fl oz/1½ cups warm water (100ml/3½ fl oz followed by the rest)
- 1 × 7g/¼ oz sachet dried yeast

✡

- 200g/8 oz strong white flour
- 300g/11 oz rye flour
- 2 tbsp caraway seeds
- 2 tsp salt
- 2 tbsp vegetable oil
- 1 tsp honey

✡

- 1–2 egg yolks, to glaze
- 1 tsp caraway seeds, for topping

Sliced rye bread is still very popular and is commonly served with salt beef, herring, smoked salmon or egg and onion. Rye was traditionally the most important grain of all crops in Germany and so naturally German bakers were great masters at baking rye breads. Although you can buy ready-made loaves in kosher delis you can't beat baking your own bread. In fact I never really enjoyed rye bread until I made this recipe.

As noted on page 68, there are two main cultural sides to Judaism: Sephardi and Ashkenazi. The latter primarily evolved from those Jews living in Germany during the nineteenth and twentieth centuries. Largely assimilated by the 1930s, the community prospered and was taken by surprise at the rise of Nazism and anti-Semitism. Starting in 1933, these policies saw Jewish doctors, shopkeepers, lawyers and businesses boycotted but it was the mass destruction of Jewish properties including synagogues, schools and businesses during Kristallnacht, 9–10 November 1938 that caused widespread alarm and the efforts of many to leave the country. Although a lot of Jews were able to flee Germany, most had to stay and 90 per cent died in the Holocaust. After the war few survivors chose to stay – most went to Israel or America – and it is only in recent years that there has been a significant Jewish community in the enlarged Germany of the twenty-first century.

Method

- Mix 100ml/3½ fl oz of the warm water with the dried yeast. Leave for 10 minutes until the yeast starts foaming.
- Place both flours, the caraway seeds and salt in a food mixer. Add the yeast mixture, oil and honey. Continue to mix together, ideally using a dough hook. The remaining warm water should be added slowly so that the dough is soft and well kneaded but not too wet.

- When the dough springs back as you touch it, it has been kneaded enough.
- Lightly oil a large bowl, and turn the dough in it so that it is coated.
- Cover with cling film and leave to rise in a warm place for 1½ hours or until it has doubled in size.
- Pre-heat the oven to 200°C/400°F/Gas mark 6.
- Punch the dough down and shape it into two 20 cm/8 inch oval loaves.
- Glaze with the egg yolk and sprinkle with the caraway seeds.
- Using a sharp knife, make five slashes across the top of each loaf.
- Leave in a warm place to prove (second rising) for 30 minutes or until the bread has significantly risen again.
- Bake for 25–30 minutes, or until the bread is deep golden and sounds hollow when the bottom is tapped. Leave to cool before slicing or freezing.

Duet of Fish Balls

Very sadly, many traditional recipes like gefilte fish are being purchased ready-made and not made from scratch. I am always being asked to teach recipes like this one at cookery school as the new generation want to learn their Ashkenazi heritage classics. These recipes were never written down and were made by adding a little of this and a little of that. Flavouring was according to one's personal taste, hence each family has their own magic ingredient. The recipe was originally carp stuffed with the minced fish. Due to the scarcity of food, Eastern European Jews used the recipe and added matza meal or breadcrumbs or ground almonds to stretch the meal, ensuring that even the poorest families had a good fish dish on Shabbat.

Variations tend to sway to either sweet or savoury depending on which Jewish community you descended from. Sweet fish balls were from the heritage of Ashkenazi Jews of western Ukraine and Poland (Polaks) and the more peppery flavour were from Lithuania (Litvaks.)

I have slightly modernised the mixture by adding spring onions and a bunch of fresh parsley to the boiled fish ball recipe and used minced salmon coated in matza meal as the fried.

Note: You will only be able to obtain fish bones for the stock from a fishmonger's; supermarkets will not sell them to you because of 'health and safety'. The best mix of fish and flavour is achieved by mincing it yourself.

This mixture can be boiled and simmered in fish stock or deep fried in a deep fat fryer. It is often served with chrain, beetroot-flavoured horseradish sauce.

Boiled Fish Balls

PAREV

Info
- Preparation Time: 30 minutes
- Cooking Time: 1 hour
- Makes: 40 small balls

Ingredients
For the stock
- 1.2 litres/1 ¼cups water
- 4 onions, peeled and sliced
- 225g/8 oz skin and bones of fish
- 2 sticks of celery
- bunch of fresh parsley
- 2 tsp salt
- 2 peppercorns
- 1 bay leaf
- pinch of sugar

✡

For the fish mixture
- 1.4 kg/3 lb mixed fish made up of haddock, cod and bream
- 1 medium onion, peeled and finely chopped
- 2 eggs
- 2 tbsp medium matza meal
- 2 tsp salt
- pinch of white pepper
- 2 tsp sugar
- drop of almond essence

✡

- Garnish: 2 carrots, peeled and made into carrot flowers

Chef's Tip: To make the carrot flowers, use a canelle knife to make four lengthways indentations, spaced evenly down the carrot. Then slice to the desired thickness.

Method
- Place all the stock ingredients in a large saucepan. Bring to the boil and simmer for 15 minutes.
- Put all the fish ingredients in a food mixer and mince together. Taste to check the seasoning before making the fish balls. The mixture should be light and slightly sticky.
- With wet hands, roll the fish mixture into balls the size of an egg. Flatten slightly, place in the stock and cook covered for 45 minutes.
- Remove the cooked fish with a slotted spoon.

To serve the stylish way: Top with the carrot flowers. The fish balls can be served warm or cold.

Salmon Fried Fish Balls

Info
- Preparation Time: 30 minutes
- Cooking Time: 15 minutes
- Makes: 40 small balls

Ingredients
- 1.4 kg/3 lb salmon, skinned and filleted
- 1 medium onion, peeled and finely chopped
- 2 eggs, lightly beaten
- 2 tbsp matza meal
- 1 tbsp ground almonds (optional)
- 2 tsp salt
- freshly ground black pepper, to taste

✡

- 6–8 tbsp matza meal
- vegetable oil, for frying

✡

- Garnish: a tiny dab of chrain, 1 ready cooked non vinegar beetroot, finely sliced or use a decorative biscuit cutter as a template to cut a top

Method
- Place the salmon in a food processor with the other ingredients and whiz until thoroughly combined.
- With wet hands roll the fish mixture into the matza meal, making balls the size of an egg or smaller.
- Heat the oil in a deep fat fryer to its highest setting.
- Put the fish in the baskets and cook in batches for approximately 2–3 minutes. Remove and leave to drain on kitchen paper. These can also be shallow fried for 2–3 minutes on each side.

To serve the stylish way: Place a tiny amount of chrain on the top of the salmon fish balls and complete with a thin slice of beetroot or beetroot shape. Allow to cool and either freeze or refrigerate until ready to serve. They can be served hot or cold.

Cheese and Onion Pie

D SHAVUOT SHABBAT **V**

Info
- Preparation Time: 20 minutes plus 30 minutes for the pastry
- Cooking Time: 55 minutes
- Serves: 6 people

Ingredients
For the pastry
- 300g/11 oz plain flour
- 160g/6 oz unsalted butter or margarine
- 1 egg
- 30g/1 oz strong Cheddar, grated
- pinch of salt and freshly ground black pepper

✡

For the filling
- 3 tbsp olive oil

✡

- 5 red onions, peeled and sliced
- 3 white onions, peeled and sliced
- 1 egg yolk, to glaze pastry

✡

- 3 eggs, whisked
- 75g/3 oz mature Cheddar, grated
- 300ml/½ pint/1¼ cups double cream
- 1 tsp whole grain or similar mustard
- 3 tbsp snipped chives
- salt and freshly ground black pepper

✡

- Garnish: 2 tbsp snipped chives

The tradition of enjoying dairy foods at Shavuot often means eating cheesecake or blintzes. I have devised a savoury dairy option in which the slowly cooked onions are meltingly sweet, contrasting with the sharper taste of the mature cheddar. Putting cheese into the pastry lifts the whole dish and gives a richer overall flavour.

You may buy ready-made pastry to speed up your cooking but homemade does taste better.

Method
- Combine the pastry ingredients in a food processor into a dough.
- Cover with cling film, flatten and place in the fridge for 30 minutes to allow the butter to harden and the gluten in the flour to relax. This will make it a lot easier to roll out.
- Heat the olive oil in a frying pan. Sauté all the onions over a low heat so that they soften and caramelise but do not burn – about 20 minutes.
- Pre-heat the oven to 200°C/400°F/Gas mark 6.
- Roll out the pastry on a work surface dusted with flour. Line a loose-based 27cm (13 inch) pie tin with the rolled out pastry. Cover with foil and fill with baking beans.
- Bake for 20 minutes. Remove the foil and baking beans and glaze the pastry with beaten egg yolk.
- Return to the oven for a further 5 minutes.
- Put the onions in the cooked pie base. Mix together the eggs, cheese, cream, mustard and chives. Season well with salt and pepper and pour over the onions.
- Bake for 30 minutes until set and golden and slightly risen.

To serve the stylish way: Snip more chives on the top and serve hot, warm or cold.

Chapter 5

Free From

—

Veggie, Diabetic and Gluten

Free From

This chapter focuses on catering for special diets including vegetarian, diabetic and wheat-free. Many other recipes in this book are also suitable and some can be made so with simple substitutions. The one time of the year when many Jewish people follow a vegetarian diet is during the build up to Tisha b'Av in July or August. This is a period of annual collective mourning for the destruction of the ancient Temple and many orthodox Jews avoid meat at this time.

There is a view that vegetarianism goes in and out of fashion based on the latest trends and medical advice. Eating a wholly vegetarian diet is not the automatic route to good health unless it is achieved by eating a wide range of different foods; nuts, beans, eggs, soya, quorn and lentils are all excellent sources of protein. A lack of iron can be challenging – this can be found in leafy green vegetables, chickpeas, baked beans, tofu, bran flakes, wholemeal bread, dried fruit and pumpkin seeds.

The Jewish Vegetarian Society is a useful source of information and has its own newsletter. More information can be found at: jewishvegetarian@onetel.com.

Free From: veggie, diabetic and gluten

- Vegetarian lettuce wraps
- Roasted root mash pie
- Spaghetti with a medley of mushrooms
- Thai pumpkin and broccoli curry
- Ratatouille lasagne
- Tapas: carrots and olives
- Crunchy leek and potato gratin served with a fennel and orange salad
- Moroccan vegetable tagine
- Orange Israeli couscous
- Vegetarian Singapore noodles
- Roasted aubergine with peppers
- Date and walnut spelt bread
- Vegetable chilli
- Lime and wild rocket risotto
- Creamy mushroom and chestnut pie with filo pastry top
- Date quinoa

Vegetarian Lettuce Wraps

Info
- Preparation Time: 20 minutes
- Cooking Time: 15 minutes
- Serves: 6

Ingredients
- 3 carrots, peeled

✡

- 300g/11 oz shiitake or baby button mushrooms
- 2 red peppers, quartered and deseeded
- 2 courgettes
- ½ onion, peeled
  1 red chilli, deseeded
- 2 cm/1 inch piece of fresh ginger, peeled and finely chopped

✡

- 2 tbsp vegetable oil

✡

For the sauce
- 3 tbsp soy sauce
- 2 tbsp sesame oil
- 1 tbsp dry sherry
- 1 tbsp cornflour
- 1 tsp salt
- ½ tsp sugar
- ¼ tsp white pepper

✡

- Garnish: 6 baby gem lettuces, separated into leaves, 12 tbsp plum sauce

This is a delicious combination of finely chopped vegetables wrapped up in lettuce and served with plum sauce. The vegetables are served hot from the wok and seasoned with a tasty sauce of sesame oil and soy sauce thickened with some cornflour. I like to serve this Chinese dish either as a starter or part of an oriental buffet. It also makes an interesting canapé if served in mini portions. The secret to presentation is to chop the vegetables as finely as possible so that it is easy to scoop them up into the baby gem lettuce.

Serve with one of the excellent kosher ready-made sauces now widely available – I favour plum but teriyaki, sweet chilli, and sweet and sour are good.

The Chinese don't combine dairy products with meat which makes the recipes easy to replicate using kosher ingredients. Chinese cookery also recognises the five taste buds – salty, sweet, sour, bitter and peppery hot – and these tastes are all very popular with the kosher palate. The art of cooking Chinese is not only to chop and blend the ingredients, but also to blend the flavours through careful matching of tastes.

As with Jews, the Chinese have numerous customs based around food and celebration of the New Year. Sometimes it is based on appearance so, for example, serving a whole chicken during the Chinese New Year season symbolises family togetherness, noodles represent longevity – be careful not to break them – and spring rolls symbolise wealth as their shape is similar to gold bars.

Alternatively food may have special significance during Chinese New Year because of the way the Chinese word for it sounds. For example, the Cantonese word for lettuce sounds like 'rising fortune', so it is very common to serve a lettuce wrap filled with other lucky food.

Method

- Finely chop all the vegetables as small as possible, making pieces of equal size. This ensures both good presentation and equal cooking times.
- Heat the wok so that it is hot. Add the vegetable oil. Stir in the carrots and cook for 3 minutes. Add the mushrooms, peppers, courgettes, onion, chilli and ginger. Cook for a further 3 minutes.
- Combine the sauce ingredients. Stir into the vegetable mixture and cook for a final 2 minutes.
- Taste and adjust seasoning accordingly.

To serve the stylish way: Place a baby gem lettuce leaf on each plate, spoon 2 tbsp plum sauce onto each leaf and fill with the mixed vegetable mixture. Serve immediately.

Roasted Root Mash Pie

Info
- Preparation Time: 35 minutes
- Cooking Time: 1 hour 15 minutes
- Serves: 6

Ingredients
- 300g/11 oz carrots, peeled and cut in batons
- 2 turnips (approx. 400g/14 oz), peeled and roughly chopped
- 23 parsnips (approx. 450g/1 lb), peeled and roughly chopped
- 1 swede (approx. 250g/9 oz), peeled and roughly chopped
- 1 sweet potato (approx. 250g/9 oz), peeled and roughly chopped

✡

- 1 bulb garlic: separate the cloves but leave the skins on
- 3 tbsp extra virgin olive oil
- salt and freshly ground black pepper
- 3 tbsp finely chopped fresh flat parsley

✡

For the cheese mash
- 1.8 kg/4 lb Maris Piper potatoes, peeled and roughly chopped

✡

- 200g/7 oz low-fat mild Cheddar cheese, grated
- 2 eggs, beaten
- salt and freshly ground black pepper

Succot falls around September/October which is when all the root vegetables are coming into season: carrots, swedes, turnips, parsnips and sweet potatoes to name just a few. This is a tasty mix, roasted until golden and then topped with a delicious cheesy mash made with mild, low-fat Cheddar cheese. It is ideal as a family meal or Sunday night supper in the Succah and a great way of achieving your five-a-day vegetable requirement.

Method
- Pre-heat the oven to 200°C/400°F/Gas mark 6.
- Place the prepared root vegetables in a pan of boiling water. Simmer for 10 minutes and drain.
- Transfer to an oven tray lined with baking parchment and add the whole garlic cloves.
- Drizzle over the oil, season well with salt and pepper and roast for 40 minutes or until soft and golden.
- Transfer to an ovenproof dish. Sprinkle over the parsley.
- Cook the potatoes in boiling water until soft. Drain well.
- Mash using a ricer or fork. Stir in the cheese and eggs and season with salt and pepper.
- Spoon or pipe the potato mixture on top of the roasted vegetables.
- Bake for a final 25 minutes or until the potato is crispy and golden.

Spaghetti with a Medley of Mushrooms

Ⓥ

Info
- Preparation Time: 20 minutes
- Cooking Time: 15 minutes
- Serves: 4

Ingredients
- 75g/3 oz dried porcini

✡

- 2 tbsp olive oil

✡

- ½ truffle if available, finely sliced (specialist Italian shops stock them)
- 2 cloves garlic, peeled and crushed
- large bunch of parsley, roughly chopped

✡

- 400g/14 oz spaghetti

✡

- large bunch of fresh basil, torn
- salt and freshly ground black pepper, to taste

✡

- Garnish: Freshly grated Parmesan, truffle oil (if available), to drizzle, or use extra virgin olive oil

Wild mushrooms and pasta are synonymous with Italian cooking, so featuring this recipe in my Italian cookery classes was a must. Very often in Italian cooking, fewer ingredients provide more flavour and this is certainly the case here, where the porcini (which are available in most good supermarkets) and a little bit of truffle oil provide a delicious enrichment to the final recipe. Having discovered a jar of truffles, I could not resist my impulse purchase and decided to include them in the recipe too. Dried mushrooms have a long shelf life, so don't worry about buying a large quantity as they do not lose their flavour provided they are kept away from sunlight and stored in a dry place within an airtight container.

The black truffle is found in Piedmont and as far south as Umbria. They are harvested from November to March and are found by a trained pig. Black truffle omelettes are a favourite delicacy, found in Assisi, and in Rome's famous Piazza Navona, you can enjoy their Tartufo Gelato (truffle ice cream).

Method
- Reconstitute the dried porcini by covering with a minimum of cold water for 10 minutes. (You use cold water and as little as possible so as not to extract too much flavour from the mushrooms. Pick them out with a spoon rather than drain them through a sieve as this leaves the grit at the bottom of the bowl.)
- Heat the olive oil in a large saucepan. Add the drained porcini and sliced truffles and cook for 5 minutes.
- Remove from the heat, add the garlic and parsley and gently cook for a few more minutes.
- Cook the spaghetti in plenty of boiling salted water according to the packet instructions or until al dente.

- Drain thoroughly then pile into warmed serving bowls.
- Pour the sauce over the spaghetti and mix well. Taste and adjust the seasoning accordingly, then add the finely torn fresh basil.

To serve the stylish way: Complete with a generous helping of grated Parmesan and some truffle or extra virgin olive oil.

Thai Pumpkin and Broccoli Curry

PAREV V

Info
- Preparation Time: 20 minutes
- Cooking Time: Approximately 25 minutes
- Serves: 6

Ingredients
- 2 tbsp vegetable oil

✡

- 2 tbsp curry paste
- 300ml/½ pint/1¼ cups coconut milk

✡

- 400g/14 oz pumpkin/butternut squash, peeled, deseeded and cut into 2 cm/1 inch cubes
- 200g/7 oz/1 cup cauliflower, cut into small florets

✡

- 450g/1 lb fresh broccoli, cut into small florets
- 1 tsp sugar
- 2 tbsp soy sauce
- 150g/5 oz/¼ cup baby corn, cut in half lengthways
- 3 kaffir lime leaves
- 1–2 large fresh red chillies, cut in half lengthways, deseeded, then cut into thin slivers

✡

- 100g/4 oz fine beans cut in 2 cm/1 inch lengths
- Garnish: 15 basil leaves

This is a typical type of curry from the northern capital of Thailand, Chiang Mai where a good selection of vegetables are combined with lime leaves, chillies and coconut milk. The secret to this dish is to cook the vegetables that take longest first before adding the other ingredients.

Jars of kosher curry pastes come in several varieties – tandoori, curry, vindaloo, tikka, madras and kebab. For this recipe, I like to use the curry one; the others will work equally well but will provide a slightly different taste.

Chabad run the synagogue and Jewish community in Chang Mai, a popular place for tourists, especially Israeli backpackers. On an average Shabbat there could be about 100 guests and as my daughter, Abbie, can confirm, the Rabbi and his wife bring together familiar Judaism and spirituality in a very hospitable way.

Method
- Heat the oil in a large wok or frying pan. Fry the curry paste, add the coconut milk and stir well for 2 minutes.
- Add the pumpkin and cauliflower and cook for 10 minutes stirring from time to time. Add the broccoli, sugar, soy sauce, baby corn, lime leaves and chilli.
- Finally stir in the beans and cook for a further 5 minutes or until the vegetables are all cooked al dente.

To serve the stylish way: Garnish with basil leaves.

Ratatouille Lasagne

Info
- Preparation Time: 30 minutes
- Cooking Time: 1 hour 20 minutes
- Serves: 6–8

Ingredients
- 1 large aubergine, cut into 2 cm/1 inch cubes
- 2 red onions, peeled and cut into wedges
- 2 red peppers, deseeded and cut into chunky strips
- 2 yellow peppers, deseeded and cut into chunky strips
- 6 cloves garlic, peeled and finely chopped

✡

- 3 tbsp olive oil
- sea salt and freshly ground black pepper, to taste

✡

- 450g/1 lb cherry tomatoes, cut in half

✡

- 5 tbsp fresh basil, roughly chopped
- 12 dried lasagne sheets

✡

For the sauce
- 60g/2 oz margarine
  70g/2½ oz plain flour
- 1 litre/1¾ pints/4 cups semi-skimmed milk, preferably organic
  125g/4½ oz half-fat Cheddar cheese, coarsely grated

✡

- 50g/2 oz Parmesan cheese

This is a tasty combination of roasted vegetables layered with lasagne sheets. I have used low-fat milk and cheese to take advantage of the goodness of dairy but without the fat. This recipe is also a great way of adding a variety of vegetables to a family favourite. Make sure that the dried lasagne you choose does not need to be pre-cooked before layering.

Recent research in the UK from the National Osteoporosis Society showed that one in two women and one in five men over the age of 50 suffer from the condition where our bones become so weak that they can fracture easily. Hips, legs and arms are the most common fractures, but it can also affect the spine and lead to shrinking in old age. Eating dairy foods such as this lasagne, packed with calcium, can help to prevent this.

Jews and Italian food have a long connected history. The very first Jews in Italy came to Rome as slaves after the fall of the Temple in Jerusalem and food historians believe many of the original kosher recipes originate from these people. Italian food is very regional and Jewish Italian food reflects this. So Jewish Tuscan food tends to include ingredients that are common in the region like lemons, almonds, pine nuts, anchovies and raisins. Further south, garlic, tomatoes, mozzarella and oregano become more prevalent.

Method
- Pre-heat the oven to 200°C/400°F/Gas mark 6.
- Mix together the aubergine, onions, red and yellow peppers and garlic. Place in an oven tray lined with baking parchment. Drizzle over the olive oil and season with salt and pepper.
- Roast for 30 minutes.
- Remove the vegetables and stir in the halved tomatoes and basil.

- Melt the margarine in a small pan, add the flour and cook for 1 minute.
- Bring the milk to the boil and gradually pour onto the flour, stirring continuously to avoid lumps then simmer for 5 minutes.
- Add the Cheddar cheese to the sauce and season with salt and pepper.
- Divide the sauce into quarters and divide the vegetables in half. Pour a quarter of the sauce into the base of a large deep ovenware dish. Cover with 4 lasagne sheets, overlapping them slightly. Top with half of the vegetables, then another quarter of the sauce. Top this with a single layer of 4 lasagne sheets followed by the remaining vegetables and another quarter of the sauce. Add the final layer of 4 lasagne sheets, spread with the remaining quarter of the sauce and sprinkle with the Parmesan cheese.
- Bake for 40 minutes or until golden and bubbling.

To serve the stylish way: Dust the lasagne with some freshly ground black pepper and some basil leaves. Serve with green salad.

Tapas: Carrots and Olives

Info
- Preparation Time: 10 minutes
- Cooking Time: 20 minutes
- Serves: 4

Ingredients
- 2 tbsp slivered almonds

  ✡

- 2 tbsp extra virgin olive oil

  ✡

- 450g/1 lb carrots, peeled and sliced thinly at an angle
- 1 clove garlic, finely chopped
- 1 tbsp chopped fresh flat-leaf parsley
- 12 Spanish green olives, pitted and sliced
- salt and freshly ground black pepper

  ✡

- Garnish: sprigs of fresh parsley

Tapas, which originated in Spain, is a variety of mini hot or cold appetisers eaten in an informal, relaxed way. As the hostess you can prepare everything well in advance, only going into the kitchen to bring out yet another of a series of tasty little starters. The word 'tapas' is derived from the Spanish verb 'to cover'. According to legend, King Alfonso X was recovering from an illness by drinking wine and small appetisers between meals. After he recovered, having enjoyed the experience he ordered all taverns to only serve wine with these tapas.

However, there are other explanations. For example, some believe that around the sixteenth century some tavern owners from Castilla La Mancha found out the strong taste and smell of mature cheese could disguise bad wine, 'covering' it and started offering cheese when serving cheap wine

Or that it was actually King Alfonso XIII who was offered some wine in Cadiz, where it was very windy so a waiter used a piece of cured ham to cover his glass to protect it from the sand. The king, after drinking the wine, ordered another glass of wine with a 'cover' on it.

Many tapas recipes are served cold or at room temperature. This one is best warm served with crusty bread dipped in extra virgin olive oil. In my opinion this recipe has the gold star as it is perfect for all occasions. Use for Shabbat lunch, Passover (omit dipping bread when serving.), or for vegetarian, parev and low-fat meals. And quantities can be easily increased if desired.

The Jews of Spain are mainly Sephardi and descend from Northern Africa and former Spanish colonies such as Argentina. One of the main cities is Cordoba which has a famous Jewish quarter. The fourteenth-century synagogue is the only one in Spain that was not defiled during the Spanish Inquisition.

Method

- Pre-heat the oven to 200°C/400°F/Gas mark 6.
- Place the almonds on an oven tray. Roast for about 5 minutes or until golden.
- Heat the olive oil in large frying pan.
- Add the carrots and cook, covered, over a ow heat for about 10 minutes, shaking the pan occasionally, until almost tender.
- Add the garlic, parsley and olives and stir to combine.
- Season, then toss the carrots over a low heat for 1 minute.
- Stir in the slivered almonds and serve warm.

To serve the stylish way: Garnish with sprigs of parsley.

Crunchy Leek and Potato Gratin served with a Fennel and Orange salad

GLUTEN-FREE RH

Ⓥ Ⓟ Ⓓ

Info
- Preparation Time: 25 minutes
- Cooking Time: 1 hour
- Serves: 6

Ingredients
- 3 leeks, trimmed and sliced
- 900g/2 lb potatoes, peeled and sliced

✡

- 1 red onion, peeled and sliced
- 250g/9 oz leaf spinach, cooked and well drained
- 2–3 cloves garlic, peeled and finely chopped
- 5 cm/2 inch piece of root ginger, peeled and finely chopped
- salt and freshly ground black pepper

✡

- 100ml/3½ fl oz vegetable stock
- 100ml/3½ fl oz double cream

✡

For the topping
- 20g/¾ oz Parmesan cheese, grated
- 200g/7 oz/1 cup walnuts, roughly chopped

✡

For the salad
- 4 tbsp olive oil
- 1 tsp honey

✡

- 5 oranges, peeled and cut into segments
- 2 orange peppers, roughly chopped
- 2 bulbs of fennel, roughly chopped

I love the combination of this delicious vegetarian dish: leeks, red onion and spinach with a sliced potato and walnut topping. It is also ideal for those on a gluten-free diet. Served with the fennel and orange salad it makes a complete meal.

When preparing leeks, ensure that you trim the root end and coarse top. The easiest way to clean leeks is to slit them lengthways and rinse under cold running water to remove any grit.

I use a food processor to slice the potatoes, which certainly puts some speed into the dish's creation, and if time is of the essence it can be cooked in advance and reheated later. The salad brings both colour and texture to the dish and requires no last-minute adjustments so that serving is a breeze.

This recipe is perfect for lunch or supper and will freeze.

The leek is the national symbol of Wales and associated with their patron, St David. One interesting story recalls St David ordering his soldiers to wear leeks on their helmets in a battle against the Saxons. This battle also took place in a leek field.

The Jews of Wales are close to my heart as my late first husband's family are Welsh. They grew up in Newport, Gwent as part of a small orthodox provincial community and kept close contacts with the neighbouring communities of Cardiff and Swansea. In a book called *My Llanelli* by Channah Hirsh, she describes the scholarly congregation as 'The Gateshead of South Wales' and the town had its own Jewish courts, kosher butchers and a Rabbinic structure.

The population peaked in 1914 at just 5,000 but this has greatly diminished as people moved to London and other larger cities. Michael Howard, the former Conservative Party leader and Home Secretary, is the son of a synagogue cantor who lived in Llanelli in the 1930s.

Method

- Pre-heat the oven to 180°C/350°F/Gas mark 4.
- Place half the leeks and half the potatoes in a large casserole dish. Add the onion and spinach and season with the garlic, ginger and salt and pepper.
- Cover with a layer of leek and another of potato.
- Pour over the stock and cream. Season again with salt and pepper and bake for 50 minutes.
- Remove the gratin from the oven and sprinkle over the Parmesan and chopped walnuts.
- Return the dish to the oven for a final 10 minutes or until the potato is cooked.
- Mix together the olive oil and honey. Place the orange segments, peppers and fennel in a salad bowl and season with salt and pepper.
- Dress the salad just before serving.

To serve the stylish way: Place a portion of gratin on a large plate with a portion of orange and fennel salad to the side.

Moroccan Vegetable Tagine

GLUTEN-FREE **PAREV** **V**

Info
- Preparation Time: 30 minutes
- Cooking Time: 40 minutes
- Serves: 6

Ingredients
- 100g/4 oz/¼ cup split almonds

✡

- 3 tbsp olive oil

✡

- 12 shallots, peeled
- 4 cloves garlic, peeled
  and finely chopped
- 5 cm/2 inch piece of fresh ginger,
  peeled and finely chopped
- 1 tbsp turmeric
- 1 tbsp dried cinnamon
- ½ tsp cumin seeds
- 1 tbsp dried coriander
- salt and freshly ground
  black pepper

✡

- 100g/4 oz green lentils
- 2 sweet potatoes (approx.
  450g/1 lb), peeled
  and roughly chopped
- 200g/7 oz baby carrots, scrubbed
- 150g/5 oz dried pitted dates,
  roughly chopped
- 1 litre/1¾ pints/4 cups
  vegetable stock

✡

- 200g/7 oz mixed colour
  cherry tomatoes
- 300g/11 oz/1 cup frozen peas
- 6 mini courgettes,
  cut in half lengthways

Every season has its special selection of vegetables so take advantage of what is at its peak when you decide to make this recipe. I have focused on the summer vegetables with baby carrots, mini courgettes, yellow, orange and red cherry tomatoes and a melange of fresh herbs: mint, parsley and coriander.

This traditional Moroccan recipe is gloriously aromatic and bursting with exotic flavours. I like to serve it with couscous garnished with fresh herbs.

In Morocco the main meal of the day is at lunchtime and typically starts with a selection of hot and cold salads and then a tagine. A cup of sweet mint tea usually ends the meal and Moroccans tend to eat with their hands and use bread as a utensil. Like Jews, Muslims are forbidden to eat pork. Much of Jewish Morocco is hidden from view, which reflects the traditional Moroccan culture; most of their large palaces are hidden in narrow streets and behind gated closed doors. Jews and Arabs lived an interdependent existence until the middle of the twentieth century with Moroccan kings protecting the Jews from harm in the interests of trade and commerce. However, all that changed in the latter part of the twentieth century and today no more than 5,000 Jews remain compared to 300,000 in the 1950s.

Chef's Tip: To peel shallots easily, drop them into boiling water for 5 minutes then refresh, drain and pull away the outer skin.

Method
- Pre-heat the oven to 200°C/400°F/Gas mark 6.
- Place the almonds on a baking tray. Toast for about 10 minutes or until golden. Remove and set aside.
- Heat the oil in the base of a tagine or use a casserole or saucepan. Add the shallots, garlic, ginger, turmeric, cinnamon, cumin

✡

For the topping
- 2 tbsp each of fresh mint, coriander and parsley

and coriander. Cook over a medium heat for 5 minutes stirring continuously. Season well with salt and pepper.
- Add the lentils, potatoes, carrots, dates and stock. Bring to the boil and then simmer covered for 20 minutes.
- Add the tomatoes, peas and courgettes and continue to cook for a final 2–3 minutes as they need very little cooking.

To serve the stylish way: Stir in the fresh herbs and garnish with the toasted almonds.

Orange Israeli Couscous

PAREV **V**

Info
- Preparation Time: 10 minutes
- Cooking Time: 25 minutes
- Serves: 6

Ingredients
- 2 tbsp olive oil

  ✿

- 4 sticks of celery, finely chopped
- 1 onion, peeled and roughly chopped

  ✿

- 2 tbsp coarsely chopped fresh parsley
- 250ml/9 fl oz/1 cup vegetable stock
- juice of 1 orange or 150ml/¼ pint orange juice
- zest of ½ an orange

  ✿

- 225g/8 oz uncooked Israeli couscous
- salt and pepper, to taste

  ✿

- Garnish: 1 orange, sliced

This is a delicious vegetarian main course dish which can be enhanced with cheese and nuts if desired or used as an accompaniment to fish or meat. Israeli couscous is called 'ptitim' in Hebrew. 'Ptitim' was invented during Israel's austere times when rice was scarce and it served the Mizrachi Jews for whom rice was a staple food.

I have flavoured this dish with oranges, so why not use Jaffas if available to continue the Israeli experience. Jaffa oranges were first grown by Palestinian farmers in Jaffa, which was then the main Mediterranean port in the mid-nineteenth century. Today they are grown all over Israel. These oranges are particularly sweet and almost seedless and their thick peel used as zest provides excellent flavours.

Method
- Heat the olive oil in a large frying pan.
- Add the celery and onion and sauté until slightly golden.
- Stir in the parsley, stock, orange juice and zest. Bring to the boil.
- Add the couscous and reduce to a low heat, cover and simmer until the couscous is tender and the liquids are absorbed – about 20 minutes.
- Taste and adjust the seasoning. Fluff up the couscous just before serving.

To serve the stylish way: Garnish with slices of orange.

Vegetarian Singapore Noodles

PAREV Ⓥ

Info
- Preparation Time: 35 minutes
- Cooking Time: 15 minutes
- Serves: 4–6, with other dishes

Ingredients
- 30g/1 oz dried Chinese black mushrooms

✡

- 1 egg, lightly beaten
- 1 tbsp sesame oil
- 1 tsp salt
- freshly ground black pepper, to taste

✡

- 3 tbsp groundnut or sunflower oil
- 3 cloves garlic, finely chopped
- 1 tbsp finely chopped fresh ginger
- 2 fresh red or green chillies, deseeded and finely sliced
- 1 x 220g/7½ oz can water chestnuts, drained and sliced
- 4 spring onions, finely sliced
- 170g/6 oz frozen peas, defrosted

For the curry sauce
- 2 tbsp light soy sauce
- 2 tbsp Indian Madras curry powder or paste
- 2 tbsp rice wine or dry sherry
- 1 tbsp sugar
- freshly ground black pepper, to taste
- 100g/4 oz creamed coconut
- 250ml/9 fl oz/1 cup vegetable stock or parev chicken stock

✡

- 225g/8 oz thin noodles, fresh or dried egg noodles

- Garnish: sprigs of fresh coriander

Noodles are very popular in southern China, particularly at New Year as they symbolise longevity. An old wives' tale says that cutting noodles reduces one's lifespan so you should not break them up when eating them. This dish can be found on the menu in most Chinese style restaurants in Hong Kong as well as in English, Australian and American Chinese restaurants. However, it is not considered a dish in Singapore.

This recipe is easy to make and the light noodles combine well with the spicy sauce. This dish is also wonderful cold and makes a lovely unusual addition to a picnic.

If you make this recipe in advance, reheat in the microwave for 5 minutes.

Method
- Put the dried mushrooms in a saucepan containing 150ml/¼ pint of water. Bring to the boil and simmer for 10 minutes. Drain, reserving the liquid to use later.
- In a small bowl combine the egg, sesame oil and reserved mushroom liquid, season with salt and pepper and set aside.
- Heat a wok or large frying pan over a high heat. Add the 3 tbsp of oil and when it is hot add the garlic, ginger and chillies. Stir fry for 30 seconds. Add the water chestnuts, mushrooms, spring onions and peas. Stir fry for another 2 minutes.
- Add all of the sauce ingredients to the wok and cook over a high heat for about 5 minutes until well combined.
- Cook the noodles according to the packet instructions, add to the wok and mix well.
- Pour the egg mixture into the wok and stir fry until the egg has set.

To serve the stylish way: Turn the noodles onto a large platter, garnish with the coriander and serve at once.

Roasted Aubergine with Peppers

PAREV **P** **V**
GLUTEN-FREE

Info
- Preparation Time: 20 minutes
- Cooking Time: 35 minutes
- Serves: 6

Ingredients
- 2 aubergines (eggplant), diced
- 1 red onion, peeled and roughly chopped
- 6 cloves garlic, kept whole
- 2 red peppers, deseeded and chopped
- 4 tbsp olive oil
- salt and freshly ground black pepper, to taste

✡

- 4 vine tomatoes, chopped
- 2 tbsp sun-dried tomatoes, roughly chopped
- zest and juice of 1 lemon

✡

- Garnish: 4 tbsp roughly chopped fresh mint leaves, 100g/4 oz pitted black olives

Finding a delicious vegetable dish that can be prepared in advance for Shabbat or Yom Tov is always good news. These ingredients blend well together and do not wilt when served the next day. In addition this recipe is low-fat and provides a fine source of vitamin C. All the vegetables are roasted and subsequently have a slightly smoked caramelised flavour. Use the finest olives and tomatoes for the best presentation and taste.

Aubergines are used in many Jewish recipes especially amongst Sephardi Jews. Examples include salads, Israeli chopped liver, Yemenite eggplant in spicy tomato sauce, baba ganoush, lamb and aubergine stews. Aubergines are easy to grow, abundant in hot climates and moreover, from a Kashrut point of view, not difficult to check for insects.

Method
- Heat the oven to 220°C/425°F/Gas mark 7.
- Line a tray with non-stick baking parchment. Toss the aubergines, onion, garlic and peppers in the olive oil. Season with salt and pepper.
- Roast for 30 minutes or until the vegetables are tender. This can be done a day ahead.
- Add the vine tomatoes, sun-dried tomatoes, lemon zest and juice, then season again with salt and pepper.

To serve the stylish way: Garnish with fresh mint and olives. Serve at room temperature.

Date and Walnut Spelt Bread

`PAREV` `SUCCOT` **V**

Info

- Preparation Time: 20 minutes plus 2 hours 30 minutes for rising
- Cooking Time: 20 minutes for rolls or 30 minutes for the large loaves
- Makes 2 large loaves or 24 small rolls

Ingredients

- 2 x 7g/¼ oz sachets dried yeast
- 1 tsp caster sugar
- 650ml/22 fl oz/2½ cups warm water

✡

- 800g/1¾ lb spelt flour
- 2–3 tsp salt
- 75g/3 oz dates, roughly chopped
- 75g/3 oz walnuts, roughly chopped

✡

- 2 egg yolks, beaten, to glaze bread

The Torah tells us that the 5 types of grain – wheat, oat, spelt, barley and rye – plus any grape or wine products are all required to be eaten in the Succah at Succot and need a special blessing. I like to bring spirituality to the Succah table so why not make this recipe for all the right reasons. This delicious date and walnut bread can be shaped either into two large loaves or into small rolls. It is perfect with hot soup or toasted and enjoyed with your favourite cheese. I have used walnuts but you can ring the changes by substituting pecans, sultanas or dried apricots.

Spelt, an ancient grain, is now having a trendy revival. Widely available in our supermarkets, the flour is pale, greyish-yellow, gritty and has a sweet, nutty flavour. It is more digestible than wheat and richer in nutrients. Spelt can be used in place of regular flour for some people with a wheat allergy but is not suitable for a gluten-free diet.

Method

- Stir the yeast and sugar gradually adding 100ml/3½ fl oz of the warm water. Leave for 5 minutes.
- Add the flour and salt and beat well, then transfer to a food mixer. Stir in the dates, walnuts and the remaining water and knead with a dough hook until the dough is smooth and elastic.
- Put the dough in an oiled bowl and turn once to oil the surface. Cover with cling film and leave to rise for 2 hours in a warm place.
- Line and grease two 1 kg/2¼ lb loaf tins.
- Knock back the dough and divide into two. Knead and shape into two loaves or divide the dough into pieces weighing 55g/2 oz each for individual rolls.
- Glaze the bread with egg yolk.

- Leave to rise for 30 minutes.
- Pre-heat the oven to 200°C/400°F/Gas mark 6.
- Bake for 25–30 minutes for the large loaves or 15–18 minutes for the small rolls. They are cooked when you tap the base gently and the bread sounds hollow.
- Leave to cool on a wire rack.

Vegetable Chilli

PAREV Ⓥ

Chilli is a favourite family meal that can be made in large quantities and put in the freezer for another day. I like to vary the vegetables to tie in with what is in season and fresh on the day. I may serve it with a puff pastry lid. This recipe is dairy-free and, without the pastry, ideal for those allergic to gluten.

Vegetable chilli is the vegetarian option of chilli con carne, the official dish of Texas in the USA. This twist evolved as a result of the increased popularity of vegetarianism in the 1960s and 1970s and the demand to eat less red meat.

In 1902 Wilbur Scoville developed a method for measuring the heat in a chilli by tasting it and giving it a value. Today this system is computerised and now measured in 'scoville' units. The sensation of a chilli can trigger the brain to produce endorphins, natural painkillers, promoting a sense of wellbeing.

Note: Chillies are as hot on the outside as they are on the inside. The veins and seeds produce the most heat. Thoroughly wash your hands after use.

I find it better to slightly undercook the vegetables so that when you cook the chilli, the vegetables still have a slight bite to them.

Method
- Heat the oil in a deep saucepan or frying pan.
- Add the onions, garlic, carrots, chillies and celery. Cook for 3 minutes.
- Add the courgettes and pepper, tomatoes, kidney beans and season with salt and pepper.
- Bring to the boil and simmer for approximately 15 minutes or until the vegetables are just soft. Transfer to individual ramekins.
- Pre-heat the oven to 200°C/400°F/Gas mark 6.
- To make the pastry lid, using a saucer or ramekin, cut the pastry into 10 cm/4 inch circles. You will need six.

- Put the pastry templates on top of the ramekins. Crimp and seal the edges.
- Glaze the pastry with egg yolk and for a spicy finish, sprinkle with chilli powder or freshly ground pepper.
- Bake for 10 minutes until the pastry is crispy and golden.

Lime and Wild Rocket Risotto

`GLUTEN-FREE` **D** **V**

Info
- Preparation Time: 10 minutes
- Cooking Time: 30 minutes
- Serves: 2–3

Ingredients
- 2 tbsp olive oil

✡

- 2 cloves garlic, peeled and finely chopped or crushed
- 1 small onion, peeled and roughly chopped

✡

- 300g/11 oz risotto rice
- 50ml/2 fl oz/¼ cup dry white wine

✡

- juice and zest of 1 fresh lime
- 750ml/1½ pints hot vegetable stock

✡

- sea salt and freshly ground black pepper, to taste
- 50g/2 oz Parmesan cheese, grated or shavings

✡

- 50g/2 oz wild rocket

✡

- Garnish: 1 lime, cut into slices

This unusual risotto dish has a fresh summery flavour, perfect as a supper dish or served as an accompaniment to salmon, sole or cod.

To make the perfect risotto you need a ratio of 1 part rice to 3 parts liquid, which usually takes the form of a complementary stock. The stock needs to be hot and added very gradually to the rice. If you are impatient and add the liquid too quickly you will not achieve the ideal result as it will be too sloppy.

Method
- Heat the oil in a medium saucepan.
- Add the garlic and onion and sauté until soft.
- Stir in the rice and wine. Cook for 2 minutes. Slowly add the hot stock ladle by ladle and the lime juice and simmer until all the liquid is absorbed, stirring the pot from time to time. This will take about 20 minutes.
- Season with salt and pepper and stir in the grated lime zest. Just before serving add the Parmesan cheese and wild rocket.

To serve the stylish way: Garnish with slices of fresh lime and a dusting of black pepper.

Creamy Mushroom and Chestnut Pie with Filo Pastry Top

Info
- Preparation Time: 30 minutes
- Cooking Time: 40–45 minutes
- Serves: 6

Ingredients
- 2 tbsp olive oil, for frying

- 2 leeks, trimmed, washed and sliced
- 2 cloves garlic, peeled and finely crushed

✿

- 750g/1¾ lb mixed mushrooms (i.e. girolle, chestnut and oyster), thickly sliced

✿

- 100ml/3½ fl oz/¼ cup dry white wine
- 200g/7 oz/1 cup cooked chestnuts, roughly chopped
- 142ml/¼ pint double cream or soya cream
- 2 tsp lemon juice
- 2 tbsp fresh thyme, leaves only
- salt and freshly ground black pepper

✿

- 8 fresh filo pastry sheets

✿

- 150g/5 oz butter, melted

Delicious for an impressive Sunday supper or as part of a buffet table vegetarian option. I love the layers of crunchy pastry flavoured with fresh thyme.

For individual portions, serve in ramekin dishes.

Chef's Tip: To freeze: At the end of stage 7, cover with cling film, label and freeze for up to 1 month. Defrost before cooking.

Method
- Heat the oil in a deep frying pan over a medium heat. Add the leeks and garlic and cook for 3–4 minutes, stirring occasionally, until soft.
- Add the mushrooms and continue to cook for 2–3 minutes, until just wilted.
- Pour in the wine, bring to the boil and simmer until nearly all of it has evaporated. Reduce the heat to medium–low and stir in the chestnuts, cream, lemon juice and half the thyme leaves. Simmer gently until the sauce has reduced.
- Season with salt and pepper to taste.
- Transfer to a deep, 1.5 litre/2¼ pint freezer- and ovenproof dish.
- Pre-heat the oven to 200°C/400°F/Gas mark 6.
- Arrange 4 sheets of filo in a single layer, brush the top side of each with some of the melted butter and scatter over some thyme leaves. Place the remaining 4 sheets in a single layer over the buttered filo ones, brush the top of these with butter and then sprinkle with thyme. Cut each double filo in half so you have 8 smaller rectangles.
- Scrunch each rectangle, and then lay side by side on top of the filling, to give a ruffled filo topping.
- Cook for 25 minutes or until the filling is piping hot and the filo pastry is golden.

Date Quinoa

GLUTEN-FREE   PAREV   (V)

Info
- Preparation Time: 10 minutes
- Cooking Time: 15 minutes
- Serves: 6

Ingredients
- 340g/12 oz quinoa

✡

- 1 tbsp olive oil
- 2 cloves garlic,
  peeled and crushed

✡

- 1 litre/1¾ pints/4 cups hot
  vegetable or chicken stock
- 150g/5 oz/½ cup fresh or
  dried dates, stone removed
  and roughly chopped

✡

- 1 tbsp lemon juice
- 2 tbsp fresh parsley, leaves only
- salt and freshly ground black pepper

Quinoa is an extremely unusual ingredient; it is the fruit of a leaf plant and classified as a seed. Originating from South America about 5,000 years ago, the Inca people used it as their staple food, followed by potatoes and corn.

Before cooking, it should be thoroughly rinsed in a strainer under running water and drained to remove 'saponin' which has a bitter taste. Requiring barely 15 minutes to cook and using a ratio of approximately 1 part quinoa to 2–3 parts liquid, this is a very healthy quick fix ingredient.

For best results sauté briefly before adding the liquid.

Quinoa is a complete protein that is also gluten-free. As it is not one of the five grains made out of wheat, barley, rye, oats, spelt or their derivatives, it has been approved by many Rabbis as kosher for Passover.

However, there are two factors to consider when consuming quinoa on Passover:

- As it looks like a grain forbidden on Passover, some Rabbinic authorities consider it may be confused with a grain and so is best avoided.
- The processing of quinoa is often done in the same location where wheat is processed and the machines may not be adequately free from chometz.

Hopefully in the not so distant future, quinoa will be fully approved for Passover and under Rabbinic supervision so that we can all enjoy it all year round.

This dish goes well with most Middle Eastern main courses and would complement Shredded Roast Lamb and Rosemary Salad on page 115 in the Modern Classic section.

Method

- Place the quinoa in a sieve and rinse well under cold water.
- Heat the oil in a large frying pan and sauté the quinoa and garlic stirring continuously until it starts to become translucent – about 5 minutes.
- Add the stock and dates. Cover and cook for about 10 minutes or until soft.
- Stir in the lemon juice and parsley and season well with salt and pepper.

Chapter 6

And Finally, Something Sweet

—

Something Hot, Something Cold, Something Chocolatey, Something to Munch and Something to Slice

And Finally, Something Sweet

When you ask people what they remember from a meal, it is always the dessert. The most revered chefs are those specialising in pastry and chocolate.

I have tried to create recipes that require as little last-minute preparation as possible so that the cook can be at the table and not in the kitchen. Kosher desserts can be a challenge because of Kashrut, as dairy-based concoctions are prohibited after eating meat. A true Jewish dessert can be both parev and dairy, making it a versatile option – even 'cheese' cake. I have included several Passover recipes as these tend to be specific and modifying them using regular ingredients does not always give the best results.

'Desserts' spelt backward is 'Stressed', which is the last thing you should be at the end of a meal with my recipes.

Something Hot

- Hot chocolate and Amaretto soufflé
- Molotov pudding
- Crunchy fruit crumble
- Plum and cinnamon pudding
- Individual apple tarte Tatin
- Stir fried bananas with butterscotch sauce
- Nutty rhubarb cake with brandy custard

Something Cold

- Italian lemon trifle
- Lychee sorbet
- Mocha crème brûlée
- Stuffed figs with walnuts
- Summer strawberry semifreddo
- Tiramisu towers
- Coconut ice cream
- Pistachio and Turkish delight ice cream
- Almost apricot cheesecake

Something Chocolatey

- White chocolate and blueberry pie
- Chocolate brownies
- Passover chocolate chip cake
- Chocolate zuccotto
- Chocolate and chestnut roulade
- Mint choc cheesecake
- Best ever chocolate sauce
- Chocolate pavlova with lemon mousse

Something to Munch

- Double chocolate cookies
- Orange and poppy seed biscuits
- Fruit flapjacks
- Pistachio and fig biscotti
- Raisin biscuits
- Italian biscuits
- Coffee toffee cup cakes
- Thin plum pastries
- Coconut and cranberry chocolate slices
- Passover apple squares

Something to Slice

- Banana cake
- Carrot cake
- Apple and cinnamon dessert cake
- Sephardi date and walnut cake
- Banoffee pie
- Honey pecan pumpkin pie
- Vanilla and dulce de leche cheesecake

Hot Chocolate and Amaretto Soufflé

PAREV Ⓓ

GLUTEN-FREE

Info
- Preparation Time: 15 minutes
- Cooking Time: 10 minutes
- Serves: 6

Ingredients
For the ramekins
- 2 tbsp unsalted butter or margarine, softened, to grease the ramekins
- 1 tbsp sugar
- 1 tbsp ground almonds

✡

For the soufflé
- 225g/8 oz plain cooking chocolate

✡

- 4 tsp Amaretto liqueur
- 4 eggs, separated
- 4 tbsp ground almonds

✡

- pinch of salt
- 4 tbsp sugar

✡

- icing sugar, to dust soufflé

✡

- To serve: 6 scoops of chocolate chip or mocha ice cream (use parev for a meat meal)

This soufflé has a delicious light chocolate and almond centre. A chocoholic dream dessert, I like to serve it with a scoop of chocolate ice cream in the centre to complete the true chocolate experience.

Soufflés are a French creation, meaning 'to puff up' which is what happens to the mixture in the oven.

The perfect soufflé can be achieved if you:

- Carefully measure and weigh all ingredients.
- Pre-heat the oven so that the soufflé does not collapse.
- Pre-heat an oven tray on to which you are going to place your ramekins so that the base heat will start the cooking process immediately.
- Make sure all equipment is spotlessly clean; any trace of grease will inhibit perfectly whisked egg whites.
- Use eggs at room temperature.
- Prepare the large or small soufflé dishes before you start making the soufflé mixture.
- Try to avoid opening and shutting the oven door once they go into the oven; they will not collapse but it does not assist cooking.
- Serve immediately to your guests who are ready and waiting.
- To prepare in advance, complete up to step 6 (just before cooking), freeze raw and cook from frozen. Add an additional 10 minutes to the cooking time or until puffed and cooked through.

Method
- Pre-heat the oven to 220°C/425°F/Gas mark 7 if you are not freezing the soufflé.
- Prepare the ramekins by greasing with butter or margarine, then dusting with 1 tbsp of the sugar and ground almonds.

- Melt the chocolate in a double boiler or microwave so that no water or steam gets into the chocolate.
- Remove from the heat and add the Amaretto, egg yolks and ground almonds.
- Whisk the egg whites with a pinch of salt until they are glossy, then add the 4 tbsp of sugar. Continue to whisk until the egg whites form stiff peaks.
- Carefully fold the chocolate into the egg whites and pour into the prepared ramekins.
- Cook for about 10–12 minutes until they are well risen and quite firm to touch. As soon as they are cooked dust with icing sugar and insert a scoop of chocolate chip or mocha ice cream into the centre before serving.

Molotov Pudding

PAREV   DAIRY-FREE   GLUTEN-FREE   P

Info
- Preparation Time: 15 minutes
- Cooking Time: 10 minutes plus 15 minutes to cool
- Serves: 8–10

Ingredients
For the pudding
- 1 tbsp vegetable oil, to grease the pudding basin

✡

- 8 egg whites
- 2 tsp potato flour

✡

- 110g/4 oz sugar

✡

For the custard sauce
- 120g/4½ oz sugar
- 8 tbsp water

✡

- 8 egg yolks
- 2 tsp potato flour
- 2 tbsp brandy

✡

- To decorate: 110g/4 oz/¼ cup slivered almonds, roasted

This is my version of a traditional Portuguese meringue dessert. Its unique texture is achieved by cooking it in a bain-marie or water bath. The secret of this recipe is to keep the mixture dry from the bain-marie water and to not let the top burn. It is parev as well as Passover-friendly so keep for all occasions. This dessert can be made in advance up to step 10, where it is allowed to cool in the oven after cooking, and enjoyed cold. The sauce will only take you a few minutes to make at the end of dinner.

I have flavoured the sauce with brandy but any liqueur or even 1 tbsp of melted chocolate would be lovely.

The name Molotov comes from the fact that the dessert is shaped liked a bomb and a Molotov 'cocktail' is the name given to improvised, usually homemade petrol bombs used to set targets ablaze rather than kill civilians. Primarily invented by the Finns during their war with Russia in the 1930s, they were named after a famous Russian general who was on the opposing side and achieved great success against tanks and armoured vehicles. Despite its Finnish and Russian connections, this dessert is definitely Portuguese in origin and can be found in most local Portuguese restaurants.

Method
- Grease a 2.4 litre/4½ pint pudding basin with vegetable oil.
- Whisk the egg whites until they are very stiff and firm.
- Add the potato flour very slowly, always continuing to whisk.
- Put the sugar in a pan and heat until it becomes golden. Watch this, it can burn very quickly.
- Add the sugar, whilst hot, to the whisked egg whites.
- Pre-heat the oven to 200°C/400°F/Gas mark 6.
- Stand the pudding basin in a larger ovenproof dish or pan.

- Fill the ovenproof dish or pan with enough boiling water to reach halfway up the sides of the pudding basin.
- Transfer the whisked egg whites to the pudding basin standing in the bain-marie, smooth the surface and cook for 10–12 minutes. Watch that the pudding doesn't become too brown.
- Turn off the oven and leave the pudding inside.
- Allow to cool for 15 minutes with the oven door open or shut, depending on the colour of the pudding, which should never be darker than light brown.
- Make the custard sauce by boiling the sugar with the water until it forms a thick syrup.
- Remove from the heat and when cool add the egg yolks, beaten with the potato flour and stir in the brandy.
- Reheat this to thicken – be careful not to let it boil too quickly or it will curdle the mixture.
- Very carefully, remove the pudding from the basin and transfer to a deep dish.

To serve the stylish way: Pour over a little custard and decorate with toasted almonds.

Crunchy Fruit Crumble

PAREV

Info
- Preparation Time: 15 minutes
- Cooking Time: 30 minutes
- Serves: 8

Ingredients
Store cupboard version
- 4 x 450g/1 lb canned fruit in natural juice: any combination of apricots, peaches, pineapple or mango, drained
- 1 tsp cinnamon
- 1 tbsp brown sugar

✡

Apple and blackberry version
- 6 eating apples, peeled, cored and roughly chopped
- 300g/11 oz blackberries
- 3 tbsp brown sugar

✡

Summer berries version
- 500g/1 lb frozen mixed berries, defrosted and drained
- 400g/14 oz fresh strawberries, hulled and halved
- 2 tbsp brown sugar

✡

For the crumble topping
- 200g/7 oz/1 cup plain or wholemeal flour
- 150g/5 oz butter/margarine
- 100g/4 oz/½ cup oats
- 1 tsp baking powder
- 100g/4 oz/½ cup demerara sugar

✡

- To decorate: ½ tsp cinnamon, 50g/2 oz roasted slivered almonds (optional)

Crumble is always a family favourite. In fact crumbles became popular in Britain during World War Two when rationing made pastry a challenge. My crumble topping rings the changes as it is both crunchy and sweet. I have given three options for the fruit filling, the choice is yours.

Serve with cream, custard or your favourite ice cream.

Method
- Pre-heat the oven to 180°C/350°F/Gas mark 4.
- Combine the ingredients of your chosen filling in a large oven-proof dish.
- Mix together the crumble ingredients and sprinkle evenly over the top of the fruit.
- Bake for 30 minutes or until the crumb topping is slightly golden.

To serve the stylish way: Dust the plate with a little cinnamon to enhance the final flavours and decorate with the almonds.

Plum and Cinnamon Pudding

PAREV ◆ RH

Info
- Preparation Time: 20 minutes
- Cooking Time: 40–45 minutes for a large pudding, 25 minutes for individual ones
- Serves: 6–8
- Can be made in advance
- Will freeze

Ingredients
- 1–2 tbsp vegetable oil, to grease ramekins

✡

- 12–15 plums, cut in half, stone removed and sliced
- 2 tbsp dark brown sugar
- 1 tbsp ground cinnamon

✡

For the almond mixture
- 150g/5 oz margarine
- 150g/5 oz sugar
- 150g/5 oz ground almonds
- 6 eggs
- 3 tbsp plain flour

✡

- To serve: ice cream, sorbet or custard, cinnamon

If you are lucky enough to have a plum tree, and you have a great crop of fruit, this is the ideal recipe. Plums come in many guises – tart or very sweet; for cooking or for eating; and in a range of rich hues from light greens and yellows to dark reds and purples. Taste your plums first as they may not need that much sugar; adjust my quantities to suit your palate and your variety of plums.

This recipe uses up a good supply, freezes beautifully and you can double the quantity with success. If you are making individual puddings, I suggest you line the base of the dishes with baking parchment circles and lightly grease with vegetable oil so that you can invert them.

Plums are now the second most cultivated fruit in the world, second only to apples. Jewish plum recipes include the traditional plum kuchen and Hungarian plum cake.

Method
- Pre-heat the oven to 190°C/375°F/Gas mark 5.
- Grease a 34 x 24 x 4 cm/14 ½ x 9 ½ x 2 inch pie or casserole dish or 6 individual ramekins with oil.
- Mix the plums with the brown sugar and cinnamon and put in the dish.
- Place all the almond mixture ingredients in a food mixer and whiz together until creamy – about 3 minutes.
- Spread this mixture over the plums and level with a spoon.
- Bake for 40–45 minutes or until golden brown.
- Serve with ice cream, sorbet or custard flavoured with a dusting of cinnamon.

Individual Apple Tarte Tatin

Info
- Preparation Time: 15 minutes
- Cooking Time: 25 minutes
- Serves: 6

Ingredients
- 150g/5 oz sugar
- 1 tbsp water

✡

- 5 apples – preferably Granny Smiths – peeled and sliced
- 2 tbsp cinnamon
- 2 tbsp brown sugar

✡

- 375g/13 oz puff pastry, ready-rolled if available
- 1 egg yolk, to glaze pastry

This is one of my family's favourite desserts, especially enjoyed on a Friday night. It is child-friendly and yet can grace the dinner party table with its stylish versatility. It's easy to make – use frozen puff pastry for excellent results – and as it uses store cupboard ingredients it can be made at short notice.

Traditionally, apples are the preferred fruit but you can always ring the changes by using pears, peaches, nectarines or plums or even a combination. This same recipe can be made as one large pie too, which is even quicker to make. It uses a little less fruit but apart from that the whole recipe remains the same.

Method
- Pre-heat the oven to 200°C/400°F/Gas mark 6.
- Place the sugar and water in a medium saucepan. Make the caramel by slowly melting the sugar to a syrup and then increase the heat and continue cooking until the sugar has turned to a wonderful golden caramel colour. DO NOT STIR.
- Immediately pour this into your individual 10 cm/4 inch oven-proof pie dishes (not loose-based).
- Mix the apples with the cinnamon and brown sugar. Carefully arrange the apple slices in a circular pattern on top of the caramelised sugar.
- Roll out the pastry if not ready-rolled. Using a 10 cm/4 inch cutter stamp out six circles.
- Place the pastry over the apples.
- Trim and crimp the edges of the pastry. Glaze with egg yolk.
- Bake for 25 minutes or until the pastry is golden.

To serve the stylish way: Invert the pies on to a serving dish with an edge to capture the apple juices. Great with brandy custard, ice cream or sorbet. Note: If you make the pies in advance DO NOT invert them until you are ready to serve, or the pastry will go soggy.

Stir Fried Bananas with Butterscotch Sauce

PAREV   GLUTEN-FREE

Info
- Preparation Time: 20 minutes
- Cooking Time: 20 minutes
- Serves: 6

Ingredients
- 6 bananas, medium ripe

✡

- 1–2 tbsp sugar
- juice of 1 lime

✡

- 2 tbsp sunflower oil

✡

For the butterscotch sauce
- 50g/2 oz margarine
- 75g/3 oz soft light brown sugar
- 100g/4 oz demerara sugar

✡

- 2–3 tbsp parev whip
- 2 tbsp brandy or other preferred liqueur

✡

- To decorate: grated plain chocolate

This is a delicious parev dessert that might encourage the children to eat fruit that normally does not appear on their menu. I wrote it for my 'Easy Chinese' cookery class and wanted to find a recipe that perfected the art of stir frying fruit as well as being quick to make. Other fruits when in season, such as peaches, pineapple, apricots and nectarines, make great alternatives. Marinating the bananas in lime and caster sugar prevents them from oxidising and ensures that they do not turn brown between peeling and serving.

To flavour the butterscotch sauce you can add one of your favourite liqueurs – rum, Sabra or brandy – for an alcoholic kick.

I have used parev whip in the sauce. This is often found in the frozen section of your kosher deli, butcher's or supermarket. Buy a few cartons and keep them in your freezer as 'freezer store cupboard' ingredients.

Method
- Peel the bananas and cut into 2.5 cm/1 inch diagonal slices. Place in a bowl and sprinkle with the sugar and lime juice. Stir until lightly coated.
- Heat the oil in a wok, swirling it round to coat the sides. Add the bananas and cook for 2–3 minutes.
- Spoon the fruit into a warmed serving bowl or place in a warm oven.
- Clean the wok with kitchen paper. Add the margarine and both sugars and stir continuously over a low heat until the sugar has dissolved. Remove from the heat for 2 minutes to cool.
- Add the whip and brandy to the sugar syrup and stir until smooth.

To serve the stylish way: For an impressive dessert serve in your finest wine glasses or brandy balloons. Pour over the butterscotch sauce and sprinkle with grated chocolate. Serve immediately.

Nutty Rhubarb Cake with Brandy Custard

Info
- Preparation Time: 20 minutes
- Cooking Time: 1 hour
- Serves 8–10 slices

Ingredients
For the cake
- 1 tbsp vegetable oil, to grease tin

✡

- 225g/8 oz unsalted butter or margarine
- 225g/8 oz/1 cup sugar

✡

- 4 eggs
- 225g/8 oz/1½ cups self-raising flour

✡

- 1 tsp baking powder
- grated zest of 1 orange
- 75g/3 oz ground almonds

✡

- 170g/6 oz/1 cup rhubarb, trimmed and cut into 2.5 cm/1 inch lengths
- 110g/4 oz/½ cup brazil nuts, coarsely chopped

✡

For the custard
- 6 egg yolks
- 75g/3 oz/⅓ cup sugar

✡

- 500ml/1 pint/2¼ cups milk or soya milk

✡

- 1 tbsp custard powder
- 2 tbsp brandy

Rhubarb is strictly a vegetable as it is the stem of a plant, and can be used for both sweet and savoury dishes. Early forced rhubarb which is grown in the North of England by candlelight is an expensive 'pink' delicacy appearing briefly in March/April. Regular rhubarb quickly follows – it is greener and thicker and will need more sugar as it is very tart. Rhubarb should never be eaten raw as the leaves are poisonous.

There are about 60 different varieties and on a nutritional level rhubarb is low in carbohydrates, high in vitamins and is also thought to speed up metabolism and aid weight loss. Rhubarb can be stored in a plastic bag in the fridge for 2 weeks and can be frozen raw (blanch for 1 minute in boiling water) or stewed.

Method
For the cake
- Pre-heat the oven to 180°C/350°F/Gas mark 4.
- Grease and line a deep 23cm/9 inch cake tin.
- Cream the butter or margarine and sugar together in a bowl until pale and fluffy.
- Add the eggs one at a time with a little flour to prevent curdling.
- Add the rest of the flour, baking powder, orange zest and ground almonds and beat well.
- Stir in the rhubarb and brazil nuts.
- Pour the mixture into the prepared cake tin and level the surface.
- Bake in the pre-heated oven for 55 minutes until well-risen and firm to touch.
- Leave to cool for about 10 minutes and then transfer to a wire cooling tray.

For the custard
- Beat the egg yolks and sugar together until pale and thick.

- Bring the milk to the boil. Take 1 tbsp of the milk and mix with the custard powder to form a paste.
- Whisk the remaining milk into the custard paste. Pour the custard milk into the egg and sugar mixture. Add the brandy. Mix together.
- Heat gently, stirring continuously until the custard coats the back of a spoon. (The custard can be made up to 4 hours in advance and reheated in the microwave.)

To serve the stylish way: Pour some hot brandy custard into a glass bowl and sit a slice of cake on top.

Italian Lemon Trifle

D SHAVUOT PAREV

Info
- Preparation Time: 15 minutes plus 2 hours chilling
- Cooking Time: No cooking
- Serves: 6

Ingredients
- 100g/4 oz sponge fingers, broken into small pieces
- 75ml/3 fl oz limoncello, or any other fruit liqueur
- juice of 2 lemons

✡

- 4 eggs, separated
- 110g/4 oz sugar
- zest of 3 lemons
- 750g/1¾ lb/3 cups low-fat cream cheese/mascarpone/non dairy cream cheese, Toffuti

✡

- To decorate: 3 tbsp roasted chopped hazelnuts

This recipe is a great dairy creation – tasty desserts of a low-fat healthy nature are not always easy to find. It is made by using low-fat cream cheese and is a yummy and refreshing finale to any meal. The hazelnut flavour combines well with the cheese and the lemon liqueur.

The average lemon contains approximately 50ml/3 tbsp of juice. Lemons yield more juice when they are at room temperature before squeezing (or place in the microwave for 10 seconds), although if they are left unrefrigerated they are susceptible to mould.

Chef's Tip: Please note that this recipe uses raw egg.

Method
- Place the sponge fingers in a bowl and drizzle over the limoncello and lemon juice. Stir and set aside.
- Using an electric mixer, beat the egg yolks with the sugar until thick and pale. Add the lemon zest and cheese and combine well.
- In a separate bowl whisk the egg whites to stiff but not dry peaks.
- Using a large spoon, mix a spoonful of egg white into the yolk mix to loosen, then fold in the rest.
- Take half the sponge mixture and divide this evenly between six small glass bowls or wine glasses.
- Repeat with half of the cheese mixture. Repeat again with the second half of the sponge mixture. Top with the remaining cheese mixture.
- Chill for 2 hours.

To serve the stylish way: Top with chopped hazelnuts.

Lychee Sorbet

PAREV   DAIRY-FREE   GLUTEN-FREE   P

Info
- Preparation Time: 15 minutes plus 2 hours 45 minutes for freezing
- Cooking Time: No cooking
- Serves: 8

Ingredients
- 4 x 400g/14 oz cans lychees

  ✿

- 2 egg whites
- 100g/4 oz sugar

  ✿

- 3 kiwi fruits, peeled and sliced

  ✿

- To decorate: sprigs of mint

Lychees (or litchis) are grown in China, India, Japan, Florida, South Africa, Hawaii, Israel and Australia. They have a pinkish brown inedible skin and a large stone. The pearly white translucent flesh is deliciously sweet and high in vitamin C. Lychees are hard to peel and quite sticky, but they can be bought in cans for my recipe.

They are wonderful in oriental fruit salads, ice cream, crumbles, pies or sorbets like the recipe below. My lychee sorbet is quick to make and an ideal dessert to complete a heavy meal. It is parev and the recipe also works well if doubled.

Australia has a large and increasing lychee industry as their climate gives them the longest growing season. The first Jews came to Australia from England in 1788 along with boatloads of petty crime convicts. Later, in 1821, more settlers arrived and by 1844 the first synagogue was built in Sydney. Gold digging enticed a further wave of Jewish immigrants to come to Australia but the last great boom in immigration was during the 1930s and 1940s when the pressure from the existing Australian Jewish community on the government ensured that tight restrictions were relaxed, allowing the entry of tens of thousands of Jews from Central and Eastern Europe escaping the Holocaust. After the fall of Communism in the 1970s many Soviet Jews moved to Australia and later in the 1980s many South African Jews arrived seeking a safer homeland. Today there are an estimated 100,000 Australian Jews with the main focus on Melbourne and Sydney.

Method
- Drain the lychees.
- Place the lychees in a food processor and whiz together. Drain again to remove a further 2 tbsp of liquid.
- Whisk the egg whites to the soft peak stage and add the sugar 1 tbsp at a time. Stir into the lychee mixture.

- Freeze for 2 hours or until just set.
- Break up the iced mixture and beat until smooth. Return the mixture to the freezer for 45 minutes to set.

To serve the stylish way: Scoop the sorbet into dainty glass dishes or wine glasses with alternating layers of sliced kiwi and decorate with sprigs of mint.

Mocha Crème Brûlée

PAREV Ⓓ **GLUTEN-FREE**

Info
- Preparation Time: 25 minutes
- Cooking Time: 2 hours 10 minutes
- Serves: 8

Ingredients
- 250ml/9 fl oz/1 cup whole milk or soya single cream

✡

- 2 tbsp coffee granules
- 2 tbsp cocoa powder

✡

- 10 egg yolks
- 170g/6 oz sugar

✡

- 700ml/1¼ pints double cream or soya single cream
- 50g/2 oz demerara sugar

✡

- To decorate: cocoa powder, strawberry slices

Originally mocha was best known as a bitter coffee bean originating from the port of Mocha on the Red Sea coast of Yemen in the sixteenth century. This area still produces some of the most distinctive-tasting coffees in the world as their coffee is always dry-processed. All traditional Yemen coffee comes from small beans and is grown without use of fertilisers, pesticides and herbicides.

The term 'mocha' has come to mean a coffee flavouring that includes a small amount of chocolate syrup or powder. Coffee and chocolate have a great affinity and crème brûlée is no exception. This is a popular dessert that never fails to impress. The secret of a perfect crème brûlée is to let it completely cool before serving. The sugar needs time to set hard to form a thin caramelised topping. It is an amazing parev dessert when made with soya single cream – light but still retaining its 'creamy smooth' texture.

Method
- Pre-heat the oven to 120°C/230°F/Gas mark ½.
- Pour the milk into a saucepan set over a low heat. Add the coffee granules and cocoa powder. Whisk until dissolved.
- Whisk the egg yolks until pale and then add the sugar. Continue whisking until light and fluffy. Add the hot milk mixture and then the cream.
- Ladle the mixture into eight 170ml/6 fl oz ramekins and place in a high-sided roasting tin.
- Fill the tin with enough boiling water to reach half way up the sides of the ramekin.
- Cook in the oven for 1½–2 hours or until set.
- Remove the ramekins from the roasting tin and set aside to cool in the fridge, ideally for a minimum of 4 hours or overnight.
- Sprinkle the top of the crème brûlées with demerara sugar.

- Pre-heat the grill to its highest setting and place the brulées under for 2–3 minutes or until the sugar starts to bubble. (Alternatively use a chef's blow torch.)
- Return to the fridge until ready to serve.

To serve the stylish way: Dust the plate with cocoa powder and decorate with strawberry slices.

Stuffed Figs with Walnuts

PAREV **D** GLUTEN-FREE **P**

Info

- Preparation Time: 20 minutes plus 2 hours soaking
- Cooking Time: 25 minutes
- Serves: 6

Ingredients

- 300ml/½ pint/1¼ cups boiling water
- 450g/1 lb dried figs

✡

For the filling

- 55g/2 oz walnut pieces/halves

✡

For the syrup

- 250ml/9 fl oz/1 cup 'tea', made with 2 bay leaves, 3 cloves, 150g/5 oz sugar, 150ml/¼ pint water, 100ml/3½ fl oz/¼ cup red wine, 2 tbsp honey, zest of 1 lemon

✡

- To serve: thick yoghurt or ice cream, dusting of cinnamon

This is my own version of a recipe that was served to me during a trip to Istanbul. It is what they called 'Turkish Viagra'. Dried figs are soaked in boiling water before being stuffed with walnuts and cooked in a beautiful red wine syrup. To enjoy it as its best, serve with thick natural yoghurt drizzled with honey.

Istanbul has the most amazing spice market that is not to be missed, but it is only one of many treasures in this ancient city that straddles the border between Europe and Asia. The European side of Istanbul has the older more historic buildings including the Neve Shalom, Istanbul's largest and most famous synagogue.

Method

- Pour the boiling water over the dried figs and leave for 2 hours.
- Hold the figs by their stalks and make a small incision in the soft end of each one. Fill the figs with the walnuts.
- Place stalk side up in an ovenproof dish.
- To make the syrup combine all the ingredients. Pour into a saucepan and simmer for 5 minutes. Sweeten the syrup to taste with more honey. Pour over the figs.
- Pre-heat the oven to 180°C/350°F/Gas mark 4.
- Bake for 20 minutes.
- Can be served hot or cold with thick natural yoghurt or your favourite ice cream.

To serve the stylish way: Place in a wine glass, top with yoghurt or ice cream and dust the top with a little dried cinnamon.

Summer Strawberry Semifreddo

PAREV D GLUTEN-FREE

Info
- Preparation Time: 20 minutes plus overnight freezing
- Cooking Time: 10 minutes
- Serves: 6

Ingredients
- 150g/5 oz sugar
- 1 vanilla pod, split

✡

- 5 large egg yolks

✡

- 600g/1½ lb fresh strawberries, hulled

✡

- 200g/7 oz double cream or non-dairy cream

✡

- light oil, to grease tin

✡

For the compote
- 75g/3 oz sugar
- 1 cinnamon stick

✡

- 2 tbsp cassis
- 450g/1 lb mixed summer berries to include strawberries, hulled and quartered, blueberries and redcurrants or blackcurrants

✡

- 1 tbsp shredded fresh mint

Semifreddo means semi-frozen and often refers to desserts like ice cream, cakes and custards. This has the texture of frozen mousse as it combines both cream and custard ingredients. Strawberry desserts are the taste of summer with their heart-shaped fruit symbolising passion, purity and healing. Go fruit picking at your local fruit farm for the best flavours as opposed to the less tasty supermarket option.

To maximise the true natural strawberry flavour always let the fruit come to room temperature before eating. Better still, leaving in the sunshine before serving will dramatically improve the flavour.

Method
- Heat the sugar, vanilla pod and 100ml/3½ fl oz water in a small pan over a low heat until the sugar has melted, then increase the heat and bring to the boil.
- Meanwhile, whisk the egg yolks until thick and pale. Boil the sugar until it reaches 120°C/230°F on a sugar thermometer (or until a ¼ tsp of syrup dropped on to a cold saucer makes a firm ball). Remove the vanilla pod, then carefully pour the sugar syrup onto the egg yolk mixture in a steady stream.
- Whisk continuously until the bottom of the bowl has cooled a little. Set aside.
- Whiz the strawberries in a food processor. Sieve into a bowl to remove the seeds.
- Whisk the cream to soft peaks and fold into the egg yolk mixture, followed by the strawberry purée.
- Line and grease a 1 kg/2¼ lb loaf tin with cling film. Pour the mixture into the tin and level the surface. Cover with cling film and freeze overnight.
- For the compote, heat the sugar, 75ml/3 fl oz water and cinnamon stick in a small pan over a low heat until the sugar has

dissolved. Turn up the heat and boil for 3 minutes. Remove and stir in the cassis. Leave to cool.

- Discard the cinnamon stick and stir in the berries and mint.
- Remove the semifreddo from the freezer – dip the base in boiling water to release. Turn out and slice with a hot knife. Spoon over the compote.

Tiramisu Towers

Info
- Preparation Time: 30 minutes
- Cooking Time: 20 minutes
- Serves: 8

Ingredients
For the biscuit
- 100g/4 oz plain flour
- 100g/4 oz margarine or unsalted butter
- 100g/4 oz icing sugar
- 2–3 egg whites

✡

For the tiramisu filling
- 3 egg yolks
- 100g/4 oz sugar

✡

- 1 tbsp marsala wine or coffee liqueur

✡

- 225g/8 oz mascarpone or toffuti cream cheese as parev option

✡

- 10 sponge fingers
- 3 tbsp very strong hot coffee

✡

- To decorate: fresh raspberries, sprigs of fresh mint, dusting of cocoa powder

If you are looking for a dessert to impress and you know that your guests like coffee, this is the one to make. Tiramisu, the classic Italian trifle, is enclosed in cylinder shaped, tower like biscuits. To get the perfect shaped towers it is worth spending a little time and care to spread the mixture evenly into the prepared rectangle using a palette or table knife.

Prepare the filling and biscuit cylinder before dinner, and assemble at the last minute to keep the towers tall and crisp.

It is worth remembering that tiramisu is made using raw eggs, so it is not suitable for the very young, pregnant or elderly.

This dessert is popular amongst all Italians and Jews alike. Rome was the centre of the Jewish Community and until 1798 the Jews were forced to live in a restricted area – the ghetto – that was still home to many Jews centuries later. Although most of the original buildings in the ghetto have been destroyed there is still a plaque outside No. 2 Via della Reginella to commemorate the Jews who were deported to Auschwitz in October 1943, few of whom came back. The synagogue at Via di Portico D'Ottavia is now a museum of Italian Jewry. Across the street there is a Catholic church with Bible scriptures in Latin and Hebrew. The whole area is well worth a visit.

Method
- Pre-heat the oven to 180°C/350°F/Gas mark 4.
- Line 2–3 trays with non-stick baking parchment. On the paper draw templates measuring 15 x 7 cm/6 x 3 inch rectangles. (Turn the parchment paper over otherwise the pen/pencil marks will come through onto the biscuit mixture.)
- Whisk together all the biscuit ingredients and using a palette knife spread the mixture thinly to cover the rectangles.
- Bake for 8 minutes or until golden brown.

- Whilst the biscuit is warm use a palette knife to lift off the parchment paper and shape each biscuit around a rolling pin to make a tube. Squeeze the sides together so there is no gap. These will set in about 10 seconds. Repeat to make 6–8 more.
- Whisk together the egg yolks and sugar until very thick. Transfer to a bowl over simmering water. Add the marsala wine or liqueur and continue to whisk until the mixture forms a thick foam – about 10 minutes. Remove from the heat and stir in the mascarpone or toffuti cream cheese.
- Dip the sponge fingers very briefly into the hot coffee, remove and set aside.
- Stand each biscuit cylinder upright on an individual plate. Put the soaked sponge fingers in the bottom of each cylinder, layer with mascarpone cheese and more sponge biscuits until the cylinders are full.

To serve the stylish way: Top with 2–3 fresh raspberries and sprigs of mint. Dust the top and plate with cocoa powder and serve immediately.

Coconut Ice Cream

PAREV **DAIRY-FREE** **GLUTEN-FREE**

Info
- Preparation Time: 10 minutes plus 3 hours freezing time
- Cooking Time: 20 minutes
- Serves: 8–10

Ingredients
- 400ml/14 fl oz/1¾ cups coconut milk
- 4 x 250ml/9 fl oz cartons soya single cream

✡

- 4 eggs
- 250g/9 oz/1 cup sugar

✡

- To decorate: 75g/3 oz desiccated coconut, toasted (optional)

This is a delicious refreshing ice cream that is ideal after an oriental meal. Its creamy texture comes from the coconut milk.

If you have an abundance of desiccated coconut left over from Passover, this is the recipe for you. It will keep in the freezer for up to one month.

Method
- Put the coconut milk and soya cream in a saucepan and heat gently. Do not boil.
- Whisk together the eggs and sugar until thick.
- Pour the coconut mixture into the eggs and sugar. Whisk together briefly and then return to the saucepan. Heat gently to thicken. Set aside to cool for 10 minutes.
- Transfer to a plastic container and place in the freezer for 1 hour or until the mixture is set about 2.5 cm/1 inch from the edges.
- Remove from the freezer and mix together using a whisk. When it is fairly smooth, return to the freezer for a further hour, then repeat the whisking once more.
- Transfer the ice cream to a rigid container, cover and freeze until firm.
- To toast the coconut, place it in a single layer in a dry frying pan and cook until just golden. Remove and set aside.
- Before serving, transfer the ice cream to the fridge for about 30 minutes to soften.

To serve the stylish way: Scoop into round balls served in a glass dish or wine glass. Sprinkle with toasted coconut.

Pistachio and Turkish Delight Ice Cream

Info

- Preparation Time: 15 minutes
- Cooking Time: No cooking
- Serves: 8

Ingredients

- 1 tbsp vegetable oil

✿

- 800g/1¾ lb mascarpone cheese
- 170g/6 oz sugar

✿

- 300ml/½ pint/1¼ cups low-fat cream

✿

- 125g/4½ oz shelled pistachio nuts
- 200g/7 oz Turkish Delight (I used rose flavoured), cut into small cubes
- 2 tbsp rosewater

✿

- To decorate: pink rose petals or 2 tbsp roughly chopped pistachio nuts

This is an unusual combination but works particularly well with a Middle Eastern meal. I have made it in a loaf tin to create a terrine but you could use individual ramekins. Lightly oil and line the tin with cling film or baking parchment so the ice cream comes out easily. The variety of Turkish delight is quite amazing so choose your favourite. I chose pink rose petals here to complete the garnish, the stylish way.

Method

- Lightly grease and line a 1 litre/1¾ pint/4 cups terrine or loaf tin with cling film that overhangs the sides.
- Using an electric mixer, whisk together the mascarpone cheese and sugar until smooth.
- Stir in the cream. Fold in the pistachio nuts, Turkish delight and rosewater.
- Fill the terrine with the Turkish delight mixture, packing it down firmly.
- Cover with cling film and freeze overnight.

To serve the stylish way: Remove the ice cream from the freezer about 20 minutes before serving. Decorate with rose petals and some chopped pistachio nuts.

Almost Apricot Cheesecake

D   P   SHAVUOT

Info
- Preparation Time: 20 minutes
- Cooking Time: 35 minutes
- Serves: 6

Ingredients
- vegetable oil, for greasing

✡

For the apricot compote
- 250g/9 oz dried apricots, ready to eat soft variety
- 2 tsp sugar

✡

For the cheesecake
- 600g/1¼ lb cream cheese
- 225g/8 oz sugar
- 2 eggs, separated

✡

- To decorate: icing sugar

This cheesecake is cooked in individual ramekins in a bain-marie (a roasting tin filled with boiling water). Any leftover fruit compote is delicious for breakfast. Prunes, dried peaches or figs can be substituted for the apricots if preferred.

On a health note, apricots are a good source of vitamin A and vitamin C and contain no saturated fat, salt or cholesterol.

When buying apricots, choose soft ones as they have the best flavour.

Method
- Pre-heat the oven to 150°C/300°F/Gas mark 2.
- Lightly oil six 10 cm/4 inch diameter × 3.5 cm/1½ inch deep ramekins and line with circle templates of baking parchment.
- For the apricot compote, place the apricots, sugar and 100ml/3½ fl oz water in a pan. Bring to the boil, lower the heat and simmer until the apricots start to break down. Add a little more water if it gets too dry. This will take about 10 minutes.
- Whisk together the cream cheese, sugar and egg yolks. Whisk the egg whites until they form soft peaks. Take 1 tbsp of egg white mixture and add to the cheese mixture, then fold in the rest.
- Put 1 tbsp of compote in the base of each ramekin and then fill with the cheese mixture to within 1 cm/½ inch of the top.
- Place all the ramekins in a deep ovenproof dish. Fill the dish with hot water to reach half way up the sides of the ramekins.
- Bake for 25 minutes or until set.

To serve the stylish way: Invert onto a plate and dust with icing sugar before serving either hot or cold.

Pistachio and fig biscotti. (Page 208)

Smoked salmon and dill frittata. (Page 7)

ABOVE Roasted beetroot with goat's cheese layers. (Page 17)
BELOW Sicilian baby aubergine salad. (Page 52)

ABOVE Sole kebabs with parsley couscous. (Page 73)
BELOW Tandoori chicken with tomato, cucumber and coriander salad. (Page 93)

Salmon teriyaki. (Page 72)

Individual tomato and basil bread rolls. (Page 39)

Tricolour minestrone, Turkish red lentil and carrot soup. (Pages 27, 34)

Mediterranean tuna stacks. (Page 106)

Something Chocolatey

Jewish links with chocolate are closely linked to the expulsion of the Sephardi Jews from Spain and Portugal in the sixteenth century and their travels to Central and South America. Up until then, the Spaniards considered chocolate a fashionable drink reserved for royalty, the rich and the priesthood and the process for making it was kept secret. But with the expulsion of the Jews during the Spanish Inquisition, many Jews took this secret with them to other countries.

Chocolate production was pioneered in Brazil by a Jewish man, Benjamin d'Acosta de Andrade, and Austria's famous Sachertorte was invented by a 16-year-old Jewish boy named Franc Sacher. In 1938 Viennese chocolatier Stephen Klein moved to New York and founded the kosher chocolate Bartons. Today in Israel there is a chain of chocolate cafés called Max Brenner, which sells its products worldwide.

White Chocolate and Blueberry Pie

Info
- Preparation Time: 25 minutes plus 4 hours to chill
- Cooking Time: 30 minutes
- Serves: 8

Ingredients
For the pastry
- 280g/10 oz plain flour
- pinch of salt
- 1 egg
- 150g/5 oz unsalted butter
- 1 tsp vanilla essence
- 30g/1 oz icing sugar

✡

- 1 egg yolk, to glaze

✡

For the filling
- 200g/7 oz white chocolate

✡

- 500g/1 lb mascarpone cheese
- 75ml/3 fl oz double cream

✡

- 200g/7 oz/1 cup blueberries

✡

- To decorate: 2 tbsp each grated white and milk chocolate

White chocolate and blueberries have a great affinity. They blend, both in flavour and colour. The pie is made with a vanilla shortcrust pastry and indulgently filled with a white chocolate cream and blueberries (or if you prefer, blackberries).

Blueberries are considered one of the 'super foods'; they are rich in vitamins A, C and E, high in fibre and low in saturated fat. They are also referred to by Rabbi Yosaif Asher Weiss in his book, *A Daily Dose of Torah*, as you should have a daily dose of blueberries, just like Torah.

'White chocolate', which is not regarded as real chocolate by purists, is actually a mixture of sugar, cocoa butter and milk solids. Unlike dark chocolate, white chocolate contains other flavouring ingredients such as vanilla in order to create its creamy confection. White chocolate does not contain any caffeine as this is found in cocoa solids and not cocoa butter.

Method
- Combine all the pastry ingredients in a food processor.
- Remove and wrap in cling film. Flatten and refrigerate for 1 hour.
- Lightly flour the work surface and roll out the pastry so that it fits a 22cm/9 inch loose-based pie tin.
- Pre-heat the oven to 200°C/400°F/Gas mark 6.
- Cover the pastry with foil, insert baking beans and blind bake for 20 minutes.
- Remove the baking beans from the pastry case.
- Glaze the base with egg yolk and return to the oven for a final 5 minutes. Remove and set aside.
- To make the filling, melt the chocolate in a bain-marie (a bowl over a saucepan of boiling water). Add the mascarpone cheese and stir until smooth.
- Remove from the heat.

- Whisk the double cream so it is slightly thickened and stir into the white chocolate mixture.
- Place half the blueberries on the pastry base and spoon the chocolate mixture over the top so it neatly covers the berries.
- Refrigerate for a minimum of 1 hour or overnight.
- Top with the remaining blueberries.

To serve the stylish way: Grate white and milk chocolate over the top.

Chocolate Brownies

Info
- Preparation Time: 20 minutes
- Cooking Time: 45 minutes
- Makes: 36

Ingredients
- 175g/6 oz plain chocolate
- 200g/8 oz margarine

✡

- 4 eggs
- 250g/9 oz dark brown sugar

✡

- 100g/4 oz plain flour
- 2 tsp baking powder

✡

- 3 drops vanilla essence
- 2 tbsp roughly chopped walnuts/pecans (optional)

These delicious fudge-like chocolate brownies are the ultimate chocolate treat. No excuse is required to either make or eat them. The secret to their success is to remove them from the oven when they are slightly undercooked as they set as they cool. Plain chocolate with a minimum of 70 per cent cocoa solids gives the best flavour.

If your chocolate brownies are getting a bit stale, give them a 10 second blast in the microwave: this will rekindle the gooey chocolate centre.

Brownies were 'invented' in the US in 1893 as a 'ladies' dessert' – easier to eat than a pie and smaller than a slice of cake and thus suitable for a boxed lunch. Variations are many, but all will satisfy a true chocoholic's passion.

Method
- Line a 22 x 22cm/9 x 9 inch square tray with baking parchment.
- Pre-heat the oven to 160°C/320°F/Gas mark 2. Heat the chocolate and margarine in a small saucepan until melted.
- Whisk together the eggs and sugar until thick and add to the chocolate mixture.
- Sift the flour and baking powder into the mixture.
- Add the vanilla essence and walnuts or pecans (if using).
- Pour into the prepared trays and bake for 35–40 minutes or until just firm to touch.
- Leave to cool before cutting up into squares.

Passover Chocolate Chip Cake

`PAREV` **P** `SHABBAT`

Info
- Preparation Time: 15 minutes
- Cooking Time: 40 minutes
- Serves: 8–10

Ingredients
- 4 eggs
- 200g/7 oz sugar

✡

- 2 tbsp Kiddush wine or red table wine
- ½ tsp almond essence
- 200g/7 oz ground almonds
- 2 tbsp cocoa powder
- 150g/5 oz plain chocolate, roughly chopped
- 100g/4 oz chocolate chips
- 150g/5 oz margarine, melted, plus 1 tbsp to grease the tin

✡

- To decorate: icing sugar, sliced strawberries

This is a great family chocolate cake recipe which is suitable for both teatime or as a dessert. It only uses Passover store cupboard ingredients and not too many eggs.

To vary the recipe try adding some chopped dates to the mixture.

Method
- Line the base of a 22cm/9 inch loose-based cake tin with non-stick baking parchment and grease the sides with margarine.
- Pre-heat the oven to 180°C/350°F/Gas mark 4.
- Whisk together the eggs and sugar until thick enough to hold a trail. Add the wine, almond essence, ground almonds, cocoa powder, plain chocolate, chocolate chips and melted margarine.
- Mix well until completely combined.
- Pour into the prepared cake tin.
- Bake for 40 minutes or until just set in the middle and firm to touch.
- Leave to cool and invert onto a serving plate.

To serve the stylish way: Dust with icing sugar and garnish with strawberries.

Chocolate Zuccotto

PAREV ⓓ

Info
- Preparation Time: 30 minutes plus 3 hours freezing
- Cooking Time: No cooking
- Serves: 10–12

Ingredients
- 1 × 400g/14 oz sponge cake

✡

- 400ml/14 fl oz /1¾ cups chocolate ice cream, softened

✡

- 100g/4 oz toasted hazelnuts, roughly chopped
- 4 tbsp chocolate drops
- 250ml/9 fl oz/1 cup vanilla (dairy or parev) ice cream, softened

✡

- To decorate: 2 tbsp Sabra or other kosher liqueur, 4 tbsp grated chocolate, cocoa powder, to dust

This is a delicious impressive ice cream layered dessert that is made in a pudding basin. The word 'zucca' means 'little pumpkin', which explains its dome shape. Zuccotto originates from Florence where it is believed to have been inspired by the Dome of Florence, the city's main cathedral. Others believe that it resembles the cardinal's skullcap.

To enjoy this dessert as its best, thaw for 20 minutes before serving.

Method
- Cut the cake into 10 cm/4 inch lengths 1 cm/½ inch thick to fit inside a 1 litre/1¾ pint pudding basin. Using a 7 cm/3 inch round cutter, make a round template of cake for the base.
- Line the sides of the bowl neatly with the cake slices. Ensure there are no gaps, overlapping the slices if necessary. Place the round cake template in the base and press in gently so there are no gaps.
- Spoon the softened chocolate ice cream into the base of the dome to form an even layer and transfer to the freezer for 1 hour.
- Mix the chopped hazelnuts and chocolate drops with the softened vanilla ice cream. Spoon into the hollow over the chocolate layer. Smooth the top, then cover with slices of cake to fit the top. Press down gently to seal the top of the cake to the sides.
- Cover with cling film and freeze for 2 hours or overnight.
- Remove the cling film. To serve, run a palette knife around the edges then invert onto a serving dish.
- Leave to soften for 30 minutes before serving.

To serve the stylish way: Drizzle over the Sabra and dust with grated chocolate and cocoa powder.

Chocolate and Chestnut Roulade

PAREV Ⓟ

Info

- Preparation Time: 25 minutes plus cooling
- Cooking Time: 15 minutes
- Serves: 8

Ingredients

- 175g/6 oz good quality bittersweet plain chocolate

✡

- 6 eggs, separated
- 110g/4 oz sugar

✡

- 2 tbsp cocoa powder
- 2 tsp vanilla extract

✡

For the filling
- 150ml/¼ pint double cream or parev whipping cream

✡

- 200g/7 oz can chestnut purée
- 4 tbsp icing sugar, to taste

✡

- 3 tbsp grated chocolate

✡

- To decorate: a dusting of icing sugar and strawberry slices

This is an easy sponge cake that is rolled and filled with cream cheese and chestnut purée. It also works brilliantly with non-dairy cream cheese.

Once you have mastered the art of making roulades, you will never consider them a challenge again. I feel that by following these three guidelines you will produce the perfect chocolate roulade: use the right size tin, whisk the egg whites so that they are very stiff and spread the filling to the edges.

Roulades always have that rustic appearance, which is part of their charm, so don't worry if they crack after rolling.

Method

- Pre-heat the oven to 180°C/350°F/Gas mark 4.
- Line a 23 x 33cm (9 x 13 inch) Swiss roll tin with non-stick baking parchment.
- Melt the chocolate in a heatproof bowl over a pan of boiling water.
- Whisk together the egg yolks and sugar until thick and creamy.
- Stir the cocoa powder, vanilla extract and melted chocolate into the egg yolk mixture.
- Whisk the egg whites until very stiff. Carefully fold into the chocolate mixture.
- Pour the mixture into the prepared lined tin and spread evenly.
- Bake for 15 minutes or until well-risen and firm to touch.
- Tear off a clean piece of baking parchment large enough to fit the roulade. Turn out the roulade onto the paper and peel off the lining paper. Leave to cool.
- For the filling whip the cream until thick. Stir in the chestnut purée and icing sugar to taste.
- Carefully spread the filling over the cooled roulade. Sprinkle with the grated chocolate. Roll up from one of the wider

ends, using the paper to help. Using a cake slice, put onto a serving plate.

To serve the stylish way: Dust with icing sugar just before serving and decorate with strawberry slices.

Mint Choc Cheesecake

D | CHANUKAH | SHAVUOT

Info
- Preparation Time: 15 minutes
- Cooking Time: 45 minutes plus 2 hours cooling
- Serves: 8–10

Ingredients
For the base
- 55g/2 oz margarine

✡

- 16 plain digestive biscuits
- 4 mint chocolates

✡

For the filling
- 750g/1¾ lb soft cream or curd cheese
- 3 eggs
- 3 tbsp icing sugar
- 12 mint chocolates, roughly chopped

✡

For the topping
- 300ml/½ pint sour cream
- 3 tbsp icing sugar

✡

- To decorate: 12 mint chocolates

This is one of those recipes that has the wow factor to satisfy both chocoholic and cheesecake fans as it combines these two magical ingredients together. Medium-fat cheese is perfect for this recipe as it has the most amazing smooth creamy texture.

Cheesecake is believed to have originated during the times of the Ancient Greeks where it was served to the athletes during the early Olympic games back in 776 BCE, and it is still as popular as ever.

When making this cake don't worry about the type of mint chocolates, as all will give a great result.

Method
- Line a 22cm/9 inch springform tin with baking parchment.
- Melt the margarine in the microwave or a saucepan. Place the digestive biscuits and 4 mint chocolates in a food processor. Stir in the melted margarine and whiz together to combine well.
- Cover the bottom of the cake tin with the digestive mixture, pressing it down firmly and evenly. Leave to one side.
- Pre-heat the oven to 170°C/325°F/Gas mark 3.
- In a large bowl whisk the soft cheese, eggs, icing sugar and 12 mint chocolates and stir until well combined.
- Add the cheese mixture to the tin, making sure the top is even.
- Bake for 30 minutes or until the cheesecake is set. Remove gently.
- Mix together the sour cream and icing sugar. Pour this over the top of the cooked cheesecake. Return to the oven for 15 minutes.
- Turn the oven off and leave the cheesecake to cool in the oven for 1 hour. Transfer to the fridge to complete the cooling process for a minimum of 1 hour.

To serve the stylish way: Decorate with another 12 mint chocolates.

Best Ever Chocolate Sauce

`PAREV`

Info
- Preparation Time: 5 minutes
- Cooking Time: 5–8 minutes
- Serves: 2–3

Ingredients
- 170g/6 oz plain dark chocolate (minimum 70 per cent cocoa solids), roughly chopped

✿

- 4 tbsp water
- 1–2 tbsp golden syrup
- 6 tbsp single cream or soya cream
- 55g/2 oz butter or margarine
- 1 tsp vanilla extract

A chocolate sauce that is tried and tested is a valuable recipe. Chocolate comes in different strengths of cocoa solids and flavours so consider these variables if you decide to alter any of the ingredients.

Although dark chocolate may appear a little bitter to eat raw, once sugar is added and turned into a sauce it can be quite heavenly.

To prevent the chocolate from seizing (i.e. going stiff and hard), it is best to slightly warm the liquid ingredients before adding them.

Method
- Put the chocolate in a heatproof bowl set over (not in) a saucepan of simmering water.
- When melted, add all the remaining ingredients and stir until smooth and shiny.
- Serve immediately whilst it is still warm or reheat gently over a pan of hot water when required.

Chocolate Pavlova with Lemon Mousse

Info
- Preparation Time: 25 minutes
- Cooking Time: 1 hour plus cooling
- Serves: 8–10

Ingredients
- 4 large egg whites, at room temperature
- pinch of salt

✡

- 55g/2 oz dark brown soft sugar
- 170g/6 oz sugar
- ½ tsp vanilla extract
- 1 tbsp cocoa powder

✡

For the lemon mousse
- 284ml/½ pint double cream, whipped to soft peaks or parev whip
- zest and juice of 1 lemon (approx. 2 tbsp)

✡

- 2 egg whites
- 55g/2 oz sugar

✡

- To decorate: dark chocolate curls/ coarsely grated chocolate

Meringue style desserts of any kind never fail to impress or please family and friends. The slight tartness of the lemon mousse blends well with the crunchy sweetness of the pavlova. Both can be made in advance and then assembled just before serving. The addition of salt helps to stabilise the egg whites and balance the flavours. For a stylish look, pipe the meringues into little individual baskets.

The dessert 'pavlova' is believed to have been created in honour of the Russian ballerina Anna Pavlova whilst she was on tour in Australia and New Zealand in the 1920s and subsequently both countries have a claim to it. Anna's dancing was compared to the light texture of the meringue. There are two secrets to making the best meringue. Firstly take as long as possible to incorporate the sugar into the egg whites. The mixture should not feel grainy. Secondly leave the cooked meringue to cool as long as possible – preferably overnight.

Method
- Pre-heat the oven to 150°C/300°F/Gas mark 2.
- Line a large tray with non-stick baking parchment.
- Draw a 22cm/9 inch circle on the paper and then turn it over.
- Whisk the egg whites with a pinch of salt until stiff. Gradually add the sugars, 1 tbsp at a time. Add the vanilla extract and continue to whisk until the mixture is very stiff.
- Sift the cocoa powder over the meringue and fold it into the mixture.
- Using a large spoon or piping bag, spread the meringue over the circle template. Form a shallow well in the centre.
- Bake for 1 hour or until dry. Leave the meringue to cool in the oven, preferably overnight.

- For the lemon mousse, whisk together the cream and lemon zest until the mixture starts to thicken.
- Add the lemon juice and whisk briefly again: don't let the mixture get too stiff otherwise it will be difficult to fold in the egg whites.
- Whisk the egg whites until they form soft peaks. Add the sugar 1 tbsp at a time. Fold into the lemon mixture. Chill for 20 minutes.
- Spoon the mousse evenly into the centre of the meringue.

To serve the stylish way: Decorate with chocolate curls or grated chocolate.

Double Chocolate Cookies

D

Info
- Preparation Time: 35 minutes
- Cooking Time: 10 minutes plus chilling and cooling
- Makes: 36 biscuits

Ingredients
- 100g/4 oz margarine

✿

- 3 tbsp clear honey
- 1 tbsp sugar

✿

- 100g/4 oz white chocolate, roughly chopped
- 270g/9½ oz self-raising flour
- ½ tsp cinnamon

✿

For the icing
- 200g/7 oz dark chocolate, roughly chopped

✿

- To decorate: 2 tbsp grated white chocolate

An excuse to make chocolate biscuits is never required but more to the point have you made enough? These are melt-in-the-mouth crunchy biscuits made with white and dark chocolate.

Chef's Tip: Store in an airtight container or freeze.

Method
- Pre-heat the oven to 180°C/350°F/Gas mark 4.
- Beat the margarine until soft and creamy. Add the honey and sugar and beat until the sugar is dissolved.
- Melt the white chocolate in a glass bowl over a saucepan of simmering water (double boiler). Be careful not to overcook the chocolate – just melted is what you want.
- Cool slightly and then stir into the margarine mixture.
- Sift the flour and cinnamon into the margarine mixture and gently fold through to form a stiff dough. Using your hands, press into a ball and flatten into a disc.
- Roll out between two sheets of baking parchment to about 4mm/¼ inch thick. Chill for 10 minutes.
- Cut the dough into 5 cm/2 inch rounds using a cutter. Roll the remaining dough and continue until all the dough is used.
- Place the biscuits on a tray lined with baking parchment.
- Bake for 10 minutes or until crisp. Leave to cool for 15 minutes.
- For the icing, melt the dark chocolate in a glass bowl over a saucepan of simmering water, stirring occasionally until just melted. Cool slightly.
- Use a teaspoon and small palette knife to gently spread the dark chocolate over half the top of each biscuit.
- Leave to cool and set on a cooling rack.

To serve the stylish way: Decorate with a sprinkling of grated white chocolate.

Orange and Poppy Seed Biscuits

Info
- Preparation Time: 20 minutes
- Cooking Time: 25 minutes
- Makes 20–25

Ingredients
- 3 eggs
- 150g/5 oz sugar

✡

- 300g/11 oz/1¼ cups ground almonds
- ½ tsp almond essence
- 50g/2 oz self-raising flour
- finely grated zest of 1 orange
- juice of ½ orange
- 2 tbsp poppy seeds

The delicious combination of orange and poppy seeds is highlighted in these almond based biscuits. If you fancy a change, lemon can easily be substituted. Poppy seeds are the tiny nutty-tasting, blue grey seeds of a yellowish brown opium plant indigenous to the Mediterranean. Poppy seeds are used to flavour breads, cakes and rolls in European and Middle Eastern cooking. In Turkey, they are often ground and used in desserts. In India, the seeds are ground and used to thicken sauces.

One of the great mitzvahs on Purim is the giving of Mishloach Manot, little food gifts to friends and family. The story of Esther tells us that the Queen was a prisoner in the palace where obtaining kosher food was impossible so eating seeds, nuts and legumes was the easiest way to overcome this difficulty. I thought that a recipe suitable to be carried in baskets using poppy seeds would be the ideal gift incorporating these elements of the Purim story.

Method
- Pre-heat the oven to 150°C/300°F/Gas mark 2.
- Line two large baking trays with non-stick baking parchment.
- Whisk together the eggs and sugar until thick.
- Add the remaining ingredients and mix together.
- Place 1 rounded tbsp of the mixture on the baking trays about 2 cm/1 inch apart.
- Bake for 20–25 minutes or until golden brown.
- Cool on the trays for 5 minutes, then transfer to a wire rack to cool completely.

Fruit Flapjacks

PAREV   SUCCOT   SHABBAT   ◆ RH   ◆ YT

Info
- Preparation Time: 10 minutes
- Cooking Time: 30 minutes
- Makes: 20 squares

Ingredients
- 1 tbsp vegetable oil, to grease tin

✡

- 275g/9 oz/1 cup golden syrup
- 200g/7 oz unsalted butter
- 75g/3 oz/½ cup demerara sugar

✡

- 400g/14 oz/5 cups porridge rolled oats
- pinch of salt

✡

- 150g/5 oz/1 cup sunflower seeds
- 150g/5 oz/1 cup sultanas

The secret of good flapjacks is to strike the perfect balance between crunchy and chewy. The gooey texture comes from the addition of golden syrup so do not skimp on this. Muesli bars and granola bars are the modern equivalent but this traditional flat biscuit is still very popular.

Substitutes for the sultanas include chopped dried apricots, cranberries or any of your preferred dried fruit.

As they include porridge oats which are full of iron, zinc and vitamin B, enjoy without too much guilt. They make ideal lunchbox snacks, will satisfy a breakfast on the run or can simply be enjoyed with a cup of coffee.

Method
- Grease and line a 20 cm/8 inch square cake tin.
- Pre-heat the oven to 180°C/350°F/Gas mark 4.
- Place the syrup, butter and sugar in a large saucepan and heat gently until the butter and sugar have melted into the syrup. Turn the heat off.
- Stir in the oats and salt.
- Add the sunflower seeds and sultanas, mixing so that all the ingredients are well combined.
- Pour the mixture into the prepared tin and spread evenly.
- Bake for 30 minutes or until golden brown.
- Place the tin on a wire cooling rack and leave to cool.
- Remove from the tin and cut into squares when completely cool.

Pistachio and Fig Biscotti

PAREV

Info
- Preparation Time: 15 minutes
- Cooking Time: 35 minutes
- Makes: 50 biscotti

Ingredients
- 250g/9 oz/1¼ cups plain flour
- 225g/8 oz sugar
- 1 tsp vanilla essence
- 1 tsp baking powder

✿

- 2 medium eggs, beaten
- 200g/7 oz/1 cup pistachio nuts, shelled weight
- zest and juice of 1 lemon
- 125g/4½ oz/½ cup dried figs, roughly chopped

Biscotti are twice baked Italian biscuits that you can enjoy any time, delicious with morning coffee, afternoon tea or as an impressive petit four to complete a gourmet dinner. The addition of pistachio nuts gives them great colour and texture – for best value buy unshelled and shell them yourself.

The origin of biscotti dates back to Roman times when the sailors discovered that if they baked their bread twice so that it was hard it would keep better on sea voyages. Somehow the idea of twice baked sweet breads or biscuits became the start of what we have today.

Method
- Pre-heat the oven to 180°C/350°F/Gas mark 4.
- Line a baking tray with non-stick baking parchment.
- Mix together the flour, sugar, vanilla essence and baking powder.
- Add the eggs gradually – you may not need it all as a stiff dough is what is required.
- Knead in the pistachio nuts, lemon zest and juice and chopped figs.
- Divide the dough into six. Using your hands roll into sausage shapes about 2.5 cm/1 inch in diameter then flatten slightly.
- Place on a baking tray, spaced well apart, then bake for 25 minutes or until pale golden.
- Remove and leave to cool for 10 minutes.
- Reduce the oven temperature to 150°C/300°F/Gas mark 2.
- Using a serrated knife and cutting at an angle, cut each 'sausage' into very thin slices.
- Lay the slices on the baking tray and cook for a further 10 minutes or until dry and firm.
- Leave to cool on a wire rack.

Raisin Biscuits

PAREV   DAIRY-FREE   CHANUKAH

Info

- Preparation Time: 15 minutes plus shaping
- Cooking Time: 20 minutes
- Makes: 36

Ingredients

- 100ml/3½ fl oz rapeseed oil
- 70g/2½ oz/¼ cup light brown sugar
- 1 tsp ground cinnamon
- zest and juice of ½ orange
- ½ tsp baking powder
- 2 tbsp brandy
- 40g/1½ oz/¼ cup raisins

✡

- 270g/9½ oz plain flour

A healthy treat. This recipe uses rapeseed oil as the binding agent for these biscuits: i.e. no other fat or eggs. And it is nut-free. Made with store cupboard ingredients, this is an ideal recipe for a Chanukah family tea due to its symbolic use of oil, and is child-friendly.

Raisin biscuits can be made in advance and stored in an air-tight container or frozen for a later date. The method is so simple – get the children and grandchildren baking with you.

Raisins feature quite predominantly in Jewish recipes from challah, tzimmes, charoset, rugelach, salads using couscous and carrots, kugels, cakes and of course biscuits.

Method

- Pre-heat the oven to 170°C/325°F/Gas mark 3.
- Line two baking trays with baking parchment.
- In a separate large bowl whisk the oil, sugar, cinnamon, orange zest and juice, baking powder, brandy and raisins. Beat together and slowly add the flour until the dough becomes soft and smooth.
- Take pieces of dough the size of a walnut and shape into round biscuits. Flatten slightly with a fork.
- Bake for 20 minutes or until golden brown.
- Leave to cool for 10 minutes.

Italian Biscuits

PAREV

Info
- Preparation Time: 20 minutes
- Cooking time: 20 minutes
- Makes: 20 biscuits

Ingredients
- 250g/9 oz/1¼ cups plain flour
- 175g/6 oz margarine or unsalted butter
- 65g/2½ oz icing sugar
- ½ tsp baking powder

✿

For the topping
- 100g/4 oz chocolate
- 2 tsp olive oil

✿

- icing sugar, to dust

These little biscuits are so easy to make that you will want to make them all the time. They require very few ingredients, all of which are store cupboard ones, and they can be made in no time at all. Have I tempted you to put your apron on?

Ideal shapes to make include: circles made with cutters, rings, horseshoes or fingers made by rolling by hand and moulding.

I have kept them plain flavoured. They can be dusted with icing sugar or dipped in chocolate. Flavourings such as ½ tsp of vanilla extract/almond extract, or 2 tsp zest of orange/lemon/lime or even 1 tbsp cocoa powder could be added to the original dough mixture if desired.

I like to serve them with coffee at the end of a meal, keep them for a special tea or add to the children's lunchbox for a treat.

Method
- Pre-heat the oven to 180°C/350°F/Gas mark 4.
- Place all the dough ingredients in a food processor or mix by hand until well combined and of a soft consistency.
- Lightly dust the work surface with flour. Roll out the dough using a rolling pin until it is about 1 cm/½ inch thick.
- Cut or shape by hand as desired. See above.
- Place the biscuits on a baking tray lined with baking parchment.
- Bake for approximately 20 minutes or until golden brown.
- Cool on a wire rack.
- For a chocolate finish, melt the chocolate over a double boiler. Add the olive oil. Dip half of each biscuit in the chocolate and place on a baking parchment to cool and set.
- For a sugar finish, dip the whole biscuit into sieved icing sugar.

Coffee Toffee Cup Cakes

PAREV **CHANUKAH**

Info
- Preparation Time: 25 minutes
- Cooking Time: 20 minutes
- Makes: 10–12

Ingredients
- 100g/4 oz unsalted butter or margarine
- 55g/2 oz golden caster sugar
- 55g/2 oz light muscovado sugar

✡

- 200g/7 oz self-raising flour
- 1 tsp baking powder

✡

- 2 medium-sized eggs
- 1 tsp vanilla extract
- 1 tsp cocoa powder
- 1 tsp instant coffee dissolved in 2 tsp hot water

✡

For the icing
- 200g/7 oz icing sugar
- ½ tbsp hot water
- 1 tbsp cocoa powder
- 2 tsp espresso coffee or strong instant coffee
- 100g/4 oz unsalted butter or margarine, softened
- chocolate-flavoured strands, for decorating

These creamy cup cakes are a perfect accompaniment for hot coffee. Serve them with your friends or family for a real special treat.

The secret to perfect cup cakes is accurate measurement of key ingredients. Make sure the cakes are completely cool before you attempt to ice them; if they are even a little bit warm, the icing will not set. Ideally make them a day in advance and keep in an airtight container overnight or freeze.

To add a little surprise to the cakes, using a melon baller or small spoon, remove an inner circle and pipe in the filling for a yummy treat. And finally, forget about the calories.

Method
- Pre-heat the oven to 180°/350°F/Gas mark 4.
- Line the muffin tins with muffin paper cases.
- In a small saucepan, melt the butter or margarine and both sugars until dissolved. Leave to cool.
- Sift together the flour and baking powder.
- Whisk the eggs and vanilla extract in a mixer then add the melted butter mixture followed by the flour, cocoa powder and coffee. This mixture needs to be smooth.
- Spoon into the muffin paper cases, about two-thirds full.
- Bake for 20–25 minutes. Leave to cool.
- To make the icing, mix together all the ingredients in an electric mixer or food processor.
- Fill a piping bag and pipe icing decoratively onto the cupcakes.
- Sprinkle with chocolate strands.
- Serve with hot coffee and a good natter.

Thin Plum Pastries

Info
- Preparation Time: 25 minutes
- Cooking Time: 30 minutes
- Serves: 6

Ingredients
- 30g/1 oz skinned whole almonds

✿

- 375g/13 oz ready-rolled puff pastry
- 2 egg yolks, beaten, for glazing

✿

- 100g/4 oz marzipan
- 1 tsp rosewater or water
- 2 tbsp roughly chopped pistachio nuts

✿

- 3–4 ripe plums
- 3 tbsp icing sugar, for dusting

✿

- apricot jam, for glazing

These versatile, elegant pastries will be just as much at home on the afternoon tea table as they will be on your dinner party table. Vary the fruit; try apricots, apples or even peaches to ring the changes.

The pastries are delicious hot, cold or warm and you can prepare them in advance. They also freeze well.

Method
- Pre-heat the oven to 200°C/400°F/Gas mark 6.
- Roast the whole almonds in the oven for about 5–10 minutes until toasted.
- Leave to cool.
- Line a baking tray with baking parchment.
- Using an 11cm/4 ½ inch cutter, cut six individual rounds from the ready-rolled pastry.
- Place the pastry rounds on the lined baking tray.
- Glaze each round with beaten egg yolk.
- Put the cooled almonds in a food processor and whiz until ground.
- Add the marzipan to the ground almonds and whiz to combine.
- Add the rosewater or water drop by drop until a soft paste is formed. Fold in the pistachio nuts.
- Roll out six equal balls of the mixture.
- Place a ball in the centre of each glazed puff pastry round.
- Flatten the ball with the palm of your hand to fill the centre.
- Cut the plums in half, remove the stone and thinly slice.
- Position the slices carefully on the marzipan pastry rounds, leaving a 1 cm/½ inch pastry border all round.
- Sift the icing sugar over the pastries.
- Bake for approximately 15–20 minutes until golden brown.
- Remove from the oven and cool.
- Melt and sieve the apricot jam to make a glaze.

- Brush each pastry with the glaze.

To serve the stylish way: Serve with custard, Greek yoghurt, cream or ice cream.

Coconut and Cranberry Chocolate Slices

 PAREV **P**

Info
- Preparation Time: 10 minutes
- Cooking Time: 30 minutes
- Makes: 16 slices

Ingredients
- 300g/11 oz desiccated coconut
- 75g/3 oz sugar
- 2 tbsp fine matza meal
- 200g/7 oz white or dark chocolate, roughly chopped, or chocolate drops
- 75g/3 oz dried cranberries
- 6 eggs

If you are looking for a quick, family favourite cake for Passover, this has to be the one. It is ideal for the matza ramble, packed lunch or mid-morning treat with a cup of coffee. In addition it contains no nuts. Just mix all the ingredients together in one bowl and transfer to a baking tray … what could be easier? I have used dried cranberries but if you prefer you can substitute chopped apricots or raisins.

The Jews of Cochin in India used a lot of coconut in their dishes. Coconut leaves were originally used to roof their houses and many smoked flavoured matzas would have been griddled or baked using dried coconut husk as fuel. Coconut oil as it was completely pure was used to light the 'ner Tamid' (everlasting light) in all the synagogues in Kerala.

Chef's Tip: For a short cut with the chocolate, use plain chocolate drops, making it parev too.

Method
- Pre-heat the oven to 180°C/350°F/Gas mark 4.
- Line a 20 x 30 cm/8 x 12 inch baking tray with baking parchment.
- In a large bowl, mix all the ingredients until well combined.
- Bake for 20 minutes until golden brown and set.
- Cool in the tin before slicing.

Passover Apple Squares

 PAREV

Info
- Preparation Time: 20 minutes
- Cooking Time: 40 minutes
- Makes: 16 squares

Ingredients
- 1 tbsp vegetable oil, to grease the tin

✡

- 225g/8 oz sugar
- 2 tsp ground cinnamon
- ½ tsp salt
- 180g/6½ oz fine matza meal or cake meal

✡

- 5 eggs, separated
- 120ml/4 fl oz/½ cup vegetable oil
- zest and juice of 1 lemon

✡

- 3 large dessert apples, peeled, cored and grated

✡

- To decorate: icing sugar

I am always looking for something different to cook over Passover that is quick and tasty to make. I find that apple recipes are always popular, especially if they are parev and can be made in advance. Pears or fresh apricots could be substituted for the apples should you prefer.

Note that this recipe has the advantage of being nut-free. At Passover, I feel especially sorry for anyone with nut allergies, because so many recipes, whether sweet or savoury, use nuts. Serve this recipe in squares and it is delicious for tea or as a dessert during Passover.

Method
- Pre-heat the oven to 190°C/375°F/Gas mark 5.
- Line the base of a 20 cm/8 inch square tin and grease the sides.
- Combine the sugar, cinnamon, salt and matza or cake meal.
- Add the egg yolks, oil and lemon zest and juice and whisk together until the mixture is thick.
- Whisk the egg whites in a separate clean bowl until stiff. Combine the egg whites with the egg yolk mixture.
- Mix the grated apple with the batter and pour into the prepared cake tin.
- Bake for 40 minutes until the mixture is firm and set in the middle.
- Cool completely before cutting into squares.

To serve the stylish way: Stack the squares up high and dust with icing sugar.

Banana Cake

Info
- Preparation Time: 15 minutes
- Cooking Time: 1 hour
- Makes: 1 cake

Ingredients
- 1 tbsp vegetable oil, to grease the tin

✡

- 150g/5 oz margarine
- 200g/7 oz light muscovado sugar

✡

- 2 eggs
- 250g/9 oz/1¼ cups self-raising flour
- 1 tsp baking powder

✡

- 2 large ripe bananas, peeled

✡

- 50g/2 oz walnuts, optional
- 50g/2 oz plain chocolate chips

The evening of the first time I made this recipe, my husband had a synagogue meeting at our house and I was hoping to try a slice of my new creation afterwards. How disappointed was I when the plate was returned empty. Subsequently this recipe has been made again and again so feel free to use it for all those occasions when a slice of cake is most welcome. It is also useful when bananas in the fruit bowl are beginning to go brown and you know that they are not going to be eaten raw. I like to keep it parev so there is no restriction on the temptation.

This recipe has fat and sugar in it, but as one banana contains all 8 of the amino acids a body cannot produce itself, don't feel too guilty when you eat it.

Method
- Pre-heat the oven to 180°C/350°F/Gas mark 4.
- Line and oil a 1 kg/20¼ lb loaf tin with non-stick baking parchment.
- In a food processor whiz together the margarine and sugar until well combined. Add the eggs, flour and baking powder and mix well.
- Using the pulse button add the bananas.
- Remove from the mixer and stir in the walnuts and chocolate chips.
- Spoon the mixture into the prepared tin and bake for 1 hour or until a skewer inserted in the middle comes out clean and not sticky. Cover with foil if the cake starts to get too brown before completely cooked.
- Leave to cool before turning out onto a wire rack.

Carrot Cake

Info
- Preparation Time: 15 minutes
- Cooking Time: 1 hour
- Serves: 8

Ingredients
- 225g/8 oz plain flour
- 175g/6 oz caster sugar
- 1 tsp bicarbonate of soda
- 1 tsp baking powder
- 1 tsp cinnamon

✿

- 2 eggs
- 200ml/7 fl oz vegetable oil
- 1 tbsp honey

✿

- 175g/6 oz carrots, peeled and finely grated
- 200g/7 oz/1 cup/1 can crushed pineapple
- 55g/2 oz walnuts, chopped (optional)

✿

- To decorate: icing sugar

This cake is very quick to make and can be put together in one bowl. It's a healthy sweet choice as the carrots and pineapple count towards your 'five a day'. You can even use wholemeal flour if preferred. For children's parties, use the mixture to make up cup cakes – these will take only 20 minutes to cook.

If you cannot find crushed pineapple in your supermarket, canned cubes or rings can be substituted and then crushed in the food processor or buy fresh pineapple and crush in the same way.

Method
- Pre-heat the oven to 180°C/350°F/Gas mark 4.
- Grease and line a 22cm/9 inch loose bottom cake tin.
- Mix together all the dry ingredients.
- Add the eggs, oil and honey and mix well.
- Stir in carrots, pineapple and nuts (if using).
- Bake for approximately 1 hour or until set.

To serve the stylish way: Dust a little icing sugar on the top just before serving.

Apple and Cinnamon Dessert Cake

`PAREV` ◆ `RH`

Info
- Preparation Time: 30 minutes
- Cooking Time: 20 minutes for the individual cakes and 40 minutes for the large cake
- Serves: 8–10

Ingredients
- 1 tbsp vegetable oil, to grease the tin

✡

- 4 eggs
- 150g/5 oz sugar
- 2 tsp cinnamon
- zest of 1 lemon

✡

- 150g/5 oz plain flour
- 1 tsp baking powder
- pinch of salt

✡

- 110g/4 oz unsalted butter or margarine, melted

✡

- 550g/1¼ lb dessert apples, peeled, cored and finely sliced
- 75g/3 oz/⅓ cup sultanas

✡

- To decorate: 1 sachet of vanilla sugar, for dusting, 1 lemon, very fine strips of the zest

One of my favourite apple cakes, this is so easy to make and always delicious; your guests will not be disappointed.

It can be made in individual ramekins or in one large loose-based tin and inverted to produce a stylish sweet creation to end a meal. This is a perfect recipe for Rosh Hashanah when apples are always on the menu both sweet and savoury.

This is a typical Ashkenazi recipe and would be found on many a Yom Tov table all over the world. It is a moist apple cake permeated with dried cinnamon and although I have served it as a dessert, you can serve it for tea or just with a cup of coffee. 'Jewish apple cakes' tend to be parev, making them permissible any time.

Method
- Pre-heat the oven to 180°C/350°F/Gas mark 4.
- Grease and line a 23cm/9 inch springform tin or 8 individual ramekins with baking parchment.
- Using an electric whisk or mixer whisk together the eggs, sugar, cinnamon and lemon zest until the mixture is thick and mousse-like – about 5 minutes. The whisk should leave a trail in the mixture.
- Sift the flour, baking powder and salt over the egg mixture, then fold it in gently.
- Slowly drizzle in the melted butter or margarine from the side of the bowl and fold in gently with a metal spoon.
- Carefully stir in the apples and sultanas.
- Spoon the mixture into the prepared tin and level the surface.
- Bake for 40 minutes or 20 minutes for the individual cakes.
- Allow to cool for 10 minutes before inverting onto a wire rack. Turn the cake the right way up.

To serve the stylish way: Dust the cake with vanilla sugar and decorate with thin strips of lemon zest.

Sephardi Date and Walnut Cake

Info
- Preparation Time: 20 minutes
- Cooking Time: 40 minutes
- Serves: 6

Ingredients
- 1 tbsp vegetable oil, to grease the tin

✡

- 4 eggs
- 55g/2 oz soft brown sugar

✡

- 1½ tsp baking powder
- 75g/3 oz unsalted butter or margarine, melted
- 200g/7 oz self-raising flour
- 1 tsp cinnamon
- 1 tsp vanilla extract
- 1 tsp nutmeg

✡

- 120ml/4½ fl oz/½ cup milk, soya milk or soya cream
- 200g/7 oz/1 cup chopped pitted dates
- 75g/3 oz/⅓ cup chopped walnuts

✡

For the rosewater syrup
- 340g/12 oz sugar
- 100ml/3½ fl oz water
- 2 tbsp rosewater

This cake is ideal as both a dessert with cream, thick yoghurt or ice cream or for tea. When serving it as a grand finale to a lavish meal, I like to add some ground cinnamon to whipped cream or ice cream or yoghurt just to complete the overall Sephardi experience.

Rosewater can be found in the specialist section of supermarkets or Greek shops. It has a very distinctive aroma and flavour and is often used as a replacement for red wine and other alcohols in cooking by Muslim chefs. It is made by steeping rose petals in water and has been used as a flavouring for centuries in Middle Eastern, Indian and Turkish cooking.

Sephardi food is extremely diverse as it combines global spices from both Mediterranean and African communities. This style of cooking is sensual, colourful and aromatic and dishes often include cinnamon sticks, vanilla seeds and scented flower waters. Entertaining is lavish, gracious and constant. Desserts such as this one are often coated with sweet syrups, cakes are made with semolina and dried fruits and nuts are high on the ingredients list.

Check the dates on your spice jars before adding to your recipe and if you feel that their pungent flavour has waned a little, dry fry them and they will come alive.

Method
- Pre-heat the oven to 180°C/350°F/Gas mark 4.
- Line and grease a 22cm/9 inch loose-based tin with non-stick baking parchment.
- In a food mixer beat together the eggs and sugar until thick and creamy. Add the baking powder, melted butter or margarine, flour, cinnamon, vanilla extract and nutmeg.
- Stir in the milk, dates and walnuts.

- Transfer the mixture to the prepared tin and bake for 40 minutes or until a skewer inserted into the centre of the cake comes out clean.
- Whilst the cake is baking make the rosewater syrup by placing the sugar and water in a small saucepan. Bring to the boil and simmer for 3–4 minutes until the sugar has dissolved.
- Stir in the rosewater. Set aside and cool.
- Pierce the warm cake with a skewer. Drizzle over the rosewater syrup until it has sunk in and been absorbed.

To serve the stylish way: Serve with thick yoghurt or cream with a dusting of ground cinnamon.

Banoffee Pie

D SHAVUOT

Info
- Preparation Time: 20 minutes plus 1 hour and 15 minutes chilling time
- Cooking Time: 2 hours
- Serves: 6–8
- Must be made in advance
- Will not freeze

Ingredients
For the base
- 400g/14 oz plain digestive biscuits
- 140g/5 oz unsalted butter, melted

✡

For the filling
- 2 x 400g/14 oz cans condensed milk

✡

- 3 bananas, peeled and sliced

✡

- 2–3 tbsp clear honey
- 500g/1 lb/2¼ cups thick Greek yoghurt

✡

- To decorate: grated chocolate

This is such a popular dessert – a combination of banana and toffee within a biscuit base. Whenever I see it on a restaurant menu I look no further. Traditionally the pie is topped with cream – I have changed this. It's the toffee and banana part that is divine, so I have written this recipe for all those who do not like thick cream but prefer Greek yoghurt.

This recipe is so popular that there is even a website about it. There are endless variations and hopefully my variation will become one of your favourites.

Method
- Place the biscuits in a food processor and whiz until they are completely crushed.
- Add the melted butter.
- Use the mixture to line a 22cm/9 inch loose-based pie dish.
- Refrigerate the biscuit base for a minimum of 1 hour.
- Place the 2 cans of unopened condensed milk in a pan of simmering water for 2 hours. Extra water may need to be added from time to time to ensure that the cans are always completely covered.
- Drain the water away and carefully open the tins.
- Mash the bananas and spoon into the thickened condensed milk. Pour this over the biscuit base and level with a knife. Leave to cool for 15 minutes.
- Mix the honey with the yoghurt and pour over the pie.
- The pie can be chilled for up to 4 hours.

To serve the stylish way: Sprinkle a little grated chocolate over the pie just before serving.

Honey Pecan Pumpkin Pie

RH SHAVUOT SUCCOT

Info
- Preparation Time: 1 hour (for the homemade pastry)
- Cooking Time: 1 hour 20 minutes
- Serves: 8

Ingredients
For the pecans
- 3 tbsp sugar
- 2 tbsp honey
- 1 tbsp unsalted butter

✡

- 55g/2 oz pecan halves

✡

For the pastry
- 300g/11 oz plain flour
- 160g/5½ oz unsalted butter
- 1 egg
- 1 tsp vanilla essence
- 2 tbsp sugar

Or
- 300g/11 oz ready-made shortcrust pastry, for the short cut version (Start at step 3)
- 1 egg yolk, for glazing

✡

For the filling
- 225g/8 oz sugar
- 1 tbsp cornflour
- ½ tsp cinnamon
- ½ tsp ground mixed spice
- pinch of salt
- 1 x 425g/15 oz can pumpkin purée

✡

This is one of those useful recipes that can be made in separate stages to fit in with your busy day. Caramelise the pecans, make the pastry (or buy ready-made), cook the pumpkin – all can be done up to 3 days in advance meaning you just have to cook the pie and decorate on the day.

The caramelised pecans are a great garnish and traditionally go well with this sweet pumpkin combination of honey and cream. It is the perfect dessert for Succot, Shavuot and Thanksgiving.

One custom that originated in Germany during the twelfth century and is associated with Shavuot was to bring children to learn for the first time. Honey was put on the slate and the children licked this from the letters with their tongues. The idea was to make the Torah learning an enjoyable experience and Torah learning 'as sweet as honey'. (Source: Rabbi Eliazar of Worms 1160–1230.)

This dessert provides all the sweetness necessary for your sweet experience either for Rosh Hashonah, Shavuot or when you choose.

Note: I recently discovered in my supermarket 100 per cent natural puréed pumpkin. One 400g/14 oz can is perfect for this pie and certainly speeds up the preparation time.

Method
For the pecans
- Line a plate with some baking parchment. Pour the honey, sugar and butter into a medium-sized saucepan. Allow the sugar to dissolve and the butter to melt.
- Add the pecan halves and stir gently. Continue to cook until the sugar starts to caramelise. Pour the mixture onto the baking parchment and leave to cool.

For the pastry
- Place all the ingredients in a food processor and combine so that a dough forms.

- 2 tbsp honey
- 3 tbsp whipping cream
- 3 eggs

✡

For the topping
- 6 tbsp whipping cream
- 1 tbsp clear honey

✡

- To decorate: caramelised pecan halves

- Remove, wrap in cling film and refrigerate for a minimum of 30 minutes.
- Lightly dust the work surface with flour. Roll out the pastry so that it fits a 23cm/9 inch deep loose-based pie dish.
- Pre-heat the oven to 200°C/400°F/Gas mark 6.
- Blind bake for 15 minutes. Remove from the oven and glaze the pastry with the egg yolk. Return to the oven for 5 minutes.

For the filling
- Whisk the sugar, cornflour, cinnamon, mixed spice, salt and pumpkin purée in a food processor.
- Add the honey and cream followed by the eggs. Blend together and pour into the cooked pastry case.
- Bake for 1 hour or until it is puffed up and slightly cracked. Cover with foil if it starts to burn.
- Remove from the oven and allow to completely cool. (Can be made the day before.)

For the topping
- Whip together the cream and honey and pipe or spoon this mixture along the top of the pie.

To serve the stylish way: Decorate with the caramelised pecan halves and serve in thin slices.

Vanilla and Dulce De Leche Cheesecake

D **CHANUKAH** **SHAVUOT**

Info
- Preparation Time: 30 minutes plus 6 hours 15 minutes cooling
- Cooking Time: 1 hour 20 minutes
- Serves: 10–12

Ingredients
For the base
- 225g/8 oz digestive biscuits

✿

- 125g/4 ½oz butter, melted

✿

For the filling
- 675g/1½ lb full-fat cream cheese
- 200g/7 oz light brown muscovado sugar
- 2 tbsp vanilla essence
- 50g/2 oz plain flour
- 175ml/6 fl oz dulce de leche
- 2 eggs

✿

For the toffee sauce
- 120g/4½ oz/½ cup sugar

✿

- 120g/4½ oz butter
- pinch of salt

✿

- 100ml/3½ fl oz double cream

✿

- To decorate: cocoa powder

This vanilla and dulce de leche cheesecake certainly has the wow factor. Make it when you have a lot of guests as it is quite rich and does serve 12 people. Dulce de leche (the name means sweet milk) is a traditional dairy product from Argentina. It is used as a topping for ice cream or fresh fruit, like bananas and as a filling for cakes like this cheesecake. Thick and intensely flavoured, it should be slightly warmed to make it pourable.

You really don't need any reason to make a cheesecake for Chanukah. However, there is a specific connection between cheese and the Festival of Lights. At this time we recall the brave heroine, Judith who helped save her people by slaying the vicious Greek general, Holofernes, (164 BCE) with the help of a little cheese and alcohol.

Holofernes had brought the Jews of Bethulia to the brink of death by seizing the town's only spring of water. The people grew desperate as they began to weaken from thirst. The beautiful Judith stepped forward and asked to see Holofernes. Taken by Judith's loveliness and charm, Holofernes invited her to an evening banquet, intending to seduce her. Judith brought a large wineskin to share with him. Charmingly, she plied him with salty cheeses, then as he grew more and more thirsty, offered him great quantities of wine to slake his thirst.

When Holofernes fell into a drunken stupor, Judith took his sword and cut off his head. When Holofernes' soldiers found his body, they were so demoralised that they fled in panic. The town of Bethulia was saved, along with the rest of Israel.

Method
- Line a 22 cm/9 inch springform tin with baking parchment.
- Pre-heat the oven to 200°C/400°F/Gas mark 6.
- Pulse the biscuits in a food processor into fine crumbs.
- Mix the biscuit crumbs thoroughly with the melted butter.

- Press the biscuit crumbs on to the bottom and 3 cm/2 inches up the sides of the prepared tin.
- Bake for 15 minutes. Remove and set aside.
- Using an electric mixer, whisk together the cream cheese, brown sugar, vanilla essence, flour and dulce de leche until smooth and well blended. Add the eggs one at a time and whisk briefly to combine.
- Pour this mixture over the cooked biscuit base.
- Reduce the oven temperature to 170°C/325°F/Gas mark 3. Bake the cake for 1 hour or until set.
- Turn the oven off but leave the cake in the oven to cool.
- Remove and refrigerate for 6 hours or overnight.
- Remove the cake from the tin and place on a serving plate.
- To make the toffee sauce, melt the sugar with 3 tbsp of water in a small saucepan until the sugar has dissolved. Increase the heat and cook without stirring until it starts to caramelise and the sugar becomes golden brown. Remove from the heat, add the butter and salt then the cream, stirring continuously until well blended. Set aside and cool for about 10 minutes.
- Pour the toffee sauce onto the cheesecake and spread evenly.
- To cut run a knife under hot water, wipe it dry and cut the cake into slices.

To serve the stylish way: Dust the plate with cocoa powder.

Chapter 7

Festivals

Festivals

The Jewish calendar is filled with feast, fasts and festivals. Even when we are commanded by God to fast to commemorate tragedy we are also commanded to feast afterwards. Our sages encourage us to feast wisely – gourmet rather than gourmand. Each festival has its symbolic dishes and favoured ingredients.

Meal times are unhurried and family-orientated. Discussion and debates both secular and non-secular are the order of the day. Children and adults eat together and guests are welcomed with open arms. In fact, it is considered most worthy to invite strangers to your table on Friday nights, Shabbat and on Yom Tov.

Each special meal begins with Kiddush and Hamotzei – the blessings over wine and bread.

I have compiled a list of festivals and their culinary connections together with suggested menu plans. The Jewish year begins with:

Rosh Hashanah (1st and 2nd Tishrei)

This date marks the beginning of a period known as the Ten days of Repentance lasting from Rosh Hashanah to Yom Kippur. Traditionally it is said that during this time God sits in judgement on the entire world. On Rosh Hashanah it is customary to eat sweet foods such as apples dipped in honey and honey cake. This symbolises our hope for a 'sweet' new year.

Other less well known symbolic foods:

Pumpkin or gourds

These have thick skins, so when we eat them or food made from them we are expressing the hope that 'as this vegetable has been protected by a thick skin, God will protect us and gird us with strength'.

Black-eyed peas (string beans)

The Aramaic name for black-eyed peas, rubiya or lubiya, sounds similar to the Hebrew word (rabah) which means to increase our good deeds in the coming year.

Carrots

In Yiddish, the word for carrots is 'mehren', which also means 'to increase'. So for this reason it has become the custom in many communities to eat carrots or fenugreek at the start of the New Year in order to wish for a good and prosperous start.

Pomegranates

There are 613 commandments in the Torah and it is claimed that there are the same number of seeds in a typical pomegranate, although I have never had the patience to check this one myself. It is also symbolic of the shape of a king's crown and if we look inside a pomegranate, even though there may be some bad seeds, there are still some good ones just as there is always some goodness inside every person.

Fish

Another example of a food eaten for prosperity and growth that we should multiply as a people and be as plentiful as the fish in the sea.

Fish Head or Sheep's Head

(These should be placed on the table and not eaten.)

It is again symbolic that on Rosh Hashanah we should be seen as the 'head' and not the tail. The sheep's head is also a reminder of the story of the binding of Isaac, in which Isaac's father Abraham is instructed to offer a ram in place of Isaac. We read this story on the second day of Rosh Hashanah.

Yom Kippur (10th Tishrei)

Yom Kippur is the culmination of the ten days of Penitence beginning on Rosh Hashanah. The day means many things. Literally the words mean 'Day of Atonement'. It is the holiest day of the year. It is the day God forgave the Jewish people for their sin of worshipping the Golden Calf. It is a day devoted to prayer. This task is taken so seriously that those who are able to are commanded to fast for 24 hours in order to detach themselves more fully from the material world and better tune in to God. It can be the longest day of the year but also the most rewarding.

Although there are clear instructions to fast, how we end the fast varies enormously by geography, age and family background. Sephardi, Ashkenazi and Mizrachi Jews all have their own customs and traditions.

My family friend of Egyptian origin breaks her fast with copious cups of black coffee and kahk which are savoury bread bracelets or round bread sticks coated with sesame seeds or cumin seeds, cheese sambousaks (cheese pastries) and a selection of salads, normally including aubergine. Another popular dish is 'ful medames', a vegetarian dish made with brown beans, olive oil, lemon juice, garlic, chopped parsley and their special tradition is to include some hummus and boiled egg as the topping. Boiled potatoes with a lemon dressing was also part of the feast, sometimes enhanced with rice. So the focus is on light but nutritious spreads of dishes to end a day of fasting.

My Persian friend likes to break the fast with breakfast style foods such as challah, cheese, egg, jam and cakes, but other Persians tend to go straight into dinner with rice, chorresht (meat stew often flavoured with saffron) and kebabs and a special drink that they only have at this time called Falloodeh seeb. It is a refreshing, energising drink made with shredded apple, rosewater, mineral water and sugar.

Moving across the world to Eastern Europe, the custom of friends with a Romanian heritage is to break their fast with cups of sweet black tea and slices of honey cake. Honey was held in high regard for its health associated attributes and many families kept beehives to ensure that they had the finest honey.

Over in Sweden, the table is set with jugs of water, wine, Coke, vegetable soup and vanilla sponge cake with lots of icing sugar. Sliced challah is plated up to be served with cheese, pickles and other deli favourites.

My former Rebbetzin, who is Italian, always has a three course meat meal, often starting with salads or soup and then followed with a chicken dish.

In Florida, USA there are many Jews from different countries. A tradition has developed of breaking the fast together as a community of friends who replace your far away family. My twin sister who lives there says there is no 'Florida tradition': it is a blend of the traditions from where they originated. In her synagogue, there are families from Israel, New York, Australia, South Africa and Europe. The communal 'Break the Fast' is sponsored by members and is quite an extensive meal offering smoked salmon, bagels, hot chicken, cold cuts, salads, rice, fresh fruit and cakes.

Closer to home, my mother said when she was young it was always cups of tea, honey cake and then a selection of herrings both pickled and schmaltz, fried fish and salads in the more traditional Ashkenazi way. But now our meal has been modernised and enhanced with salmon, quiches, salads, jacket potatoes and fruit platters.

So as with many Jewish practices, there is no clearly defined ritual for that first all-important meal after the fast. It varies from one continent to another. Climate and ingredients native to specific areas play a vital part in the recipes that families enjoy – often with great relish.

Succot (15th–21st Tishrei)

Succot is a Hebrew word meaning 'booths'. It is an autumn harvest festival recalling the forty years the Israelites wandered in the desert after the Exodus from Egypt. Today the holiday is celebrated by the building of a Succah – a temporary hut-like dwelling in the synagogue, and often in our homes. The Succah is made of greenery and harvest produce laid over a frame through which the sky is visible. It represents harvest fruits and the frail huts the Israelites lived in. We decorate the Succah with the seven species indigenous to Israel mentioned in the Old Testament. These are wheat, barley, grapes, figs, pomegranates, olives (oil) and dates (honey). From this, many of these ingredients are popular on the Succot menu.

Any dish incorporating one's harvest produce or own region is appropriate for Succot. Typical recipes include stuffed vegetables, fruits, main course pies like my roasted root mash pie. They symbolise abundance or wealth with which we have been blessed. Ashkenazi favourites include kreplach, and stuffed cabbage (holishkes). Sephardi festive dishes include couscous with seven vegetables and various toppings and vegetable casseroles flavoured with lots of aromatic spices such as tagines. One-pot dishes like these are also easy to transport into the Succah. According to the Talmud the table should be decorated with pomegranates as they too are symbolic of plenty, and a bottle of wine.

Simchat Torah (22nd Tishrei)

The words 'Simchat Torah' mean 'rejoicing in the law'. This is the annual celebration to mark the completion of the reading of the five Books of Moses and the first part of Genesis (1st book of the Torah). Our Torah reading cycle has been completed and re-begun. Simchat Torah is a very joyful occasion. The scrolls are taken from the Ark and paraded round the synagogue seven times, often accompanied by flag waving, dancing and even a L'chayim (drink) or two.

Chanukah (25th Kislev–3rd Tevet)

This is a joyous festival that commemorates the rededication of the second Temple way back in 165 BC. We are told that after the Temple's desecration there was insufficient oil to sustain the lights on the magnificent golden candelabra which was supposed to be lit at all times. Only a tiny jug of oil was found with enough for one day. The oil lamp was filled and lit. A miracle occurred as the oil lasted for 8 days until new supplies could be found.

As oil is the feature of the miracle, fried foods play an active part in the culinary celebrations. Latkes and doughnuts are a great favourite. Sephardi Jews have loukoumas – deep pastry coated in honey and sesame seeds with syrup. They also enjoy sambusaks which are puff pastries filled with cheese or meat and deep fried. Israelis make sufganiyot which are doughnuts injected with delicious fillings such as custard, cream, chocolate and of course jam.

Tu B'shevat (15th Shevat)

Tu B'Shevat is the Jewish New Year for trees. It is a day for planting trees and other greenery, and for reminding ourselves of our duty to care for our planet. One tradition is to bring spirituality to the dining table in the format of a Seder focused on new fruits. Some communities have the custom to eat fifteen different fruits corresponding to the fifteenth Shevat, whilst others eat twelve different fruits to correspond to the twelve Tribes of Israel.

Purim (14th Adar)

The Purim story is told in the biblical book of Esther. The Jews of Shushan in Persia were singled out for destruction by the wicked Haman. The timely intervention of the Jewish Queen Esther saw Haman's evil plan thwarted. Today Purim has evolved into a fun holiday for children and adults. Purim parties and carnivals are held and a good time is had by all.

Many dishes are sweet and sour to recall how sweet it was to conquer adversity. Traditional foods include hamantashen which are triangular pastries filled with poppy seeds, jam or chocolate. Hamantashen means 'Haman's pockets' in Yiddish. Some say Haman wore a three-cornered hat, which is why the pastry is triangular.

We have a Seudah (Purim Feast) on the day of Purim. At this meal, many serve an especially long braided challah, symbolic of the long rope used to hang Haman.

Vegetarian and Middle Eastern dishes are popular at Purim. This is because Queen Esther allegedly ate only seeds, nuts and legumes to keep kosher and the story is set in Persia.

Passover (Pesach) 15th–22nd Nissan

Passover celebrates the Exodus from Egypt and our freedom from slavery. It is called Passover (Pesach) because the Angel of Death 'passed over' Jewish households, sparing Jewish children from the destruction meted out to the stubborn Egyptians.

The festival lasts for eight days during which no chometz (fermented grain) may be consumed. Houses are rigorously cleaned to remove any trace of chometz. Ordinary flour is replaced with ground almonds, potato flour, matza meal and most recipes contain eggs.

It is traditional to eat matza (unleavened bread) on Pesach. This is because when Pharaoh finally agreed to let the Jews leave Egypt they had insufficient time to prepare food for the journey resulting in the production of unrisen bread.

On the first two nights of Passover we hold a Seder. This ritualistic family occasion includes the retelling of the story of the Exodus as if we were there. The Seder table has a special plate holding symbolic foods, which are part of the story.

- Burnt Shankbone: this commemorates the sacrifice made the night the Jews fled Egypt.
- Karpas is a green vegetable, usually parsley (though any spring green will do). Whilst karpas may symbolise the freshness of spring, others say people eat it to make them feel like nobility or aristocracy. Some families still use boiled potatoes for karpas, continuing a tradition from Eastern Europe where it was difficult to obtain fresh green vegetables. We dip the parsley into salt water which represents the tears shed during slavery.
- Charoset is a sweet salad of apples, nuts, wine and cinnamon that represents the mortar used by the Hebrew slaves to make bricks.
- Burnt hard-boiled egg: the roasted egg (baytsa) is symbolic of the festival sacrifice made in biblical times. Eggs are also symbols of mourning.
- Salt water symbolises the tears and sweat of enslavement, though paradoxically, it's also a symbol for purity, springtime, and the sea, the mother of all life.
- Maror are bitter herbs using horseradish or onion. This symbolises the bitter lives of the slaves before the Exodus.

- Matza. Perhaps the most important symbol on the Seder table is a plate that has a stack of three pieces of matza (unleavened bread) on it. The matzot (plural of matza) are typically covered with a cloth.

Yom Ha'atzmaut (5th Iyar) Israel Independence Day

This celebrates the establishment of the modern State of Israel and we enjoy eating a selection of Israeli foods such as falafel, hummus, pitta bread, Israeli salad and tahini.

Shavuot (6th and 7th Sivan)

Shavuot means 'weeks' and celebrates the giving of the Torah to the Jewish people. The word 'weeks' records the seven weeks it took, according to tradition, to travel from Egypt to the foot of Mount Sinai where, traditionally, Jews received the Torah (Jewish law). Dietary laws were included – until these were fully understood, only dairy produce was eaten. For this reason dairy foods such as cheesecake and blintzes (cheese filled pancakes) are still Shavuot favourites.

Tisha B'av

This sad fast day, normally in August, completes a three-week period of collective Jewish mourning for the destruction of the first Temple and other historical tragedies. During the three weeks leading up to it you may not have a party, marry or cut your hair. For the last nine days eating meat, drinking wine, and wearing new clothing is forbidden, except on Shabbat.

Festival Menus:

Pesach Milk

Roasted red pepper and carrot soup
Duet of fish balls – boiled fish balls/salmon-fried fish balls
Italian matza salad
Almost apricot cheesecake

Pesach Meat

Tapas: carrots and olives
Passover beef lasagne
Red and green summer salad
Coconut and cranberry chocolate slices

Shavuot Dinner

Tricolour minestrone
Tomato and basil bread

Plaice fillets with mushrooms
Lebanese tabbouleh
Banoffee pie

Rosh Hashanah Milk

Hot or cold borsht, or:
Carrot and apple soup
Salmon crumble
Sicilian baby aubergine salad
Apple and cinnamon dessert cake

Yom Kippur: Taking the fast

Wild mushroom and leek soup
Chicken paella
Individual apple tarte Tatin

Breaking the fast

Carrot cake
Banana cake
Lemongrass fish cakes with lime mayonnaise
Salmon teriyaki
Pomegranate kasha salad with honey dressing
Crunchy papaya salad
Thin plum pastries

Succot Milk

Italian tomato and bread soup
Moroccan vegetable tagine, or:
Roasted root mash pie
White chocolate and blueberry pie

Succot Meat

Sweet potato and chestnut soup with garlic croutons
Date and walnut spelt bread
Whisky chicken
Tropical fruit filo pie

Formal Dining

Dainty cherry tomato tartlets
Italian chicken spirals, or:
Sea bream with saffron and coriander
Hot chocolate and Amaretto soufflé
Pistachio and fig biscotti

Chanukah Tea

Raisin biscuits
Mint choc cheesecake
Coffee toffee cup cakes

Friday Night Dinner

Chinese chicken and sweetcorn soup
Hazelnut-stuffed turkey with brandy sauce
Roasted aubergine with peppers
Orange Israeli couscous
Mocha crème brûlée, or:
Crunchy fruit crumble

Shabbat Lunch

Jerusalem kugel
Vegetarian lettuce wraps
Smoked aubergine pâté – Moutabel
Stuffed mushrooms with hazelnut gremolata
Tzimmes chicken
Chocolate and chestnut roulade

Purim Seudah

Purim challah
Mini spinach and pine nut pies
Mini corn fritters with guacamole
Ratatouille lasagne, or:
Sesame fish with udon noodles
Orange and poppy seed biscuits
Chocolate brownies

Glossary

A book of this nature has numerous terms that are not necessarily widely used in everyday language. The glossary will help with this.

ASHKENAZI – The word is derived from the Hebrew word for Germany and is a generic term for Jews who derive from Eastern France, Germany and Eastern Europe and their descendants. Most Jews in America are Ashkenazi.

BAGEL – A ring-shaped bread roll, made from a yeast dough which is first boiled and then glazed with egg, and baked. Popular flavours include onion, rye, pumpernickel, cinnamon and raisin.

BLINTZES – Thin pancakes, Russian in origin but similar to French crepes, stuffed with various fillings and often topped with sour cream.

BORSHT – A Russian style soup that can be served hot or cold usually made from beetroot. Variations include sorrel and cabbage borsht. It is often served with sour cream and boiled potatoes.

CHABAD – An ultra-orthodox sect specialising in outreach work bringing disconnected Jews back into the fold.

CHAG – The Hebrew word for festival. 'Chag Sameach' or happy holiday is the usual greeting between all Jews.

CHALLAH – A plaited bread loaf traditionally made with egg yeast dough and used for Shabbat and festivals.

CHAROSET – A mixture of chopped fruits, nuts and spices combined with red wine and eaten during the Seder service on Passover.

CHOLENT – A traditional meat and vegetable stew prepared before Shabbat begins, left to cook slowly overnight and then eaten for lunch.

CHOMETZ – Leavened foods and ingredients forbidden at Passover.

CHRAIN – The Yiddish word for grated horseradish and beetroot relish traditionally served with white fish.

COMPOTE – A French term that has been adopted by Jewish cooks which refers to a mixture of dried fruits that are sweetened and then cooked.

EINGEMACHT – Traditional Passover preserve of German origin usually made from apricot, beetroot, spices and nuts or carrots.

FALAFEL – A deep-fried chickpea croquette of Middle Eastern origin that is served as an hors d'oeuvre or stuffed into the pocket of pitta bread with lettuce and tahini or hummus.

GEDEMPTE – Stewed or braised.

GEFILTE FISH – Gefilte is the German word for stuffed and refers to a mixture of ground fish, matza meal and eggs and shaped into balls which are then poached or fried.

HALACHA – The legal part of Talmudic literature, an interpretation of the laws of the Scriptures.

HAMANTASHEN – Triangular pastries filled with poppy seeds, jam, prunes or other mixtures and served at Purim time to resemble the three-cornered hat that Haman used to wear.

HAMOTZEI – Blessing made before eating bread.

HASSIDIC – Orthodox Jewish movement originating in Eastern Europe (currently Belarus and Ukraine) in the eighteenth century. Their practice emphasises the spiritual and joyful elements of Judaism.

HOLISHKES – Sweet and sour cabbage leaves stuffed with meat and rice.

HUMMUS – A Middle Eastern dip made from chickpeas and sesame seed paste (tahini).

KASHA – Buckwheat groats usually served as an accompaniment to meat, but also in soups, salads or as a breakfast cereal.

KICHEL – Biscuit or cookie.

KIDDUSH – The Blessing or sanctification made over wine on Friday night, before Shabbat lunch and on festivals. It also refers to the wide range of light sweet and savoury delicacies served buffet style after the synagogue service.

KNEIDLACH – Also called matza balls: dumplings made of matza meal and served in chicken soup.

KNISHES – Stuffed dumplings filled with potatoes, meat, cheese or rice and then either fried, boiled or baked.

KOSHER – The Hebrew word that describes the dietary laws. From a root meaning 'fit', 'proper' or 'correct'. Jewish dietary laws are the laws of Kashrut. Also used to describe food products with Rabbinic Supervision which may have been prepared in accordance with ritual laws.

KREPLACH – Pockets of paste-like dough that are stuffed with meat, cheese and boiled or fried like ravioli and served in soup.

KUGEL – Potatoes or noodles combined with an egg and oil mixture and baked in the oven like a pudding. Usually served as a vegetable or when sweetened with raisins, sugar and apples, as a dessert.

LATKES – Small pancakes made from grated potatoes fried in oil traditionally eaten on Chanukah.

LEKACH – Dark honey cake traditionally served on Rosh Hashanah and Yom Kippur.

LOKSHEN – Egg noodles, traditionally served in soup or used in kugel.

MANDELBROT – Twice-baked crisp almond biscuits/cookies originating in Germany.

MATZA – Unleavened bread traditionally eaten during the eight days of Passover.

MATZA CAKE MEAL – Matza that is ground extra finely and used for baking and stuffings during Passover.

MATZA MEAL – Matza that is ground finely and used as a substitute for flour during Passover or as a coating or thickening agent instead of breadcrumbs. It can be purchased either fine ground or medium ground.

MEATY – Recipes containing any meat ingredients or derivatives including poultry, beef, lamb and stock.

MIKVEH – A ritual bath containing purified rain water used for spiritual cleansing.

MILKY – Recipes containing any dairy ingredients including milk, butter, cheese and cream.

MITZVAH – Technically this: it is a God-given commandment listed in the Torah. However, it has come to mean a good deed done for the advantage of others.

MIZRACHI JEWS – Jews from the Middle East. The word 'Mizrachi' is derived from the Hebrew word for Eastern.

PAREV – 'Neutral' food that contains no meat or dairy products and could be eaten with either a meat or dairy meal. Fish is parev but Ashkenazi Jews do not eat fish and meat on the same plate.

PAREV CREAM – A non-dairy cream substitute.

PITTA BREAD – Middle Eastern flat hollow round bread that can be filled with falafel, hummus, tahini and salads.

PLAVA – Egg-based plain sponge cake often flavoured with lemon zest or almond essence. It is eaten over Passover.

SCHMALTZ – Rendered chicken fat taken from the top of the chicken soup and used instead of butter, margarine or oil.

SEDER – This means 'order'. It is the Festive Meal eaten on the first two nights of Pesach and has this name because the rituals performed are always in a specific order.

SEPHARDI – Jews from Spain, Portugal, North Africa and the Middle East and their descendants. The word 'Sephardi' is derived from the Hebrew word for Spain.

SEUDAH or Seudah Shlishit – This is the Hebrew and Yiddish for a third meal customarily eaten on Shabbat and Purim afternoon.

SHABBAT – The seventh day of the week on which God rested from His creation of the world. A day of rest and spiritual enrichment and good food.

SHABBAT SHALOM – This is the traditional Shabbat greeting between fellow Jews literally wishing a 'peaceful day'.

SIMANIM – Symbolic foods eaten on Rosh Hashanah to give good fortune.

STRUDEL — A pastry made of very thin sheets of dough and filled with a variety of sweet and savoury mixtures.

SUCCAH — This is a temporary dwelling place that we eat in during the holiday of Succot.

SUMAC — This dark red spice comes from the berries of a wild bush that grows in all Mediterranean areas, especially in Sicily and southern Italy, and parts of the Middle East, notably Iran. It is an essential ingredient in Arabic cooking, being preferred to lemon for sourness and astringency.

TAHINI — Sesame-seed paste usually served as a dip or with falafel in a pitta.

TALMUD — Ancient Rabbinic commentaries analysing and interpreting the Torah.

TORAH — Technically the Torah is the first five books of the Old Testament: Genesis, Exodus, Leviticus, Numbers and Deuteronomy, sometimes called the Pentateuch. However, the word Torah is often used to refer to the entire body of Jewish teachings.

TZIMMES — A mixture of sweet potatoes, prunes, carrots and assorted dried fruits that are often sweetened and sometimes cooked with meat.

VARNISHKES — Noodle dough filled and shaped into bows, traditionally served with kasha.

VORSPEISEN — Selection of Ashkenazi starters.

WORSHT — It is a salami sausage served in slices.

YESHIVA — A religious senior boys school often involved in the training of academic and community Rabbis.

YIDDISH — A mixture of German and Hebrew language spoken by Ashkenazi Jews using the Hebrew alphabet.

YOM TOV — This is used to refer to all major and minor Jewish holidays and festivals. Jews greet each other with a 'Good Yom Tov' when they meet at this special time.

Index